M000302712

Portrait Photo of Father Bolduc
- commissioned by Mrs. Beemster

Father Hector Bolduc

Defender of the Catholic Tradition

by

Thomas E. Summers

Wolverine Press

2023

To order additional copies, please visit:

www.amazon.com

Contents

Book Dedication

I would like to dedicate this book, *Father Hector Bolduc—Defender of the Catholic Tradition*, to Archbishop Marcel Lefebvre who founded the priestly Society of Saint Pius X.

After nine years of struggling to become a good priest in liberal seminaries, Father Bolduc found Archbishop Lefebvre's seminary in Ecône, Switzerland. I think a sample of the diary entries during the first two weeks of Father Bolduc upon entering the Ecône seminary in October of 1973 explains why I dedicate this book to the good Archbishop:

> "I was in the house only a few minutes when I felt right at home, it is fantastic being in a real seminary. My soul really has been lightened, I can see now more clearly how far from God I had strayed because of the modernistic and satanic influences in the 'new' seminaries. How beautiful it is to hear the *Salve Regina* sung nightly. There is a lovely statue of the BVM right outside my door with a votive candle lit. I have pledged to say my rosary before it every night for all those who are looking for the Tridentine Mass and for my parents."

It warms my heart to know that Father Bolduc was lost and struggling before he found the seminary in Ecône and that afterwards, with the Archbishop's help, he founded so many chapels and harvested so many souls for God.

Thomas E. Summers—biographer.

Forward

As a youth, we were taught by our religion teachers that our life's objective was to know, love, and serve God and therefore save our souls. How we accomplished that was using the same truths from the apostles as explained by the infallible teachings of the Catholic church. These teachings have not changed since the beginning of the Church, that is until the 1960's with Vatican II. Civil society was also experiencing foundational shaking events at this time with a presidential assassination, riots, and the moral fiber of the nation that was deteriorating quickly. What you will find in this biography is that Hector Bolduc spent the majority of his life in preparation to fight for Catholic Tradition. Then in that one, decisive choice, that outpouring of all of his energy into one activity, he became a priest to fight to save Catholic Tradition[1]. He had the right skills, energy, and total commitment to fight for the Catholic truths of all time.

During the 1960's, I was intent on becoming a priest but was warned off by a Monsignor that the present seminaries were not teaching the truths of the Catholic faith. I couldn't believe it, but I trusted the Monsignor and then went on to teach Catholic grade school students. My eyes were then opened wide as the teaching sisters were instructing the students that Jesus was not really God among other errors.

I had heard about the Traditional seminary in Écône and in September of 1973, left for there. Upon arrival, I was welcomed by Fr. Urban Snyder and then introduced one by one to this array of new "first year" seminarians. All seemed like normal amiable good souls who were now taking their first steps towards the abnegation of self which is required in the priesthood of Jesus Christ. Outside of the fact that all were complete strangers to me, there was actually nothing unusual

---

[1] For more understanding of why Father Bolduc spent the rest of his life fighting for Catholic Tradition, see Archbishop Marcel Lefebvre's "Open Letter to Confused Catholics"

about these introductions until Fr. Snyder came to Hector Bolduc. His face was so full of light and his look was so extrovertedly friendly but had a countenance of sternness and determination, that I was immediately taken aback by a sense of deep surprise and alarm. This was the look of one from far away already who was seeking only success in God. It was so fierce as to be alarming.

Fr. Bolduc was dutifully ordained at the end of that first seminary class year. (June 29, 1974) having been studied and assessed by the able judgment of Archbishop Lefebvre and his panel of professors and counselors. Among many things what stays ever most firmly with me is the memory of Hector Bolduc. It was everything just short of shocking.

After my own ordination on June 29, 1978, I was assigned by Archbishop Lefebvre to assist Fr. Bolduc in his priestly apostolate. The Archbishop said that he was assigning me to "work under Father Bolduc—he gets things done." He had borne this burden for four years almost alone. For the next 18 months, we were working "shoulder to shoulder, arm to arm" to satisfy the spiritual needs of the Catholics of the United States and Mexico. I would have the opportunity to find out just what lay under that Hector Bolduc face mask. This turned out in the end to be a futile search and my assessments of him were all failing to comprehend enough. After this short time, I was transferred to Phoenix, Arizona.

My true comprehension of that Hector Bolduc regard—that "fix in his eyes" full of resignation to the Divine Will and Determination to accomplish the saving of Catholic Tradition—was finally realized upon reading this marvelous and well researched biographical study of the life of Hector Bolduc by his friend and collaborator in saving souls from Parma, Michigan, Thomas Summers.

This reading of Fr. Hector L. Bolduc's life is entirely postmortem in which the certain and final meaning of Fr. Bolduc's life is brought to light. As the Summers' study shows, in effect Fr. Bolduc was called already in youth in the family and on the farm to serve God and his church and through, in, and with Christ Our savior to serve his fellow man.

In reading this post mortem account of the facts of Fr. Bolduc 1) on the farm, 2) in the military, 3) in various religious orders as he was led by God, 4) in various scholastic institutions and other seminaries, 5) in his travels to Christian sites of historical renown famous to our Faith and lastly 6) in completely extra-curricular activities such as huge bike rides across huge distances for no apparent reason but to exercise his virtue. 7) in his childhood hobbies which, when developed into his adult life. would help sustain his most auspicious generosity in his Priestly Apostolate buying property for churches, purchasing all kinds of church goods and fixtures of devotions such as sacred statues and sacred portraits.

Begging the indulgence of the reader but in reading and rereading that Summers' biographical life of Hector Bolduc I wept again and again and exclaimed to myself that I surely was just now understanding that fearless intrepid soul whom I found to be inscrutable and enigmatic. He was the right person with the right skills at the right time to fight tirelessly to save the Catholic faith from ruin. He and the other priests fought the established Catholic hierarchy to keep that precious pearl that we in the timeless Roman Catholic faith now practice.

Fr. Bolduc was my friend, associate, boss and superior in religion from 1978 when I was ordained until 1984 when he temporarily went into sabbatical mode for a much-needed rest and recovery and regrouping.

I would be remiss if I did not mention those other Catholic persons, both lay, priests, and religious, who along with Father Bolduc, spent their complete energies ensuring that Catholic Tradition is here 50 years after Vatican II.

I expect all who read this life of Hector Lutgar Bolduc will be edified and thankful that Father Bolduc was here to help save the Traditional Catholic faith.

—Rev. Fr. Terence Finnegan
Our Lady of Quito parish
May 3rd, 2023
Phoenix, Arizona

P.S. On this very day in St. Mary's, Kansas, is being realized the dream of Fr. Bolduc which he could not obtain while in this world. The Establishment and Consecration of the Most Beautiful Edifice in honor of the Immaculate Virgin Mary, Fr. Bolduc's Heavenly Queen. It is noteworthy that Fr. Bolduc signed all letters to his fellow Catholics and to priests with the signature, "In Mary Immaculate."

Preface

Why is there another book on someone's life? Is this a fair question? A lot of us have led good lives, maybe not as priests, but we did the best we could. I think the answer is that Father Hector Bolduc was not only an amazing person, but he was a leader in the movement to return to the traditional Catholic faith in the United States. Father's spiritual assets are the many people that he assisted in some way to reach Heaven. His material assets were many: churches, farm, and lands here in the United States and in Canada, plus antiques, relics and art that he obtained over his life.

After Father's passing in 2012, the Board of Directors of Father's corporation had meetings yearly to manage and eventually dispose of the material assets. During one of these meetings, in 2017, it was suggested that if we ever wanted to write a biography of Father Bolduc, it would be necessary to capture memories of Father Bolduc from his friends before they forgot them or passed away. In all, over one hundred people were contacted, and they enjoyed reliving some of their memories of Father. After that, Ernest Bolduc, Father's older brother, shared Father's diaries with me. Hector had kept them since 1947 when he was eleven. For sixty-five years, each day he would write a page of information about happenings. It always included the weather, any natural sights he observed, and the highlights for that day. In all, there were twenty-one thousand nine hundred fifteen daily entries! I took notes as I read the diaries, so quotations from the diaries contain his exact words as well as I could decipher them (his handwriting was not always legible).

After the interviews and the diaries, an awesome picture of Father's life emerged. Still left for others to research are the two hundred plus copy paper boxes of correspondence and the detailed journals and ledgers in which Father kept his very personal notes. Sometimes, interview notes conflicted with diary entries. This happens as time passes; memories are not always perfect. Articles in newspapers or magazines, unfortunately, were not accurate at times. Diary entries of Father's were always written in a timely fashion and are therefore most likely more reliable.

In addition to diaries, Father kept separate journals, records, or ledgers. He would refer to them when he wanted to expand further on a subject, usually of a private nature. One example is: "See Journal 65, page 243 for more detail." The diaries from 1947 (age eleven) to 1951 (age fifteen) have not been located.

One of the secondary benefits of this research was learning firsthand about the "pioneers" in the Traditional Catholic Movement in the early 1970's and their struggles. I am hoping that my children and grandchildren will read about these struggles to preserve the Catholic Faith and appreciate what they have received from persons such as Father Bolduc.

The one person that made this book of memories possible was his older brother, Ernest Bolduc, who provided many of the articles and memories, and much of the support to complete this work. It could not have been done without his valuable and excellent help.

I would like to apologize in advance for any slights that may be felt. I tried to describe as best I could in my weak English, the story of Father Bolduc with all charity

In addition to this book, the materials used to do the research will be available on the internet. These include all the source publications, the audio sermons, the videos of Father (sermons, PBS special on the Bolduc family, funeral, speeches), and his description of the visit with Padre Pio. Please refer to Appendix G for access instructions.

Thomas E. Summers—Parma, Michigan

Bolduc family picture. Front row L-R Anita Felixine (9-12-1937 age 18), Robert Joseph (10-17-1944 Age 11), Barbara Dorothy (9-3-1942 Age 13), Ora Theberge (5-27-1902 Age 54) Hector Charles (10-9-1901 Age 54), Helen Lillian (4-15-1946 Age 10), Laurette Leda (7-14-1941 Age 15), (Back row L-R) Armand Antonio (4-9-1939 Age 17), Hector Ludger (6-21-1936 Age 20), Maurice Frank (5-18-1931 Age 25), Roland Henry (6-7-1923 Age 33), Kenneth Patrick (3-17-1922 Age 34), Charles Arthur (10-12-1925 Age 30, Theresa Elaine (6-16-1929 Age 27), Ernest Gedeon (10-12-1933 Age 22)

Chapter One
The Bolduc Family

On January 1, 1952, a fourteen-year-old named Hector Bolduc, the son of a New England farmer, wrote a diary entry about his New Year's resolutions. The entry was the first of more than twenty thousand diary entries that he would make over his lifetime. These diaries document the life of a man, who as a Catholic priest would help preserve the Latin Mass and traditional Sacraments across America.

William Wordsworth wrote in the poem "My Heart Leaps Up," that "The Child is father of the Man." To understand Father Bolduc, especially his work ethic, and to fully appreciate his apostolate as a man of God, we need to understand the family, the childhood, and the land he came from.

The Bolduc family was raised in northern New Hampshire, a state composed mainly of mountains, forests, and lakes. Bitterly cold in the winter and punishingly hot in the summer, this topography and climate breed tough, self-sufficient people who go by the state motto: "Live free or die." New Englanders are aptly described in the 1942 book, *We Took to the Woods*, as people who practice "hard work, honesty, persistence in the face of adversity," and who have "the ability to make do with the resources on hand, a lack of pretension, [and] the clarity of vision to call a spade a spade."

New Hampshire is known as the "Granite State." Much of the land is untillable due to the large amount of granite just under the topsoil, and the Bolduc farm was no exception. The farm had been established by federal grant in 1779. It spanned three hundred acres between the small towns of Gilford and Laconia and bordered beautiful Lake Winnipesaukee. But of the three hundred acres, only eighty were tillable.

Being a farm boy farming on the forty-third latitude, young Hector Bolduc filled his diary with farm life, especially the weather. Although the summer could be very hot—Hector talks in his diaries about haying with the heat being one hundred ten degrees in the shade—it was the cold, snow, and rain that affected their livelihood the most, as this diary entry shows: January 5, 1952—"Got more snow today than we have had in five years. One foot of snow."

Other entries express worries such as: Did they have enough ice cut to keep their food cold during the summer? Would the rain ruin their hay? Was it cold enough for the sap to run? The ability to answer these questions correctly determined the survival and prosperity of the Bolduc family.

The Bolducs were a deeply Catholic family and believed in an extremely limited government. The priorities in their family were: faith, family, country, and community. The name, Bolduc, is a French version of a name from the Netherlands: 'sHertogenbosch, a city in Holland meaning "The Duke's Forest."

Hector Bolduc grew up with twelve siblings. His father, Charles Hector, "Pop," was born in Canada on October 9, 1901 and emigrated with his father to Laconia, New Hampshire, in 1915. His mother, Aurore [Ora] Theberge, was born in Laconia on May 26, 1902. Charles Bolduc and Aurore Theberge married on January 30, 1921. They had fourteen children and Pop gave each a nickname: Ken (The President), Roland (Bud), Charles (Sam), Theresa (called Crow due to her dark hair), Marie (who died at the age of two months in 1929) Maurice (Jink or Joe), Hector (Cocktail), Armand (Punk), Barbara, Ernest (Cherry), Anita (Pig), Lauretta, Bob, and Helen. Everyone in the family used the nicknames. Ken was the President because all decisions went by both Pop and him. Hector was "Cocktail" because he loved eating fruit cocktail. They called Ernest "Cherry" because he'd climb the cherry trees to eat them clean of fruit.

Hector seemed to be closest to his brothers Ernest, Armand, Sam, and Bud. They are most mentioned in his diaries. He also had a soft spot for his sister, Theresa, who was nine years older than him, who he said was the most like his mother. Although she moved to Connecticut when Hector was fifteen, she remained a big part of his life. She drove from Connecticut to New Hampshire for many Thanksgivings, Easters, and dinners in between. For all the Bolduc children, the farm remained home for generations.

The farm, purchased by Pop from his father in 1927 when he was twenty-six years old, required the family to work together. The family rose at 4:00 am to start work in the dairy barn. Everyone helped milk the cows, even the children as young as age four or five.

Pop delivered milk and other farm products daily; the kids would take turns going with him. They would stop at the Rexall store and get an ice cream cone. Sometimes, Pop would have to hook up the Belgian horse team to deliver milk since the drifts were fifteen to twenty feet deep in spots. On days like that the deliveries could take five and a half hours.

The Bolduc family lived off the land and appreciated every aspect of the changing seasons: each season brought its own beauty and work. During winter, families would go down to the lake and cut chunks (36"x18"x12") of ice and store it in a shed. These chunks of ice were very heavy. They would put a row of sawdust, then ice, and then more sawdust until the shed was full. This would hopefully take care of their refrigeration needs for spring, summer, and fall. Even with all that ice, they still needed more cooling for the milk, and would lower twenty-quart milk cans into water wells, which was quite a job because of the weight of the milk can.[2]

In early spring, with horses pressing through enormous drifts, the children harvested sap from the maple orchard that crowned the farm. After the last frost, they planted plenty of corn for the dairy farm. In late summer they harvested hay from three farms in the surrounding area to feed their eighty head of cattle. Initially, the Bolducs did all the hay by hand, but eventually bought a side delivery rake and a hay loader. The children convinced their dad to get a tractor—that it was time to modernize the farm. Shortly after the arrival of the tractor, Pop came out to see the big tractor stuck in the field. He got out the Belgian horse to pull out the tractor and commented that it

[2] *Laconia Evening Citizen* 1/14/15 – Keeping the Old ways – ice, harvesting ice on Squam Lake (source 89)

did not matter how much horsepower the tractor had as it took only one horsepower to get it out!

Pops learned from a farm specialist about crop rotation to conserve the soil. Young Hector, a member of Future Farmers of America (FFA), understood the concept and agreed with his dad's dFecision: "A man came up today to talk to Pop about a farm conservation program. Pop is going to do it. I'm glad" (August 10, 1953).

The Bolduc Farm was essentially self-sufficient. Ora Bolduc once told Pops: "You take care of the farm and I will take care of the house." But Ora was often out in the fields and gardens right alongside the kids and Pop.

Besides the corn and hay fields, the Bolducs had prolific vegetable gardens. Name the fruit or vegetable, it was planted there in great abundance—raspberry bushes, popcorn, beets, carrots, cucumbers, tomatoes, sweet corn, peppers, pumpkins, squash, and potatoes. A short New England growing season meant starting seedlings in the house when outside the fields still looked like winter. Planting, weeding, and harvesting the gardens was a massive task. To illustrate the vastness of the harvest: in 1953, the Bolducs picked one hundred sixty raspberry bushes! After harvesting, every piece of produce had to be preserved in some way. The family canned around one thousand quarts of food each year, but they used other methods of preserving too. Bins in the cellar were used, in which potatoes, carrots, beets, and apples stayed cool and unspoiled. Some vegetables and fruit would be buried with sand, others with straw. By springtime, some of the vegetables would get soft, but they were tender also.

Vegetables weren't the only food in the cellar. Freshly butchered beef would hang in the cellar to cure. When the family needed meat for the day, they would scrape mold off the carcass with the back of a knife and cut a piece for the main meal. Ora would wash the meat in baking soda to remove all contaminants. Pork was more complicated. After butchering a pig, the family would freeze the meat in the cold New Hampshire winter. They had to hope that it would not thaw out before they could use it all.

Nothing was thrown away. If the meat was close to going to waste, Ora would preserve the rest. A quart or two of canned meat would feed the entire family. And if the produce was going bad, she would make sure the needy neighbors received some food. Especially during the Depression and World War II, the families whose children teased the Bolduc kids for smelling like a dairy farm would get food delivered. Ernest would complain: "If you grow it, you need to use it. Why do we have to feed the neighbors?" Their mother would answer: "Just go and leave it under their front porch. They will find it." Because of this goodwill, the neighbors would help with the harvest and with the year-round chores.

Besides the harvest, the animals had to be fed and watered. Just maintaining the fences was a massive job. Other chores around the farm included cleaning out the stalls from the cattle and fowl, hauling and spreading the manure, cutting and hauling wood, picking stones, fitting a field for planting, and picking up loads of sawdust for bedding.

Painting and repairing the buildings was a never-ending job. If anyone had a little time, Pops would find some maintenance that needed to be done. And there was always milking cows, cooling the heavy twenty-quart cans in deep water wells, and, of course, delivering the milk to the townspeople. Keeping the farm took many hands but helping always meant a good meal. Often there were twenty people or more at the dinner table, sharing the fruits of their labor. "We had plenty of food. We always had an extra plate or two at the table," Ernest Bolduc recalled. "There were people that came up to me that said they didn't know how they would have made it if it hadn't been for [our] parent's generosity."

On a farm, being able to repair or build whatever is needed is an essential skill. Hector installed equipment, painted and plastered his own bedroom, built a horse stall and feeder, repaired farm machinery, moved a garage, worked on an electrical installation, fixed a stairway, patched a tin roof in a strong wind, and restored water pumps. The farm could not afford to hire out the handyman chores, so everyone learned on the job.

If he wasn't working on the farm, Hector was protecting the livestock and gardens. He would shoot his gun at targets and varmints. He had no love for those animals that stole chickens or ate the vegetables. One woodchuck he hit multiple times but never killed. He nicknamed him "Old Iron Sides" after Hector shot him with an arrow, but Old Iron Sides was able to get into his hole, arrow and all.

Hector had the same work ethic at this age as he did throughout his life. He accomplished more in a day than most people do in three days. He never spoke about the amount of sleep he got but during these times it could not have been that much seeing all the activities in which he was involved.

It was this environment that helped form Hector Bolduc into the man he was. When Hector mentioned that he was a Bolduc, people in Laconia, Gilford or the other small towns knew he was a good and honest person. Everyone agreed that the Bolducs knew how to work.

"We were born to work on that farm," Hector Bolduc's older brother, Ernest, said in an interview in 2022. You might think these circumstances—long days, necessary chores, no vacations from the daily routine—could lead to resentment. But the way that Pop and Ora Bolduc integrated their Catholic faith with the necessary work of farm life kept the spirit of their children grateful and generous.

As in many good Catholic families, Ora was the heart of the home. Ernest related that his mother's love was unconditional. She showed it in the everyday tasks that she performed for the family. Her housework was systematic. According to a PBS special about the Bolduc Family in 2017, each day had its task: Monday was wash day; Tuesday, ironing; Wednesday, mending; Thursday was for mopping floors. She began every day by starting a fire in the family's old 1880 wood burning kitchen oven. She never did get used to the electric range and used the oven for storage.

Ora was a good cook and would make anything the children asked for. She did not have any recipes, just "a pinch here and a pinch there." Often when the children's favorite dish of fried potatoes was served, Pop would complain that there were no boiled potatoes (his favorite dish). Ora would smile and tell him that the children worked just as hard as he did, and they deserved their favorite kind of potatoes too.

Mrs. Bolduc's homemaking went far beyond chores and meals. She prayed for her family unceasingly. She always had a handkerchief in one of her apron pockets and a Rosary in the other. Every spare moment she would be saying her beads. "We were raised by a saint," Ernest recalled. "I never heard my mother swear. She needed to pray for at least one of us at any point in time." When Ken, Bud and Sam all went to serve in World War II—one in Germany, one in the Pacific theater, one in the air force—Aurore promised a Rosary every night to bring them back. They all returned.

Pops was the spiritual head of the family. Like many Laconia and Gilford residents, every week, the family went to Sunday Mass. But in Lent, they traveled every Wednesday to the church to say the Rosary and again on Fridays to pray the Stations of the Cross. Often, they would get stuck on the way to church during this muddy season. Someone would have to go home, get the horse, and pull them out.

Sometimes the children wondered out loud why they had to go to church for these devotions when they could easily have stayed at home and said them in the living room. Pop never gave an answer. When Pop was close to death, Ernest asked him again why they had to go to church during Lent. And his father answered: "I was not a very good Catholic when I was young, and my mother (Ernest's grandmother) died in 1927. I was twenty-six years old, and I still wasn't a good practicing Catholic." On her death bed, she made her son promise that he would bring up his kids Catholic and they would go to church every time they were supposed to. He remarked: "And now you have the answer."

Sugar shack

At the Gilford Sap house 1983 Father and Brother
Anthony(Mark Schaeffer)

An excellent example of Pop's commitment to raising his children in the Catholic faith is found in the maple orchard that still supplies sap to the Bolduc Syrup House.

Pop began making syrup with his own father, Gedeon, in 1917. By purchasing the farm, Gedeon and Charles Bolduc had also inherited the orchard from the original land grant farmers. That family, the Jewetts, had begun tapping maple trees in 1779. In May of 2020, sap was still being harvested from the remaining trees, making the Syrup House the longest continuously-producing maple syrup operation in the entire world.[3]

There were nearly five hundred trees in the syrup operation in the 1950s, some of the maples grew so big that three people together could not get their arms around one. Over the years, the Bolducs have kept records on all their syrup yields. At its peak, the syrup house produced five hundred gallons of syrup.

Before plastic lines replaced the buckets and taps, thousands of gallons of sap had to be harvested from the maple trees bucket by bucket. Hundreds of buckets had to be taken twice a day to the sap house where a wood fire, fed by hand-split pine wood, boiled the water out of the sap to get a fine maple syrup. Trudging through the snow, often on snowshoes, the Bolduc children began helping as soon as they could walk without spilling a pail. Sometimes they used a horse and sleigh to collect the line. It was hard work, but the children could not get home fast enough after school to get the chores done and then get over to the sap house. They loved the process.

Syrup work was important work. Sugar operations usually would finish in early April right around Holy Week. In Gilford and Laconia, school children were given half a day off on Good Friday to honor the Passion of our Lord. At the Bolduc Farm, the children were busy on Good Friday. From noon to 3:00 pm they hauled buckets and boiled sap as usual. But not a word

---

[3] PBS special on the Bolduc family – 2017 (Video 6) - featured many unique families in the United States that had a special story to tell about how life was in the United States. The Bolduc family members that were interviewed were Ernest, Robert, Armand, Anita, granddaughters (Sandy Bolduc Froman, Roberta Tracy).

was spoken during those hours. They meditated and prayed while they worked. Pop led them in this practice, and when the necessary work was done, he brought his family to the church for confessions and Good Friday services.

Pops always stayed true to that deathbed promise to his mother. Even though work on the farm was demanding, God always came first.

Even though Pops worked hard, he still found time to enjoy his family and to bring a good laugh to others. Every night after dinner, he would bring out his violin and the family would sing many songs around the fire. He taught his children the value of taking care of those around them. A smoker for many years, he stopped in a single day. He stood up after smoking, started to cough and then fell on the ground. His sons helped him up. He opened the stove and threw the cigarettes into the fire. That was the end of his smoking.

Once the farm was well established, Pop added an unusual way to earn income for the farm: he convinced several of his friends to invest in racehorses and then would race the horses for them. Wiry and small, Pops had the frame and size of a jockey. Eventually, other family members would travel to race-tracks out of state to see Pops race and sometimes win.

At the Bolduc farm there seemed to be visitors most days— either relatives from Canada, married children stopping in for supper, neighbors, or people just stopping by to see the new colts. In 1953 there were twenty-four guests for New Year's Day dinner. Somehow, Ora always seemed to have prepared enough food. Her cooking kept the family coming back for birthdays, anniversaries or just to help at the farm.

Because of her care, the Bolduc children always made Mother's Day and her birthday special events. One year for her birthday she received "a telephone table, a set of handkerchiefs, a flowerpot, and a catsup dispenser. Family came with kids, and we had so much ice cream." Hector made it a point to pick "May flowers" for his mother every year.

Family life at the Bolduc Farm did not end as the children grew up, got married, and started their own families. Hector's diary notes the love and care the family members had for each other and for the homestead.

In the early 1960's, when a planned highway bypass threatened the maple syrup operation, Pop's boys tried to help him fight the eminent domain case in court. When they lost against the government, Pop's sons stood by him as the highway company clearcut the crest of Boyd Hill and burn his beloved maples. "It was the only time I saw my father cry," Armand Bolduc would comment about that fateful night in August of 1964.

When the hay needed to be harvested, the tractor repaired, the barn shored up, the Bolduc men would be there. They would work their day jobs to support their wives and children, after work they would pick up their kids from school and go do a round of chores. Sunday brunch saw many grandchildren around the kitchen table.

This carried on to later years after Hector Bolduc purchased the farm: Budd, Ernest, Armand, and Sam seemed to be continually working on the crops, animals, machinery, or buildings. Their care did not stop with that property. They took care of "Gramps," Gedeon Bolduc, as well as he grew older. The Bolducs were known for always lending a helping hand to their neighbors. New England Catholics, they truly knew how to take care of each other.

Hector was a Bolduc, through and through. He loved the United States and the government and how it was founded. He loved the farm and the woods and was satisfied by putting in a hard day's work. And like his brothers, Maurice and Ernest, he walked back and forth to the Gilford Public Elementary School, two miles one way and two miles, uphill, back.

In other ways, however, Hector was very different from his brothers. He didn't just love the Constitution. He studied it. He memorized the Declaration of Independence and could recite other founding documents. He spent hours replicating the Declaration in tiny writing on printer paper.

Hector was also the tallest in his family. On the long walks home from school, he would sometimes get in fist fights.

Ernest would take short cuts to avoid the kids who bullied him for smelling like the farm, the same kids who would come for meals at the Bolduc's. But Hector wouldn't dodge through the woods. He'd throw a punch or two and a suggestion that the bullies' families ought to work a little harder for themselves.

Ironically, Hector had a reputation for avoiding chores. With twelve children weeding in a garden or picking rocks from a field, it was easy for one to disappear. Ernest related: "Sometimes our dad would catch him and punish Hector, but the punishment was never severe enough. Pop would ask Hector, 'Where did you go, we were all working and all of a sudden, I look up and you're gone?' Hector said he did not know, and Pop threatened: 'One of these days I'll follow you and figure out where you go.'" Their father once spent the whole afternoon looking for the little devil and when it came time for dinner, there was Hector, expecting to be fed, just like he had worked all day. Hector must have sometimes sneaked away to his secret location in the woods, where he liked to pick flowers for his mother and to read. Once, alone in the woods, he passed out, a problem he never shared with his parents and that he grew out of. But other times, Hector's disappearing act involved actually spying on the rest of the family working. It was a habit he ended only in high school. Pop said, "I didn't know where you were." Hector replied that he knew where his father was and how much time he spent there.

One of the few early pictures "Confirmations" L-R Armand, Anita, Hector

Chapter Two
School Days

Hector never went to a Catholic school but his parents always put the faith first, ahead of chores, eating, sleeping, and recreation.

Elementary school was a great joy for him. The grade school he attended had two grades to a classroom, so Hector could work ahead and do both classes at the same time. Miss Haddock taught third and fourth grades. When she married Mr. Davis, who also taught at Gilford Elementary, Hector joked that Mr. Davis went fishing and caught a haddock. He adored his teachers because they were showing him how to be successful in life. His drive for success perplexed people. He seemed to always be in trouble, not for misbehaving but because the people he met could not believe that a child his age could do all the tasks he took on. They were put off by all his knowledge and skills.[4]

One of Hector's secrets was his memory. He would memorize everything he could, for example, all forty-seven pages of "Evangeline," the poem by Henry Wadsworth Longfellow. He would recite for hours. Hector could memorize easily because he looked for the stories within the texts and he loved the topics he chose. The other key to his wide knowledge was that he tried to experience as much as he could of life firsthand.

Hector's life in high school was typical for a young man of that age living in a rural community. He worked on the farm. He got a job. He attended Laconia Public High School. He did not play sports:

> January 29, 1954: "School. We played Bradley and Bedford. Sure wish I could play."
> January 30, 1954: "Worked in the barn"

---

[4] I only had one interview with Armand since he deferred to Ernest for most of the information. Shortly after the interview over the phone, Armand passed away.

January 31, 1954: "Sunday. Church."

Hector stood over six foot tall in high school, but he was not able to take part in basketball at school: the farm and a job in town kept him too busy. He would attend basketball and football games and comment on what the score was at each game. Nature, family life, hobbies and reading did not leave much time for athletic activities or spending time with friends.

Hector worked nights and weekends at Larry's Market for his last three years of high school, after his farm chores were complete. He found other ways to make extra money too. He raked blueberries at a neighboring farm for seventy-five cents an hour, and picked tomatoes for one dollar an hour. He purchased two pigs with the money he saved, twenty-four dollars, raised them and had them butchered at a cost of five dollars. Then he sold two hundred seventy pounds of meat. He also bought a calf from Pop.

Unlike some of his older brothers, Hector would graduate from high school. In August of 1952, Hector's junior year started, and he said in his journal: "Can't wait for school to start."

From his high school courses Hector learned what he thought was interesting and important. As a result, his report card didn't always reflect his abilities: "Got report cards. English C, sociology C, Agriculture B." He recognized that he was capable of much higher marks: "Should have done much better in English."

The only class that Hector mentioned in his journal is the Future Farmers of America (FFA) class. Some of the local activities of the FFA were planting thousands of trees, attending educational meetings, and taking trips to see local crops. Press clipping[5] also noted that for the vocational agricultural team of Labonte, Hector Bolduc topped the first division of the tree planting contest at the Forestry Field Day. Another local FFA activity was a dance: "I went to the FFA dance at the recreation area. I did not dance. I sold tickets."

---

[5] *Laconia Citizen* 1/1/1953 Vo-ags champs in tree planting (source 76)

Twice Hector was selected as one of five students to travel by train to the yearly FFA conference in Kansas City. As a sign of the changing times, while attending the State convention he noted: "I met Barbara Booth, the first girl that I know of that is in the FFA." During this trip to Kansas, Hector, as he would throughout his life, visited local historical sites and important persons. On this trip, Hector went to President Truman's home, unannounced, and introduced himself to the retired President.[6]

This sudden excursion was consistent with Hector's interest in politics. Even at a young age, Hector paid attention to what was happening in the world, especially in the political arena. He really despised communism as seen by this diary entry from March 5, 1953: "Joseph Stalin died—Thank God. The world has long awaited this wonderful moment." When King George VII died in England and Queen Elizabeth was crowned, he not only thought she was going to die soon but also that her being Queen was bad for Scotland.

During Hector's high school years, the Korean conflict was happening and there were truce talks. It is apparent from his diary entry that he did not put much faith in the talks: "The truce is finally signed. It is almost unbelievable. After all these years of that useless truce talk." Hector would carry this interest in politics and governmental systems for his entire life.

Another life-long interest that began in his teenaged years was collecting. Hector began by collecting old newspapers, some of which dated back before the War for Independence. He would view travelling historical collections—"Went to Laconia to see the shawl that Lincoln was wearing when he was assassinated"— and would always try to barter or outright buy artifacts that weren't even for sale. "Buying rings from a friend for three dollars; sold a loon feather; got a 1900 Indian head penny; bought two Indian head pennies from Trader Butterfield."

He collected anything and everything. Family members helped his love of artifacts:

---

[6] See note from Ernest Bolduc on 8-20-2021, Independence, Missouri

March 3, 1953: "Pop got an ambulance that was drawn with horses—I wanted it for my antique collection."

April 4, 1953: "Sam came up and brought me a load of antiques. Boy, were they ever nice. He got them from a friend."

Hector called his collection his "treasures," but it wasn't the value of the items that primarily attracted him to collecting. Hector admired antiquity and loved to be able to touch the physical remainders of history. He was also aware that history is made in the present. This was evident in his soliciting the autographs of famous living people. He would mail a request with a return envelope and ask for a note and then a signature from them.

March 27, 1953: "Received a letter from Mr. and Mrs. Dwight D Eisenhower today."

January 16, 1954: "Received a letter with the autograph of Herbert Hoover."

In May of 1954, Ernest commented on the plane crash that Ernest Hemmingway survived. Hector noted: "Was more than glad to hear that Ernest Hemmingway and his wife were safe and sound. He is truly a great writer. I must get his autograph."

Whatever Hector couldn't experience or see firsthand, he read. He loved to read. In his diary, he would make a note, on a rare empty day, that he read all day up in his room. His diaries mention listening to rain, especially on a tin roof. It was a special treat to read a couple of books with rain tapping on the roof. He also read newspapers and old documents in the farm attic:

February 2, 1952: "I have been shooting my bb gun ever since I got it. Went up in the attic to read some of the Jewett's old diaries. I found an old round trunk up there."

February 6, 1954: "Chopped wood. Worked in the barn. Pop bought a wonderful typewriter. I always wanted to learn how to use one."

Hector used this addition of a typewriter to the Bolduc farm to aid in his research and writing. His first typed paper was the last paper he wrote as a high school senior. May 28, 1954: "Finished my paper—it is thirty pages long." It was a theme on the history of famous gems. None of his high school papers would survive, but Hector's interest in gems would remain, especially how diamonds, rubies, sapphires and emeralds connected the history of ancient dynasties to the majesty of the Church.

Somehow, between all these extra activities, Hector still found time for entertainment around the farm and in town. As a young high school boy, he cut down small saplings and built a stockade with multiple cabins, wagons, and animals. He learned magic tricks and practiced them with his family and neighbors as his audience. He used his carpentry skills to build props. In the rural community of Gilford, the local carnivals were a must-attend event. At one carnival, he won two big lamps and two stuffed dogs.

Hector's family had a new television set in 1952, but he often went to the movie theaters in Gilford and Laconia. Hector did not just attend movies; he wrote reviews in his diary. The movies were of many different genres: "Red Badge of Courage," "Last of the Mohicans," "The Miracle of the Lady of Fatima," "Pony Rider." He would record comments such as: "One of the best movies I have ever attended" or "Not worth seeing." He also attended any play he could find in the area.

Hector never simply consumed entertainment as a distraction from work. He always offered an opinion, either in conversation or in his diary.

May 15, 1953: "Went down to a neighbor and watched the Wolcott–Marcinia fight on TV, I never saw such a fixed fight. It is a disgrace to the world of boxers."

January 14, 1954: "Went to a play at H.S called 'I remember Mama.' It was truly one of the finest plays I have ever seen."

Most of Hector's entertainment and relaxation was found on or around the Bolduc farm itself, however. In spring, family members would make their kites and find a good wind in an empty field. April 18, 1953: "I gave my red one [kite] to Lauretta. It went the highest. Anita's broke loose and got stuck in a tree."

Kites weren't the only thing Hector launched into the skies of New Hampshire. According to Ernest, during the 1950's, Hector made a rocket and shot it one night on top of Boyd hill next to where Immaculate Conception Chapel is today. The rocket was six feet tall and about 10 inches in diameter.[7] Many saw this fiery flame in the sky and officials were never able to find out what it was. It shot up in the sky about one hundred seventy-five feet per the officials.

In summer, Hector would go fishing at one of the local lakes. On one trip with his older brother Budd, they caught fifty-four perch. On other trips, the catch included pickerel (walleye), bass, and the unwanted sunfish. Hector would also go off swimming and boating during some of the really hot spells especially after working on the farm. He would often comment on the glory of God's nature and in the case of swimming: "the water was sure beautiful."

During the winter, he would go skiing, skating, and walking. He often recorded these walks and enjoyed these activities at night with a full moon and a light snowfall.

> December 16, 1953: "Was very nice on the pond with the moon and stars and me there all alone."
>
> August 20, 1952: "Saw my first pure white deer—a 4-point buck. First ever."
>
> March 31, 1955: "Saw a robin today."
>
> May 10, 1956: "Picked a large four-leaf May flower from my secret patch."

With the distances from farm to farm and his other time demands, Hector was not able to spend much time with friends. At fifteen years old, he writes in a nostalgic way about friendship:

December 19, 1952: "School. Went to a basketball game. I saw Larry Brown. I hadn't seen him for two years. He is one of my best friends. I will never forget him."

As for girls, Hector associated with them in school or at a dance, but he never seemed to date. "Had dancing in the gym today. I danced with Mary Jane Haddock. She is a very nice

---

[7] See Letter from Ernest – source 88

girl." "I played an April Fool's joke on Lorraine Bourgault. Was she ever mad." He made this entry about girls in 1952: "When I grow up, I want to be a bachelor. I have gone out with only one girl in my life and that was when I took Pat Abbott to the seventh-grade reception at Laconia High in 1948."

He cherished friendships and never took them for granted even at a young age. His diary includes remembrances of two friends he lost in two separate accidents.

December 8, 1953: "School. It is three years ago today that my very good friend Henry Newton Corriveau was shot and killed. I was shocked to hear of the death of my very good friend Walter Cutler Garaner III who was killed playing Russian roulette. He was close to me."

Learning about the uncertain nature of life through these losses made high school graduation especially poignant.

> June 11, 1954: "Last day of school. Class day today. A very sad affair. Class pictures."

> June 12, 1954: "Lots of work on the farm. Went to the banquet and the Senior prom. Had a wonderful time. I'll never forget the beauty of it all."

> June 14, 1954: "Tonight I graduated. It was such a sad affair. I cried throughout the entire affair. They were all wonderful kids. Just can't wait for 1964 and the tenth-year reunion."

Hector received a tie clasp and cuff links as his graduation gift. Seven days later, he turned eighteen. The next phase of his journey towards the priesthood began.

Chapter Three
Transitioning to a Career (1954-1959)

By the time Hector graduated, four of his brothers had served in two major twentieth century conflicts: World War II and the Korean War. Initially, his own aspirations lay beyond the military. On February 10, 1954, he wrote: "Saw Mr. Casewell today about attending University of New Hampshire. Sure hope I can go. Have planned it for a long time."

A Bolduc tradition of military service had already become important to his family, however. A few months later, Hector writes: "Pop and Mom want me to join—instead of being drafted. I will have to join the Army or National Guard. I would rather go into the Army and be killed the first day than join the National Guard. If I'm forced to join the Guard, I will be nothing but a coward."[8] What caused this contempt for the National Guard is unclear, as Hector's respect for the United States, at home and abroad, was unfailing.

Youthful points of view aside, Hector began to develop the skills that would set him apart in the Army. He practiced shooting the guns he bought. He went deer hunting though he never took any quarry. He once caught two live raccoons while hunting but planned to let them go. Hector didn't enjoy taking life unless the animals were undermining buildings, eating poultry, or causing havoc in the garden.

Hector also seemed to prefer archery to firearms. He became proficient enough to join a Laconia club where he volunteered to maintain the archery field course.[9] He invested fifteen dollars and eighty cents in a new fiber bow, which was equal to one hundred fifty dollars in twenty-first century currency.[10] The Laconia club competed with other clubs and

---

[8] See 6/7/1954 diary
[9] 9/5/1954 diary
[10] 10/10/1954 diary

Hector often ranked first in tournaments. He participated in this club until he left for the Army.

In the last days of 1954, Hector filled out his Draft Question-naire. He would wait nearly four years—ironically the length of bachelors' degree—for the military to call his number. He spent those years working in town, farming with his father, studying and preserving history, enjoying his hobbies and building his antique collection

Now beyond high school, with more time to work, and a bit more money to spend, Hector continued to expand his "collection" of treasures. He reached out for items he thought valuable. On April 18, 1955, he noted: Albert Einstein, whose autograph I have been trying to get for four years, three months and twenty days died today. I wrote him one hundred six-ty-three letters, which he never answered. Nearly twenty years later a friend would secure this for his collection. On January 20, 1973, we see that he was eventually successful in his quest: "John S. was there while I was gone and left me the autograph of Albert Einstein which I shall treasure forever."

Hector's name would become better known through various dealers nationwide: they would call him when they had an item they thought might interest him. However, he mostly collected from people who were local and who knew his love of history and artifacts. He wrote on November 11, 1955: I bought a one hundred seventy piece coin collection from Gerard for ten dollars and twenty cents. The coins were mostly flying eagles cents, large cents and two-cent piece.

Hector also saw the value other collectors overlooked. He attended auctions and went to antique shops. He purchased old books, housewares, jewelry, guns, and diamonds.

Due to a love of all history, Hector continued his atten-dance at the Thompson P. Ames Historical Society meetings. The meetings had speakers on subjects ranging from firsthand accounts of European travel to discussions on local Gilford history. Historical Society dues were two dollars in 1955 and each member was requested to bring a twenty-five cent gift to the annual Christmas party. As part of his historical work,

Hector brought a replica of the Declaration of Independence for display at the Independence Bank at Lakeport, New Hampshire.

Hector also collected things that could not be paid for. Somewhere in the hills surrounding the Bolduc Farm, he'd found gold. He panned for it in the early spring when the water levels washed the gold from a secret source. He wrote on March 21, 1957: "Found some gold in a stream. It was real." Hector immediately went to a jeweler and verified its authenticity.[11] A day later he wrote: "Panned for more gold today—got about 1 ½ ounces." March 26, 1957: "Now have 2.25 ounces." In 1957, that much gold was worth about $80.00, which, adjusted for inflation, would equal over $800 half a century later.

Hector was close with his family and trusted his brother, Ernest, with keeping his "treasures" safe, but Hector never revealed the location of the stream with the gold or of the secret caves he'd found in childhood. The place in the woods, where he'd fainted alone, was also never found. Although Hector's health improved, with the lessening of those spells, the hard work and lack of sleep made him susceptible to colds and flus. The year he graduated high school, he had a nine-day hospital stay with pneumonia and was sick enough to sign up for medical insurance as a young man. In 1957, he was ill every month from September through November. His diary leaves no hint as to how he spent his time sick in bed. One can guess he was catching up on years of sleep deficit. Most likely he caught up on dreams as well. He was still writing poetry and the diary has some of those poems. On his twenty-first birthday, Hector wrote a poem and then reflected:

"Dreams, I yearn for thee. And yet I never see thee come or go. You pass like some sweet touch of magic breeze and stop an instant here and there and then move on to leave me when I woke still wondering, little dream from where didst though come? where hast thou gone? will you return? Signed Hector Bolduc, June 21, 1957."

---

[11] Interview with Ernest Bolduc – source 76

It seems that friendship with people Hector's own age would mirror his dreams, coming and going. A week after his birthday, Hector wrote: "Went to a wedding—Roberta Beaudoin and Ralph Corriveau. Ralph is a very close friend of mine." Ralph was the older brother of Henry Corriveau, Hector's childhood friend, who had died so suddenly at age thirteen.

His mother remained his rock through this time of waiting to serve. Her birthdays, her vacations, her weeks of preserving, her rare hospital visits all making it into the daily charting of Hector's diaries.

It was during this time that Hector began making friends with older ladies, a tradition that would be lifelong.

> June 2, 1957: Mrs. Keating died today. She was seventy-two. One of my best friends and one of the finest women I have ever known.
>
> June 6, 1957: Visited Mrs. Galusha.

He enjoyed talking to these ladies, learning about the local history they knew. He valued the stories they told and liked to cheer up their lonely hours. Often, he did odd jobs and made sure their homes were well-maintained.

The farm work was always present and time consuming. Hector worked with Pop and his brothers that still lived at home and even some of the brothers that were married would help out in the busy season. The seasonal work was especially heavy in summer.

The syrup producing time in early spring required long hours. When the five hundred plus gallons of syrup were finally in the jars, the family had to clean the buckets that had been used for gathering the sap from the trees, storing them for yet another year:

> April 21, 1956: Washed 333 buckets.
>
> April 25, 1956: 582 total buckets.[12]

Like any other child raised on a farm, Hector had been driving the farm trucks on the property and to the mill since he

---

[12] 4/25/1956 diary

was around twelve years old. A license might seem superfluous, but it was necessary. When Hector was over twenty years old,[13] he took one driving lesson and passed the test.

Hector continued to work at Larry's Market, cutting meat, usually working after sunset to maximize his usefulness on the farm. The managers took time to teach Hector proper meat cutting technique. This was noted on his skill inventory when joining the Army. Hector also learned general contractor skills during these pre-Army years: he helped his brothers Budd and Sam, who were in the construction business, with their projects.[14] He learned project management, cost estimating, carpentry, plumbing, cement, and electrical work—skills which would later serve him well.

Despite their busy days, the Bolduc brothers were always active in local politics. His brother Armand was on the Laconia Council for over thirty years and served as Laconia mayor from 1984 to 1985. Family members went to town meetings to voice their opinions on zoning, school improvement, and election issues. Hector also was on a public safety committee that met periodically.

During the 1956 election, Hector was a strong Democrat, as can be seen by this entry on Election Day: "I certainly hope that the Democrats win the larger majority in the senate and the house." And this entry two years later, "Stevenson (a Democrat) is our candidate. He will be our next president." After the election, he had a broken heart symbol with the statement "Eisenhower is again president." As the Democratic party swung further and further left, Hector would move to the Republican party.

Hector continued to attend Mass and receive the sacraments regularly. His diaries reflect more than the casual commitment to faith: Hector prayed the Rosary in public with his family. During the 1956 hunting season, he attended a three-day evening mission at Our Lady of the Lakes. In the monotony of pulling nails, spreading fertilizer, hauling wood, and picking

---

[13] 10/29/1956 diary
[14] 9/12/1954, 10/19/1955, 7/7/1958 diaries

rocks, where other young men with a mind like Hector's might have begun questioning the place of faith in daily life, Hector's diary shows that he became more focused on his Catholicism:

> March 29, 1958: "Pray for the souls of the world that have been engulfed in sin. Russia will be converted—Our Lady of Fatima."
>
> August 22, 1958: "Sawed a load of boiler wood and a load of stove wood. 'Blessed be thy Holy Name.'"
>
> October 8-9, 1958: "Pope Pius XII has suffered more strokes. Hauled manure. The Pope is very ill. We must pray."

One entry that Hector did not note in his diaries, but might have if he'd known, was that on March 28, 1958, Elvis Presley joined the US Army. Elvis was *the* important "artistic" happening of this time period. Elvis was the "King of Rock and Roll" and was taking the country by storm.

Hector loved the arts. He watched operas on TV. He listened to classical music on the radio. He purchased a record player and spent Sunday afternoons listening to vinyl and playing cards. When he could, Hector traveled to listen to the Baltimore symphony orchestra perform and then journaled about it. Hector knew Elvis was a threat, so he started a national "I Love Ludwig" club: an association aimed at keeping people attuned to real music. He wrote on December 17, 1958: "Today is Ludwig van Beethoven's birthday."

Hector would continue his efforts at preserving classical music during his time in the Army. Hector would also take one last homegrown skill to the Army, and unexpected one at that: ballet.

Hector loved dancing and had participated in ballroom dance throughout his high school years. He saw no conflict between working all day and taking a dance lesson at night. At the age of twenty he writes:

> December 26, 1956: "Attended a meeting of the Belknap Bowmen [archery]. I was chosen chair of the Dance Committee."

And exactly a year after his first dance lesson: "I took my first ballet lesson tonight—it's wonderful." Hector invited his sisters to his dancing lessons and drew ballet dancers in the margins of his diaries.[15] Even while in military service, the juxtaposition of life and dance continued: December 28/30, 1958: "I was informed today that I will leave for Hanau tomorrow. Rehearsed for a Ballet. Borrowed S's tights. Spent most of the day typing out forms and information for my Top Secret Clearance." A military journalist eventually embellished Hector's dance lessons into an entire career in an article in an Army publication called *The Spearhead*:[16]

> Hector started studying ballet at the age of seven in his hometown of Laconia. From the time he graduated from high school in 1954, he decided it was time to turn professional. So, he headed for New York and joined the famed Metropolitan group. Hector danced with the Met until he joined the army in February. Seven months of the year, he traveled around the nation with the Met's touring company. The remainder of the year was devoted to more study in dancing, music, and languages. Through his association with the Met, Hector Bolduc personally met several of the greats in the world of opera including Maria Callas.

While Hector *did* dance until he "joined the army in February," there was never a week where he was not tapping maple trees or repairing a barn or attending his local parish church. The article [in *The Spearhead*] is an excellent example of journalistic exaggeration, but Ernest Bolduc confirms that dance was important to Hector. It may have been an unlikely hobby for a future priest, but there is still a suitcase full of dance tights and shoes somewhere in the Bolduc Farm collection.

---

[15] 2/27/1958 diary
[16] *Spearhead* 10/16/1959 page 4.(Source 48)

Father Bolduc and Elvis

Chapter Four
Army (1959-1961)

Hector filled out his draft questionnaire in the last days of 1954 and was directed to take his Army physical at Manchester, New Hampshire, on April 24,1958. On January 22, 1959, he went to Manchester again to take the ACB [Army Classification Battery] test and "passed with flying colors." He left for the Army on February 6, 1959, and arrived at Fort Dix in New Jersey for basic training.

Typical activities at the start were PT [physical training], marches, crawling under barbed wire, inspections, infiltration techniques, typing in the Commanding Officer's building, and classes on "why [they] should adapt to the military." More enjoyable activities included movies every other day and antiquing with off-base passes. Hector was assigned to be a squad leader and drilled with the honor guard. By March, Hector developed a lung infection which put him in the hospital for a week, which he found dull. On March 28,1959, during his stay at the hospital, he wrote: "Wrote a lot of letters. Gloria Jean Wright is our night nurse. Miss Florence Nightingale of B-24."

At the front of the 1959 diary, Hector had some observations on the army: "The army is like a big game of chess. Each piece is important and does his part. The Queen is like the General— the most powerful piece. The King is the Government, the pentagon—when it is lost, the game is lost. The knights and the bishop are the officers. They have power but are limited in their authority to use it. They can move only in certain areas. They are restricted to certain avenues. The pawns are soldiers. Each piece occupies a certain strategic position. Sometimes he may do no more than fill a vacant place. However, if he were not there, the position would be of great importance as it would be vulnerable to the enemy and if toppled, would afford a strong foothold to the enemy therefore threatening the safety of the entire board. The men (pawns) are shifted about to the taste of the officers who in turn are responsible to their superiors. Each piece contributes its little bit to the game, each in his own capacity, regardless of how important, is equally responsible for the eventual outcome of the game."

He was made a private in four months.

After two months at Fort Dix, Hector was transferred to Fort Chaffee in Fort Smith, Arkansas. He had a two week visit home: "At last I have mom's cooking. Boy, I will certainly eat now that I am home. Food at Dix was particularly good indeed, but Mom is still the World's best cook."

On April 1, 1959, Hector reported to Fort Chaffee. Activities involved learning how to use the 105 Howitzer (artillery used heavily during the Second World War), machine guns, and the M1 rifle, dubbed by Patton as "the greatest battle implement ever devised." The recruits also went on extended field exercises, also called bivouacs. In the middle of June, Hector made this note: "Left for Bivouac. Spent the day killing ticks."

At twenty-two years old, Hector was probably one of the older men at Fort Chaffee. Ever the prankster, he had a lot of fun with the other young trainees, reminiscent of college dorm mischief he'd never had:

"Water fighting and boxing match."

"Locked McClendon in a locker and got caught."

"We had a ball in the barracks—shaving cream fight, pillow and towel fights."

"I retained my title as towel champ after defeating Hendericks."

The camaraderie of the young men was interrupted by politics and segregation. Hector marked note of it: "Went to Fort Smith—the city—with Louis and Ely. We had quite a time. Charlie Lewis couldn't enter any eating places or theaters because he was colored."

Hector was given security clearance which would be needed with his future assignments. His next assignment was guided missile training in Fort Sill, Oklahoma.

On July 8, 1959, Hector received his assignment to Friedberg, Germany. He had one week to see some movies, go antiquing, and to mail boxes of treasures home. He sat through a week of classes on "indoctrination overseas and defense against every propaganda" and a seminar on "Going to a foreign country."

Then, halfway through July, Hector noted: "Left for the USS H.W. Butner. Arrived Pier 4 NY harbor. I have a bunk near the ceiling. Ship is opposite the Statue of Liberty and Empire State building. On July 16, 1959, just past two pm, the whistle [on the boat] blew a shrill long moan, and we began to edge out of the pier. The flag rose above us and the band on shore struck up 'Gonna take a sentimental journey.' Everyone let out a loud yell. Near the water, the Statue of Liberty stood out like a green Greek goddess."

The most beautiful part of the trip was the evening prayer. Hector described this: "As the chaplain's voice came over the box, the whole ship fell quiet—so still, you could hear the waves slap against the hull. Slowly the ship rolled back and forth under the stars and every head would bend in prayer. With the word 'amen,' the ship popped back to life as if someone had awakened from a dream."

The 108 Company A 2nd Howitzer division would spend ten uneventful days at sea. On the ship, Hector's responsibility was "directing traffic to the mess hall."

On July 24, 1959, Hector wrote: "We pulled into Bremerhaven [Germany] harbor in the early afternoon. Long before we got there, we could make out the church steeples against the sky. Quaint pink roofed buildings dotted the landscape and people were swimming at beaches along the shore. The 61st army band was on hand to greet us as we docked, many people came to watch. They waved and wished us a pleasant stay. The men are strikingly tall, strong, and handsome. Most of them were wearing shorts. The Germans from what I saw of them seem like a beautiful people."

There had been talk on the voyage over about Elvis Presley being at Friedberg. Hector had assumed The King of Rock and

Roll would be the archenemy of any lover of classical music, especially a person like Hector who was instrumental in founding the "I Love Ludwig" Beethoven clubs. But soon, Hector and Elvis were together talking about classical music and rumor has it that he taught Elvis how to sing the "Ave Maria." Elvis bunked next door to where Hector stayed. Later, Elvis moved off base and Hector would visit him at his house.

When Elvis died in 1977 at the age of forty-two, Hector, then a priest and forty-one years old himself, was interviewed about Elvis:[17] "Father Bolduc recalls that he was a roommate of Elvis's for six months while both were stationed in Germany with the U.S. Army. The two were assigned to the Ray Barracks in Freidburg. Father Bolduc was assigned to the 27th artillery and Elvis to the 37th tanker unit of the 3rdArmored division 32nd Armor. He (Elvis) was very personable, Father Bolduc said. He also said Elvis was an extremely fine person. Father was invited to Elvis's wedding but was unable to attend. Father later spent a day with Elvis and his wife at Graceland in Tennessee. The two men exchanged cards and letters about twice a year. Father recalled that Elvis was a man of deep feeling, noting that Elvis had eventually moved off base. There are several pictures of the two of them together. Father pointed out that they both became sergeants, but Father was first to be promoted. Father Bolduc remembered the generous donation made by Elvis to the 'I like Ludwig Club.' Despite Elvis's rock and roll tastes, he still was considerate of the sentiments of others."

Hector practiced with the Honor Guard and had frequent parades and inspections. The soldiers also prepared for armed conflict in army "games." There was daily practice with various weapons such as the 105 Howitzer, 30 cal. machine gun, battle tanks, grenade throwing. and 30-mile marches. After being readied for conflict, his main job was the office clerical functions of typing, filing, preparing for inspections, and administering the calendar of events. He was also responsible for vehicle maintenance. His monthly pay was seventy-seven dollars. On the first of September, he took a driver's license test and

[17] *The Laconia Evening Citizen* August 17, 1977 (Source 100)

was one of two that passed. He also went to his first German language class.

On December 29,1959, he left for Hanau, Germany for his new assignment. One of the first activities was a war games enactment in the field for two weeks where two armies simulated attacks on each other. Some soldiers were shot and killed, some were gassed, some generals were assassinated as a practice for the possible real conflict. He was now classified as a clerk for post operations. That was not his only job, as he performed guard duty with the other men in the unit.

On February 6, 1960, there was a diary note: "All my detail notes on Operation Winter Shield can be found in my green booklet (read this as a journal) #4."

I cannot imagine how many different private journals Hector had and wonder where they are now. I have had a chance to read what I believe is journal #5 which covers 1960 and 1961. Some of the material is very private and personal but other information gives an interesting look at Hector's army life.

His journal entry of March 24, 1960, relates his attitude upon entry into the Army around February, 1959: "I realized right away after talking to some of the men that I am going to have to take a very positive attitude toward the Army, even though it will be in direct defiance to my fellow servicemen and contrary to the opinions of most—otherwise I will lose all respect for myself and those things upon which I have always placed so much importance."

He continues on April 27, 1960, in discussion with a man named Tony: "A man is not just a member of the male sex that walks around with bulging muscles. That is just a distinction at birth. Babies are born, men are made. A man is judged by his ability to adapt himself to the situation which surrounds him and the manner in which he confronts and solves these situations. His intelligence is not how much he gets on his CT test nor how much he got on his last report card. No, his intelligence is how well he puts to use those things he has learned. Who would you respect more—a man with a dozen college degrees and unlimited expanse of knowledge, who wasted his life away, or a simple humble man who used all his ability (although limited) to further himself and succeed in raising himself just a little bit in life?"

I found the following journal entry very predictive of how Hector handled challenges in his life—he took them head on and usually succeeded. On July 24, 1960, Hector wrote:

"Well, it finally happened. For weeks now, the men of the Battery have been planning to take action to correct some of the injustices [committed by an abusive sergeant] in the battery. For weeks, we collected information such as D-F's (Disposition forms) and statements and made them into a booklet. We drafted a letter putting forth our feelings and circulated it among the battery. It was signed by eighty-three of the men (75%) and we submitted it to the I.G. (Inspector General). […] If I do say so myself, it was a masterpiece. A great deal of work went into it. Every item on page five was checked by me against the Court Martial Manuals to be sure we were not endangering ourselves in any way. [...] It was a major moral victory for me." (Hector goes on to describe the process where he was interviewed for 2 hours as the spokesman for the battery and the outcome was good.) (Further down) "All references to this matter, including photographs, extra copies of the letters, DF's, etc., may be found in my file reference, envelope #66. It is presently being kept in <u>safe keeping</u>."

His diary entry on August 25, 1960, it has two words—"Court Martial." I asked the Armed Services to send Hector's service record and was surprised to see that his rankings for conduct and efficiency were almost perfectly "excellent" except on July 21, 1960, when Hector had his only "good" ranking in conduct. This could be a result of the Court Martial on August 26, 1960, for stealing a bowl and a knife set valued at twelve dollars and ninety cents from the PX in Germany. He pleaded not guilty. There was some disagreement to the wording of the charge, but when it was reworded to his satisfaction, he pled guilty. His sentence was that he had to pay fifty dollars and be restricted to base for fifteen days.

I asked his brother, Ernest, what this was all about.[18] Ernest said, "Every now and then, he did something foolish like this and I once asked him why and his answer was to prove the court actions were not always fair. He explained people murder and get life with no parole, and a few years go by and they are paroled and out again. Doing small things like he did in Germany have a bigger penalty than a murder. I told him that I had to agree, however, let someone else prove that to be true, and his answer was that he lived it and it was not hearsay. Later in life he pointed out O.J. Simpson as an example of this unfair legal treatment."

Hector had a great love for humor of all kinds and had a friendly, enjoyable laugh. This journal entry on October 30, 1960, is typical of his practical jokes on others: "I must say that I never had so much fun as I had with the game with Smith. He had been drinking and I did not hesitate in taking advantage of the situation. Smith is a fairly good pool player while I am very poor having only played a few games before. To beat him, I knew that I would certainly have to play contrary to the rules. As fast as Smith would make a ball, I would take it out and place it on the table. As a result, he sometimes sank the same ball three or four times. In the last game, he only had one ball left. I had all mine in and was trying for the 8 ball. Just as he sank his last ball, I placed the #2 ball on the outer edge of the table. He saw it, scratched his head shrugged his shoulders and played it. I scratched on my next shot, and he won, not knowing that he had made three times as many balls as I had."

In his job as company clerk, Hector was responsible for organizing many of the activities such as inspections, marches, war games, and meetings: "Four generals and a dozen colonels were here today for a visit. The inspector general was here to investigate letters written by the whole battery. The main ob-

---

[18] Ernest's transmittal letter dated 2/28/2018 (source 115)

jective of the troops in Germany is to try to stop the Russians from coming through the Fulda Gap if war comes."[19]

One of Hector's greatest achievements in Germany took place during the last 3rd Armored Division Marksmanship competition when he twice won first place for his unit in four events: rifle, pistol, carbine, and machine gun divisions. He is the only Army person known to have ever captured top honors in all four events.[20]

During his stay in Europe, Hector visited France, Spain, Morocco, North Africa, Berlin, Greece, India, and Turkey. His knowledge of languages was a big help during his tour. He spoke German, French, and Flemish fluently and could work with Italian and Spanish.[21]

For a concert for German—American relations week, Hector served at the entrance door as a translator.[22] He also shared his knowledge of rare gems by giving a talk on diamonds at the Officer Club.[23] In the Army newsletter, The Spearhead, it is stated:[24] "The real 'gem' of his handcraft collections is his jewel collection. In it are represented some of the world's most precious stones—all, sad to relate, imitation."

Hector's interest in gems began in his hometown of Laconia, New Hampshire. With the price of gems what it was, he quickly decided that collecting the original was out of the question. So, resorting to the next best thing, he contacted a gem cutter and placed an order for replicas made of forged crystal or quartz. Each replica conformed in dimension, weight and color to the original gem. Since about two hundred fifty hours were required to cut, grind, and polish each stone, Hector's collection was years in the making. He lectured before several clubs on the subject and traveled thousands of miles to view famous collections. After his arrival in Europe, one leave was spent in Bombay viewing the collection of the Giawar of

---

[19] 7/22/1960 diary
[20] *The Laconia Evening Citizen* 6/3/1961 (Source 41)
[21] *The Laconia Evening Citizen* 6/3/1961 (Source 41)
[22] 5/23/1960 diary
[23] 4/25/1960 diary
[24] *Spearhead* Vol. 7 #4 January 27, 1961 (source 42)

Baroda. The collection took eight hours to view since it is so vast. Another leave was spent in Rome where he viewed the Papal gem collection in the Vatican."

Hector was chairman of the orphans committee, which he founded soon after arriving in Friedberg.[25] He would often visit the children in the local orphanage. A close friend of Hector's was Domenick Lazzaro. Domenick remembered Hector's work with the orphanage: "Over the years, Hector and I were in the same unit (47th artillery) and were in the same barracks. Hector did a lot of charitable activities for the orphanage, for instance, after a fire in the orphanage." Later in his stay in Germany, he organized the unit to build a swimming pool for the orphanage.

On March 4, 1961, Hector and a friend set out on a thirteen-hour train ride to Konnesreuth, Germany to see the stigmatist Theresa Neuman. He had received a letter of recommendation from Father Curran. Unfortunately, they could not see Theresa at that time, as she was in agony.

On April 3, 1961, he returned to see her, and described his visit as "one of the most awesome things I have ever seen." Hector wrote an article about Theresa Neuman for his "book."

On July 11, 1961, Hector, with three friends, visited Theresa again: "I took her hands in mine and touched the scabs on the hands. I examined them very closely. I asked her to remember us in her prayers and she said she would pray for us all.[see paragraph below.] She gave me a card for my mother that she had signed."

In January of 2020, Ernest Bolduc sent me the actual journal referenced in the previous paragraph. It was my first look at a journal and what was in it. It appears to be journal #5 having entries for the years 1960 and 1961. To give you an example of the detail in the journal versus the diary, here are journal entries for his visits to Theresa Neumann:

For the visit on April 3, 1961:

"On Good Friday, March 31, 1961, I went to Konnesreuth, Germany to visit the famous Theresa Neumann.

---

[25] *The Laconia Evening Citizen* 6/3/1961 (source 41)

[Hector had arranged to use an army truck and took seventeen men with him, including Domenick Lazzaro.] There was already a large crowd gathered about her home when we arrived. I went to the little Gasthaus where we had stayed when visiting the month before, and looked up a man who is married to Theresa Neumann's niece."

"After the services, we returned to the little cottage directly across from the church and joined the long line of people who were waiting to see the "Miracle of Konnesreuth." Soon the entire square was filled with people. Many had umbrellas as it was raining quite hard, but we had none, so we just stood there getting soaked. I did not mind at all as I had been looking forward to seeing her for so long. About half an hour later, a small window on the second floor opened and Hector Naber, the village priest who is ninety-one years old, addressed the crowd and gave a summary of Theresa Neumann and informed us on how the viewing was to be conducted. Shortly afterwards, the door to the cottage opened and nuns could enter. A steady stream followed from the right of the door and up the narrow staircase. As we were going up the staircase, we met several ladies coming down who were crying. As I entered the room, the first thing I saw was Father Naber seated on a chair at some distance from the bed. In the far corner of the room, near a window, stood a large bed covered with white sheets and on it, Theresa Neumann sat slightly hunched over. It was quite a sight to behold. She wore a white shawl over her head, and it was stained with large spots of blood where the wounds from the thorns were bleeding. Blood was seeping through the white smock that she wore on her shoulders and arms. Her hands were outstretched, and I could clearly see the holes in them. Large clots of blood formed around the wounds and blood dripped freely from them onto the white bed spread. Two large rivers of blood about 2 inches wide ran from her eyes down to her chin and down the sides of her neck. Blood dripped from her chin to the bed. Her eyes appeared to be closed. Her lips were moving slightly, and she seemed to be murmuring exceptionally low. Her face was twisted in agony, and she seemed to be in great pain. We were there only a few minutes but in those short minutes, I have never been so close to God. I shall never forget that experience as long as I live. There is no question in my mind that her stigmatism is genuine. I am sure that someday the name of Theresa Neumann will rank among the saints in the Holy Catholic Church."

The journal entries for the next visit started on July 7, 1961:

"We arrived on Sunday and went to church and then found out that visiting could not occur on Sunday, so we enjoyed a delicious dinner at a small inn (Gasthaus) overlooking the square where is located the church and house of Theresa Neumann. While enjoying our meal, we noticed two gentlemen, one a priest, who were eating at the table next to ours. They spoke French and not having spoken French for quite some time, I thought it would be nice to converse with them. At the same time, I might be able to find out something about Theresa Neumann, as I have made it a practice of speaking to everyone who might know something about her. Ironically enough, one of the gentlemen turned out to be a Monsieur Ennemond Boniface, who is considered the greatest living authority on Theresa Neumann and has authored several books on her which are considered par excellent. We talked on and on and I learned a great deal on Theresa Neumann.

"Mr. Boniface volunteered to send a copy of his book (a French translation) to my mother. Before leaving, he took several photographs of us standing before the Church at Konnesreuth. Not being able to visit Theresa Neuman, I decided to show the town and the famous church, the Kapella, which is located only a kilometer from the Czech border, to Jimmy and Lorenzo. We thought it best to leave the truck behind and walk to the church. We hiked through the back woods and fields. We finally reached our destination, and all enjoyed the lovely church. It is richly decorated with gilt and gold. It has six lovely onion shaped towers. We walked back to Konnesreuth, stopping on the way to eat wild berries and to put fresh flowers on an icon [religious picture] we found hanging on a tree by the road. We stopped at the Gasthaus house prior to our departure for refreshments, beer and water, and returned to Vilseck. Our meal consisted of fried potatoes, schnitzel (veal steak), salad, bread, butter, cheese and water, and coffee.

"We arrived back at Konnesreuth [on the eleventh] early in the morning. At 1300 we (Jimmie McFadden, Tom Soden, and Peter Marcuika) were asked into Theresa Neumann's home. I spoke for some time with her sister and then we finally were motioned into her room. She was standing and met us at the door as we entered. She greeted us and I answered in German. She remarked that she recalled the American soldiers who had placed the cross on the church. I asked to examine her hands and she held them out to me. The holes were covered with thick scabs that seemed pink underneath and were, to an extent, transparent, for as I passed my hand under the wound, I could see the change in the light. Her hands seemed cold and hard as rocks. I felt the scabs and they were secure and there is no question that they were real as when I moved one, the skin around her hand moved also. I mentioned that my mother would be very happy that I had visited her and upon hearing of my mother, she reached on a small table and opened a fat black wallet or pouch made of leather. From this, she selected a lovely photograph card printed in English of the Sacred Heart and gave it to me for my mother. On the back, she had written a few words and signed her name. The words she wrote were: 'United in Holy Prayer, Theresa Neumann.' I know my mother will treasure it always.

"Lt. Jennings, my battery commander, had asked me to ask her to remember him in her prayers and I told her that we all would like her to remember us in her prayers. She replied that all would be remembered in her prayers to God. I had three rosary beads [five-decade rosaries] with me, and I placed them in her hands. She held them for a moment, said a prayer and returned them to me. I then thanked her, shook her hands, and left.

"I cannot begin to explain the strange feeling I had upon entering her room. Before going to her home, I had stopped at the Church and prayed that God would give me the strength to face such a holy person. I had a thousand questions to ask her. Upon entering, I completely forgot everything. Tom, McFadden, and Pete stood by and never spoke a word except for 'auf wiedersehen' upon leaving. Miss Neumann and I spoke in German. Her face was as white as snow. I shall never forget this experience. Perhaps, I shall never be so close to anyone so holy all my life."

During his army tour, Hector attended college classes by mail. On June 2, 1961, he finished his last college test.

On July 24, 1961, Hector left Germany for his next assignment in Fort Ord, California, and arrived in New York harbor via boat on August 2, 1961.

At Fort Ord, he was assigned as company clerk at HQ Company. This assignment was very similar to the one in Germany, but Hector seemed to spend more hours trying to get the work done. On October 30, 1961, there is this diary entry: "Can't seem to get caught up. Worked from five am to twelve pm." It sounds like good preparation for his next career—the priesthood—when he would have only three or four hours of sleep on many nights.

Hector enjoyed the weather and scenery in Fort Ord, California, which is only fifteen miles from Carmel. He often traveled there to enjoy the swimming and scenery: "Spent the afternoon at Carmel beach sunning and wading. Stayed late into the evening and watched the sun go down. Worked on my book."[26] The book he refers to may be his journal.

Many of the activities in which Hector participated in Germany, he also enjoyed California. He writes: "Went to Hofbrau in Monterey and had a wonderful evening listening to German Singing. One man in a German costume played the

---

[26] 12/31/1961 diary

accordion. Everyone sang—we stayed until 0230 am."[27] Visits to antique shops and movies were also enjoyed during this leave,

Hector's faith seemed to be moving in the right direction during his Army years. He continued to attend Sunday Mass, received the Sacraments, and attended activities of the Holy Name Society.[28] He writes of practicing religious activities that were new for him, such as fasting and attending the Stations of the Cross.[29]

As his tour of duty was coming to an end, Hector began to miss his good friends and memories: "Strange, after waiting thirty-eight months, and now that my army career is coming to an end, I almost hate to see it come. I have been very melancholy the past few days. Even went so far as to dig out my old diaries and read past experiences."[30]

On April 4, 1962, Hector left the Army and headed back to his home in New Hampshire. In Hector's 1965 diary, he noted on February eleventh that he "received discharge papers from the U.S. Army—6 years total—honorable discharge."

Hector had formed many friendships in the Army and would correspond and visit with these people over the years.

---

[27] 1/20/1962 diary
[28] 12/14/1959
[29] 12/23/1959 and 3/7/1962 diary entries
[30] 4/1/1962 diary

Padre Pio and Father Bolduc

Hector in Germany with Tom Soden (from Demenick),
Most likely the couple is the Hittle's

Chapter Five
Post Army (1962-1964)

Once discharged from the army, Hector contemplated his next occupation and resumed his normal civilian activities of helping on the farm, antiquing, attending Thompson Ames Historical Society meetings, as well as taking up most of his other pre-army activities.

Once he was home, family life took a large part of Hector's interest: "Ernest married Doris on May 5, 1962, with three hundred fifty in attendance at the Holy Rosary Church. The whole family was involved in the preparations and decorations." In September, he wrote of a sister's marriage: "Anita married to Norman. Visited. At the reception, two people fainted, and one was taken to the hospital."

On New Year's Eve in 1962, the family gathered and enjoyed the New Hampshire weather and each other's company: "We went skiing. We took a lot of pictures. Afterwards, we went on a few rides on the toboggan near Morin's. Went to the Olbers for dinner and stayed there all evening to usher in the new year. We all had a terrific time with the balloons."

Another journal entry recorded that Hector's mother was given the "Mom of the Year" award at a gathering of two hundred people: "Had a wonderful testimonial for Mom."[31]

The celebration of the 150th anniversary of the founding of the town of Gilford was to happen in 1962 and Hector was put in charge of the celebration.[32] He started visiting more people and sites and gathered information for his book on the "Gilford Story." He also went to the pest house and dug to see if there were really people buried in the back field. He found a skeleton and the remains of a coffin six feet down.

Hector had a coin prepared to commemorate the Gilford celebration. The coin was bronze and slightly larger than a

---

[31] 3/30/1963 diary
[32] 5/7/1962 diary

silver dollar. On one side, the coin bore a symbol of the figure of achievement, holding aloft the wreath of progress. The reverse side showed a scene of the Belknap Mountain range, with Lake Winnipesaukee and the Gilford shoreline in the foreground. The coin was the first in the town's history and was offered for sale as a souvenir piece.[33] Hector mentioned on August 11, 1962, that he "is selling a lot of coins." Two weeks later, they had a parade for the 150th celebration with a float that took weeks to build and decorate.

His interest in politics never waned, and whenever something happened in the political arena, Hector had some comments or suggestions to make. Whether local, national, or international, he always had a few remarks concerning it recorded in his diary. On January 22, 1964, he commented on a letter that he had sent to his legislators: "Mailed my requests for legislation banning the communist party by a constitutional amendment to Reps and Senators."

Three days later: "Visited a Mr. George Lincoln Rockwell at the motel. He is the Nazi commander in the US. The ugly rat. We had an interesting talk."

Three days later: "Went to see Mr. Varney re. zoning ordinance." At this time, Hector was typing letters, getting signatures, running off one thousand new letters to be handed out, and attending strategy meetings. At a town meeting on March 11, 1964, the diary had this comment: "We gave John W. a run for his money. He was so mad, he was literally seeing red. The zoning issue was postponed. We had two lawyers and a stenographer present."

On September 5, 1962, Hector wrote: "Town meeting tonight, a black Tuesday as the dreaded zoning plan was adopted tonight 257-215. After one hundred fifty years, Gilford starts a downhill slump. The bypass highway through our property was approved." The results of this decision are seen in the August 14, 1964, entry: "Tremendous bonfires tonight as the state workers are burning Pop's maples in front of the house.

---

[33] *Laconia Evening Citizen* 8/11/1962 Coin – Gilford 150th Anniversary (Source 35)

The whole of Boyd hill was ablaze. It was really quite beautiful." Pops cried over the loss of his beloved "sugar bush." This was the only time the boys had seen their father cry.

Hector continually added to his gem collection, either by purchasing "good deals" or digging them out of the earth: "Went to Osipee, where we went rock hunting in the mountains. We found a large quantity of gem quality stones in a narrow hole in a huge boulder that we called 'balancing boulder.'"[34] Again: "Went to my old brook where I found gold a few years ago and found several good-sized pieces in quartz."[35]

On February 26, 1963, Hector was notified that he had been selected for the Peace Corps.

In June of 1963, Pope John the XXIII had died and Paul VI was elected Pope. Hector relaxed for a few weeks before taking off on a trip during which he "watched the Pope's coronation on TV."

On June 10, 1963, Hector left for a three thousand-mile bicycle trip. In preparation for the trip, passports were obtained, and a new bike purchased: "Bought a new bicycle—161 marks. Has light, horn, saddlebags, air pump, lock, etc."[36]

He went to Germany and visited the Hittles and other friends. One of the activities at the Hittle's was making gummy bears—"We finished the washers on the twenty thousand gummies today."[37] He went to the orphanage to see how they were doing. Then went to Konnersreuth and visited Theresa Neumann's grave."[38]

On July 16, 1963: "Left Mulheim at 05:30. Covered 160 miles. Lovely castle and churches in Marburg." At times, he had to take a train or a ferry to cross certain terrain. Whenever possible, he would sleep in the fields or in a farmer's lean to. He toured churches, enjoyed the countryside, met and talked to many people, spent parts of rainy days in the library, and went to church whenever possible. He was not able to go to Mass for

---

[34] 11/25/1962 diary
[35] 4/17/1963 dirary
[36] 7/10/1963 diary
[37] 6/20/1963 diary
[38] 6/30/1963 diary

two Sundays due to the lack of active churches in the Scandinavian countries.

His travels took him to Germany, Denmark, Sweden, and Norway. The trip ended on July thirty-first back in Mulheim, after he had traveled approximately three thousand miles. He then started writing an article for the paper back home about his trip.

Before leaving Europe, he visited his old army base and then traveled to Paris to see opera houses, Notre Dame, jewel collections and to see the Mona Lisa. He visited once again with Mr. Boniface, who had written a book on Theresa Neumann: "Mr. Boniface gave me an autographed book and many souvenirs of Theresa."

After visiting France, Portugal and Spain, he traveled by train to Italy. There he visited Foggia and St. Giovanni Rotundo where he saw Padre Pio:

"September 14, 1963: We were up at four to go to Padre Pio's five am Mass. Many people. After Mass, I went to the sacristy and touched my beads to his hand. Sent many cards home. I went to Foggia but decided to return and spend the weekend at St. Giovanni Rotundo. Sent a wire to Ernest [Bolduc]. Attend Padre Pio's benediction. Touched his hand afterwards. We sang by his window later that evening. Climbed the mountain behind the Villa."

"September 15, 1963—Sunday: attended Padre Pio's five am Mass. Went to the basilica of St. Michael the Archangel on Mount Angel with a priest. We drove in a taxi. The only church in the world whose altar is not consecrated because it was consecrated by St. Michael himself when he appeared to St. Laurence. Also saw the imprint of St. Francis of Assisi. Visited the grave of Padre Pio's parents. Attended his benediction. Visited the hospital. Spent the evening with a friend from Africa."

"September 16, 1963: Went to Padre Pio's Mass again today. He put his hand on my shoulder while going up the steps. Served Mass and attended Benediction. We all gathered to sing good night to Padre Pio."

"September 17, 1963: Attended Padre Pio's Mass and Benediction. Saw the stigmata very plainly this morning. Entered the heart of the church during preparation for Benediction because Miss Pyles light had burned out and she wanted a new one. Great grace and blessing."

"September 18, 1963: Attended Padre Pio's Mass. Today is the anniversary of St. Francis of Assisi's stigmata. This noon, I went into the convent and kissed Padre Pio's hand. I spoke to him and asked him to bless my mother. He was very happy today. He blessed a small gypsy boy and patted him on the head. There is a beautiful scent about Padre Pio, especially his hands."

"September 19: 1963: Attended Padre Pio's Mass and benediction. Saw him in the sacristy, etc. I held a small baby while he blessed him. He was very happy. There is a most wonderful odor about him. Received my telegram and money. Received from the Abresch store a picture of myself and Padre Pio."

"September 20, 1963: Padre Pio's 45th anniversary of the stigmata. Met Mr. Senea—an author on Padre Pio. Attended Benediction and had him bless my photos, etc. Kissed his stigmata. Padre Pio's wounds bled today."

Hector started immediately to document his visit to Padre Pio and completed a thirty-three-page double-spaced document.[39] In this document, you can see Hector's detailed approach to studying any subject. The document is very inspiring and well written. One hindrance to his visit was that he did not speak Italian so some conversations between Padre Pio and others were not understood by him. One can see Hector's

[39] See source 36 – *Padre Pio Stigmatist* written by Father Bolduc

love of the "instruments" of God and his deep analytical, methodical approach to anything he tackled.

A good part of Hector's trip after the visit to Padre Pio was spent visiting friends and touring locally in Germany.

On November 22, 1963, while still in Germany, Hector received some horrific news: "Went to Mulheim and saw Herr Hittle. Returned to the hotel in Frankfurt and a few minutes after arriving, I heard the unbelievable shocking news that President John F. Kennedy has been shot and killed a few minutes ago. I cannot believe it. It's true."

Hector arrived in New York on November 28, 1963, over five months after he had left the United States. He later spoke about different parts of his trip to various organizations in New Hampshire, Massachusetts, and New York using a slide show.

Hector started attending meetings of the Infants of Mary with his sister Lauretta. At one meeting, he gave a talk on Rome and Europe.[40] He joined the Catholic Young Adults Club (CYAC) with his sister Lauretta. On the ninth of April, he gave a talk on Theresa Neumann.

The Second Vatican Council started in 1962. Hector commented on May 8, 1963: "Lauretta, Helen and I went to a Children of Mary meeting where we heard a talk on the Ecumenical Council by Msg. Paradise of Manchester—very good."

Hector and his sister Lauretta seemed to be a team going to the CYAC and lectures. On February 11, 1964, he wrote: "Went with Lauretta to Belmont and had a wonderful instruction class by Father Bracg. Excellent." He had also started attending daily Mass: "Went to church as we do every morning."[41]

In early 1964, Hector and his brothers, Budd and Sam, worked to reorganize the interior of St. Helena's Catholic chapel at Weirs. There was a description of the redesigned chapel in a March 1, 1964, article in the *Laconia Citizen*: "Unique chapel with altar in center allows for greater participation in the Mass. Pews made by the Bolduc brothers are on all four sides. This is in conformance with the new liturgy brought out in the Ecu-

40 2/13/1963 diary
41 3/28/193 diary

menical Council [Vatican II]. Everyone present will be able to see the priest better.

"The overall project was conducted by the Bolduc brothers – Charles and Roland and their staff. Hector Bolduc is shown in the picture. Plans call for the tabernacle to be located off the altar and suitably adorned. The altar marks the crossroads of God and Man.

"A great need today is to restore the altar in every sense of the word, most of all spiritually, to its God-given meaning. The first altar faced the people: Christ dying on the Cross. When the people once more face the altar in full faith, they will know that their return to the altar is their return to God."

Hector had been exposed to religious sisters and they had a positive influence on him. He had this to say about one of his speaking engagements: "Went to Belmont and spoke to the Altar Society—had a swell time. Sister Agatha is one of the most honest, natural persons I have ever met. She is so simple that it is impossible for her to hide anything or be deceitful. In this respect, she has a wonderful gift of God."

Hector's mom was a continually good religious influence on the children as seen on Good Friday in 1964: "Early in the morning, as has been mom's custom for years, we all kissed the feet of Christ on the crucifix as we came down the stairs."

Hector attended Catholic Christian Doctrine classes during this time. On March 20, 1964, they discussed evolution. He also became a third-degree member of the Knights of Columbus.[42] One event of Knights that he participated in along with one thousand five hundred attendees was "You are now a witness."

The first hint about a religious vocation in his diary was on July 27, 1964, the month before he left for the seminary: "Father Curran visited me at the castle. I saw him about my documents and application." Then, on August 10, 1964, he related: "Sent all of my material off to the Marian Fathers."

On August 27, 1964, Hector noted: "Left for Stockbridge, [Massachusetts] and arrived at the Marian Fathers on Eden

---

[42] 4/5/1964 diary

Hill in good time. Saw the Father Provincial and he discussed my application. Went to Church. Picked plums. After supper, Father Provincial called me and told me that I had been accepted and that I must report for Sunday. I am very happy. May God help me and with his grace, God willing, I will one day serve him as a priest in the Marians."

Mr. Gary Pauly, a fellow member of the Father Bolduc corporation (Traditional Catholics of New Hampshire), related that Father Bolduc told him that his visit to Padre Pio was helpful in knowing what order to enter for the priesthood: "As I remember, Padre Pio told Hector that he would join the Marist priests."[43]

After being accepted to the Stockbridge Seminary on Thursday, he came home on Friday, sold his Buick for one hundred fifty dollars, had his will notarized, packed on Saturday and left for the Seminary on Sunday, August 30, 1964.

Ernest Bolduc recalled the trip to Stockbridge, where he left Hector:[44] "Hector called me on Friday night in 1964 and asked me if I could bring him to Stockbridge, Massachusetts, on Sunday. I said I could, but asked him, 'Are you going to do something there and then come back?' Hector said no, he was going to stay there. While driving there, I said, 'What in the world are you going to do there?' He said that he did not want to get everybody excited. He was going to Stockbridge to study for being a priest. I thought I was going to wreck the car. I asked him why he decided to become a priest? Hector said, 'Well, I grew up, and got an education. I've traveled the world, and been to every big country in the world. I've collected all my life. I've dated fantastic women, but I never got excited about dating them. I had no desire to go any further with women. I have all this collection. I don't worry about where I'm going to eat tomorrow, I have enough money for the rest of my life. Now I need to do something for everybody else. I need something challenging; I love God. I want to do something for everybody else.'"

---

[43] See 5/28/2020 email from Gary Pauly
[44] See 2/25 letter from Ernest (source 101)

Chapter Six
Marianist Novitiate, Stockbridge Massachusetts/ Maryland (1964-1965)

The date was September, 1964, almost two years after the start of Vatican II. Hector's first week at Stockbridge with the other three new applicants (two for brotherhood and one for the priesthood) was a retreat preached by Father Fidelis. The four were inducted formally into the Society of Marian Fathers and began their postulancy. Hector noted: "It was a beautiful ceremony. When we left the chapel, it was dark and there were a thousand stars out. Father Provincial had used the expression from St. Bernard during the sermon 'and look to Mary as thy star.' Our spiritual director, Father Fidelis, pointed out Mary's star to us—the North Star. The ceremony and sermon were both inspiring and I felt very good."[45] Shortly after the retreat, two of the Postulants left for home.

The Marianist's Stockbridge location was like the mother house. Education and formation would take place at other locations, the first of which was in Brookeville, Maryland.[46]

There were trips back to Stockbridge for various events, but Hector's education began in Maryland. While in Stockbridge, Hector sought out a famous artist—Norman Rockwell.[47] Ernest Bolduc related that Hector was a very close friend of Norman's. Hector loved to visit Norman at his studio. The Marian fathers were on the hill there and Rockwell lived next to the main street at the bottom of the hill. Hector had several of Rockwell's prints that are signed by the artist.

Hector was now close to many historical sites in Stockbridge and enjoyed to visiting them: "On my bike ride I saw the home where President and Dolly Madison lived when the British burned the capital." On December 2, 1964, he wrote:

---

[45] 9/1/1964 diary
[46] 9/10/1964 diary
[47] Ernest Bolduc notes (source 88)

"Visited the FBI building in Washington. We also went to the National Archives and saw the original Declaration of Independence, the Bill of Rights, and the Constitution."

He loved that he was at the center of the political world of the United States. He was able to meet important people and attend significant events: "Went to President Johnson's inauguration. I met and spoke to Senator Robert Kennedy. My first Presidential inauguration." On January 20, 1965: "We were allowed to send cards home today—a special consolation."[48] He wrote on January twenty-seventh: "We first went to Washington for a tour of the White House. Then we climbed the Washington Monument. Then we went to the Bureau of Printing and Engraving to see money made. Then on to the Smithsonian. Saw the new Rubens and the Rembrandt (man in a fur coat). Both excellent."[49]

Hector began to learn not only Catholic teachings but watched and learned teaching techniques from some of his teachers. Hector, when he became a priest, had an excellent approach to his sermons and teaching methods. On July 15, 1965, he commented on some of his teachers: "We had classes in the morning with Father Fidelis and Provincial. I really have learned to appreciate their experience and skill in teaching others. Unlike Father X, they speak on our level and don't incorporate their own theory, ideas or philosophy into the matter being taught. They can get to the heart of the matter quickly and efficiently."

Father Fidelis recommended to Hector that he get his affairs in order before he professed. Hector flew home for three days on July 19, 1965, to inventory his assets, finalize his will, and stop his insurance. Hector noted in his diary that his weight was down from one hundred sixty pounds to one hundred fifty-two pounds, which was quite light for his six-foot frame.

An interesting note in the diary may characterize Hector's life (see underlined below): "Our conference concerned the last two letters to the Priests in the churches of Laodicea and

---

[48]   1/20/1965 diary
[49]   1/27/1985 diary

Philadelphia. The smug religious, lukewarm, no advance. We must strive forward. <u>One cannot stay dormant, either he goes ahead or he goes backward</u>." (Emphasis added.)

The diary, for the first time, begins to reveal some of Hector's inner spiritual thoughts. After the second young man left, Hector prayed: "I pray that God will grant me the strength to persevere."[50] Being the only novice for the priesthood left, he was accepted by himself in the order of Marian congregation—clerics regular: "The seminarians from Washington came down to sing and participate. Also present were Father Provincial (Joseph), Fathers Fidelis, Gerald, Larry, Ronald, and Roland. I was presented my medal, my constitution, my cassock, and collar and sash. Had a party afterwards."[51]

The higher-level seminary was in Washington, D.C., which was close to an hour away. Trips back and forth were common: "Went to Washington and visited the seminary. I am surer than ever that great things are in store for the Mercy of God shrine. One day, a great shrine will rise there. How great is God's goodness. Our Lady had led me to here because of my devotion to Padre Pio and Theresa Neumann. She has plans for me in the future of Stockbridge. I am sure of it. God give me the grace to persevere."[52]

Hector's spirituality began to deepen. He was on fire with zeal for his religious vocation and for progress in sanctity. He wrote: "St. Michael protect me and keep watch over the Church of the Master. Thank you, Lord, that I was born a Catholic. Were it not but for Your divine grace, I may have been or be an ignorant hypocritical Protestant. Never permit me to close my eyes at the end of the day without thanking you for this great grace."[53] A month later, he wrote: "I am trying hard to increase in the virtues of charity and humility. These are two of my weakest points and will undoubtedly be a stumbling block on the way to perfection. I must also make a greater effort to concentrate my thoughts during periods of prescribed med-

---

[50] 9/6/1964 diary
[51] 9/14/1964 diary
[52] 9/15/1964 diary
[53] 9/29/1964 diary

itation and avoid distractions."[54] On November 29, 1964, the seminary had the first Mass that was all in English. The novitiate had daily classes on the Bible, singing, the Mass, and other subjects. Weekly they had days of recollection and conferences with Father Fidelis and other priests.[55]

Hector did have some health problems throughout his growing up years and was in pain more than the normal person. He handled it quite privately: "Jesus give me strength. I ask you not to take the pain away, only give me the patience, the grace, and strength to bear it."

During Lent it is customary to abstain from something in order to mortify yourself. It should be something that you are able to give up and hard enough that it is a sacrifice. On Ash Wednesday, March 3, 1965, he wrote: "My mortifications during Lent will be—no bread, butter, desserts, salt, pepper, or card playing. Also, better relations with my fellow novices especially Father Gerald." And the next day, having trouble with his resolutions, he prayed: "O Jesus, give me the strength to uphold the fasts I have undertaken during this Lenten season." The Provincial visited with each of the seminarians on a regular schedule to give them inspiration and to hear how they are doing: "I had my canonical visit with Father Provincial today. Very instructive and informative."[56]

There is a certain decorum that is expected in a novitiate, which is a quiet atmosphere to allow for prayer and meditation. A certain amount of fun is acceptable, but it seemed the young men were exceeding those limits: "Father Fidelis gave us an admonition for breaking silence and warned he would appoint a monitor and give warnings of dismissal. He also admonished us for too much fun-making and laughter. Both were well deserved."[57] This was most likely not the first warning, as Father Fidelis is using the word "dismissal."

Nightly, Hector examined his conscience and made progress in some of his weak areas:

---

[54] 10/3/1964 diary
[55] 12/10/1964 diary
[56] 3/31/1965 diary
[57] 4/7/1965 diary

"Have had no incidents involving anger or bad temper this week—big improvement."[58]

Hector had ready access to friends and priests for discussion of spiritual questions. Quite often, as often as every other day, he discussed items of interest with one or the other: "Went to Washington to confession. Had a long talk with Father John and Fran. Had a conference with a Father Connell regarding vocations—very good."[59]

There were many card games (e.g., Canasta, Gin Rummy), pool, volleyball, ping pong, and croquet games for recreation with his fellow students and seminarians. Having a bike available allowed Hector to get some exercise and explore interesting sites: "Bike ride to the old, abandoned mansion and poked around the ruins. We found many old graves."[60] One of the projects Hector undertook when time was available was to catalogue all the library books by making up an index card for each book. This was to take him almost a month. Much free time was apparent in the daily schedule.

Hector never was anywhere for an extended period of time that he did not enjoy gardening, harvesting vegetables and fruit, or fixing something like a leaky roof or a surface that needed scraping and painting. He was the seminary's new handyman whether it was electrical, plumbing, roofing, structural, or landscaping. He had his bow and arrow along at the seminary, and as a result, there were fewer varmints on the property.

Hector read a new book every three or four days, most of the books being spiritual such as The Lord, Apparitions at Lourdes, or Father Damian. Interestingly, he still mentioned that he was often working on his "Padre Pio" book since he visited him in 1963. This book ended up being a thirty-page double spaced excellent commentary on Padre Pio. Hector worked on a lengthy history of the Marian Fathers and his other class projects included a report on St. Theresa of Avila.[61]

---

[58] 5/8/1965 diary
[59] 5/19/1965 diary
[60] 11/2/1964 diary
[61] 2/3/2965 diary

On September 3, 1965, Father Fidelis informed Hector that his next training location was to be Saint Procopius College in Lisle, Illinois. On September 15, 1965, with almost the whole family in attendance, Hector took another step towards the priesthood: "Oh my Jesus, I give myself entirely to you. I took my simple vows at a Mass beginning at ten am. A beautiful ceremony. The boys sang very well. We had a fine lunch afterwards."

The next day, Hector flew to his next home in Illinois.

I called the Marian Fathers in Stockbridge, Massachusetts, in February of 2018. The receptionist told me that there was a priest that was close by that may remember Hector Bolduc. Father Seraphim answered the phone and related that yes, he remembered Hector Bolduc. I was astounded that he remembered Hector Bolduc since it had been over fifty years ago that Hector had entered. Hector did make an impression on everybody he met—some good and rarely, not so good. I explained why I was calling, and he wanted to know what happened to Hector and I informed him that Father had died in 2012. He told me that they only kept records for seminarians that made their perpetual vows and therefore would have no records on Hector Bolduc. He then reminisced that Hector caused trouble in the community because of his very strict attitude towards the faith. It made me smile seeing that Hector started at a young age defending Tradition. It made sense that he was faithful to the true teachings of the Church seeing his upbringing and his visits to Padre Pio and Theresa Neumann.

Chapter Seven
St. Procopious College, Illinois (1965 – 1966)

On September 20, 1965, Hector had his first day at St. Procopious College at Lisle, Illinois. The Marian Hills Seminary was located fifteen minutes from the college in Clarendon Hills. St Procopius is now called Benedictine University. The Marian Hills seminary in Clarendon Hills has been abandoned. In 2018, the statistics for the Marians in the United States show a depressing trend: Forty one priests, nine brothers, twenty-four seminarians, and forty-nine novices and postulants. There are only nine religious houses and residences.[62]

The subjects that Hector took were Rhetoric, History of Greece, Botany, Theology and Latin. The course in Latin was his toughest subject and required some help from other students: "A boy by the name of Fran gave me a Latin lesson, my weak subject. Worked on Latin till late. Jesus, Mary, Joseph, look down upon me and assist me that I may persevere and conquer this subject."[63]

His midterm grades arrived: Latin C, Botany B, theology B-, History of Greece B+, Rhetoric C.[64] His final semester grades were about the same except Theology which was brought up to an A and he ended up with a 3.1 Grade Point Average. On February 7, 1966, Hector is seen improving in Latin: "Our Latin tests were returned today and I got a perfect score. Father John was ready to declare a holiday."

There were many enjoyable activities for Hector at this seminary. Gardening and planting fruit trees continued to be one of the favorite pastimes for him.

They had TV and were able to watch it whenever time allowed. Pope Paul VI visited America and Hector was able

---

[62] Wikipedia – Marianists
[63] 9/24/1965 diary
[64] 11/27/1965 diary

to watch it on October 4, 1965: "Long Live the Pope! Everyone talking about Pope Paul's visit. Biggest thing ever to hit America. Brother Jeff and I watched it on TV—we were thrilled every minute."

He continued to devour books, sometimes commenting that he read "a number of books today." On that Thanksgiving, 1965, he watched the *Sound of Music* on TV, viewed some art treasures from the Vienna Collection, and saw the movie *My Fair Lady*. The seminarians played pool, cards, and outdoor games. Chicago was close enough that he was able to see many productions such as the Messiah.[65]

The arrival of family letters was the highlight of the day. Hector was not allowed to go home for family affairs and weddings. His sister Helen married in early October 1965, and he made small mention of it: "Helen married today." He was able to go home for a two-week Christmas vacation and made a trip up to Stockbridge: "Was up early and drove to Stockbridge Mass and visited Father Provincial and all the other priests and brothers. So nice to be home again. Helped Father John decorate the hall again till late this evening. Had a wonderful talk with the Provincial. Spent most of the day in bed."[66]

That Hector continued to advance spiritually is seen only in the prayers that are included in the diary, but he does make comments in the diary to mention whether the Mass is in Latin or English,[67]

There were events at the College that were starting to disturb Hector: "I went to the Library at St. Procopius to see an art film. It was terrible. God is evident in our midst that we need not seek him in the make believe."[68]

While home over Christmas vacation, he mentions that the reception of Communion is unusual: "Went to the first Mass at the new church today (In Stockton, Massachusetts). Thirty men present, eight received communion."[69]

---

[65] 12/10/1965 diary
[66] 12/21/1965 diary
[67] 2/8/1966 diary
[68] 11/10/1965 diary
[69] 12/22/1965 diary

On January 7, 1965, Hector made the first note in the diary about talks to superiors concerning issues at the seminary: "Had a counseling with Father Stanley this evening. We went over, and he okays, my next semester schedule. We discussed many topics and I feel much better knowing that things have been aired and I think there will be much gained from it. A letter from my Provincial was quoted. Started on my monthly retreat today."

His intent is to solve this problem, of which he never definitely states the nature, by working together with his fellow seminarians: "Had a talk with Brother Jeff and Brothers Joe and John. We are all going to do our best to settle the dispute which is at hand."[70]

In early March, 1966, the Father Provincial arrived to address the issues: "Father Provincial arrived this afternoon. Father started counseling this evening. Jesus, Mary, and Joseph, guide us all during this trying period."

From March 1966 to the end of the semester, the diary has frequent mention of the problems at the seminary: "Chapter concluded. I had a long talk with the Provincial this afternoon. I asked him to consider Brother Jeff's case. I also spoke with him about several problems here in the house. I had other long talks with Father Stanley and Brother Jeff. I think much has been accomplished and much more will be accomplished." That same day, there were conferences: "In the afternoon, Father Stanley called all the clerics into his room for a talk. There was confirmation on some points and absolute denial on others. There was little satisfaction reached on some of the points although I believe some good resulted. Several untruths were told on the part of some of those present and there seemed to be a plague of poor memories."[71] One of the problems was not isolated to the seminary building but had spread to St. Procopius College itself: "At least one Marian seems to be the center of ridicule at school because of his heavy smoking and drinking habits."[72]

---

[70] 2/23/1966 diary
[71] 4/16/1966 diary
[72] 4/20/1966 diary

Just before the school year ended, Hector had a talk with the Provincial and resolved to send the summary of the issues to Rome: "Bed with this terrible cold. Father Provincial was here for visitations. Very disappointed with my visit with him. He saw me for only five minutes and would not let me out of bed to get the material that I wanted to show him. Will have to wait and speak to my provincial and send this material to Rome."[73]

He had seen the Vatican II *Novus Ordo* Mass and on December 5, 1965, he experienced another rite of the Mass: "We went to Chicago and attended an Eastern Rite (Melkite) Mass by Monsignor. I really enjoyed it. We received under both species. It was the first time in my life that I had ever tasted an alcoholic beverage. "

In all my time with Father Bolduc, I never saw him drink any "spirits" except the wine during Mass. On December 27, 1964, I learned why: "A custom on the feast of St. John is to drink blessed wine from the chalice. I passed up the wine as it was not mandatory, and I am under a vow."

His diary contains beautiful prayers every few days. They are sometimes very practical: "St. Theresa, please remember me in tomorrow's test" or "Father George, look down upon your congregation and bless it with the unity which it so sorely lacks"[74] or "We won the B-ball game last night. Thank you, Mary, you answered my prayers."[75] Other prayers were asking for spiritual strength: "Ash Wednesday—received ashes here at Clarendon Hills. Mary Immaculate, hear the prayers which we are sending up to your blessed Son and intervene in our behalf."[76] On Palm Sunday in 1966, "Jesus, I love you. Saint Theresa, please watch over me."

Hector taught CCD class at a local church. He gave talks on his trips to Europe and the Catholic doctrine of it, which were greatly appreciated: "I spoke at the CCD class this morning for

---

[73] 5/21/1966 diary
[74] 1/27/1966 diary
[75] 2/19/1966 diary
[76] 2/23/1966 diary

Mrs. Ernest. The class gave me a lovely card and a box of chocolates."[77]

Hector had been informed that his next training would be in Washington, D.C., so he sent his trunks out there. There was not a lot of fanfare on Hector's leaving. On May 27, 1966, is a very low-key entry in his diary: "Sent my two trunks to Washington. I left on [the] train after saying goodbye to the Fathers and Brothers."

He arrived in Boston and was picked up by Ernest and taken home for a short family visit. At home, he received his final semester grades which were much improved: Latin C, Roman History B, Rhetoric A, Zoology A, Philosophy A, and Theology A.

I called St. Procopius College, now called Benedictine University. The receptionist told me that they had a historian who might know about Hector's stay there. Father Flint came on the line and said that they closed the seminary in 1968. They are an order of Benedictines but did also train diocesan seminarians for the priesthood. He did find Hector Bolduc in the 1965-66 yearbook in the college seminary section.[78] Hector had been sent there to be trained by the Marian Fathers. He referred to Hector as a MIC (Marians of the Immaculate Conception). Father Flint said there were a few people that remembered Hector but had nothing positive or negative to relate. Father Flint concluded that Hector may not have been a very memorable person. I corrected him in his mistaken conclusion and told him a few stories to emphasize the point that Hector was extremely memorable.

After a few weeks of visiting and some much-needed manual labor on the farm, Hector left for Stockbridge, where he was to conduct five one-week vocation camps for boys. As usual, Hector was glad to be at his spiritual home: "Thank God I am here."[79] He also wrote: "Beautiful singing and lots of smiles—thank you Mary."

[77] 2/13/1966 diary
[78] Yearbook pages. Turns out the identified Hector Bolduc was not Hector Bolduc. (Source 109)
[79] 6/12/1966 diary

Each of the boys camps were well attended with some twenty to forty boys. As would be expected, there were many athletic activities such as baseball, golf, mountain climbing, ping pong, and swimming. Hector had his thirtieth birthday during the first camp and often joined in some of the games and races. In the relay races, he might have not considered his age because he tried to keep up with the boys with some bad consequences: "Mike and I joined in the races, and I was exhausted to the point of vomiting. The boys got a good laugh."[80]

In addition to skits and athletic activities, the vocation camps took the boys to various religious houses within driving distance and had Bible vigils and days of recollection during the week. One other activity was skits in which Hector took an active part: "We practiced a musical skit written by Father John on the [President] Johnson beautification program. I have the part of Mrs. LBJ. Boy, what fun. How wonderful it is to be here where there is such happiness."[81]

In the years to come, Hector received letters from the campers and was editor for the *INFO* magazine that is sent out to the campers.[82] On July 11, 1967, Hector commented that he inserted *INFO*s into two thousand five hundred envelopes.

---

[80] 7/5/1966 diary
[81] 6/20/1966 diary
[82] 10/12/1966 diary

Chapter Eight
Xaverian University (1966-1967)

Upon arriving in Washington, Hector spent the first week in retreat. The retreat master, Father Selski, talked with Hector regarding his leaving St Procopius in 1965 with some unfinished business: "I had a long talk with Father Selski today concerning my report to the Provincial and to the Superior General. It was a very fruitful encounter. This evening at the conference, Father Sielski spoke on the importance of observing the rule. This was undoubtedly brought on by the discussion we had on that subject concerning the laxity of its observance in the St. Casimir province and the desire of some reformers there to alter it to their pleasure."[83]

After the retreat, Hector renewed his vows on the feast of the Assumption: "I renewed my vows today. The vows must be my life. If I never transgress them, there is no doubt that I will obtain their end which is self-sanctification."[84] Hector would attend classes at Xaverian college.[85]

The classes to which Hector was assigned were French, Latin, English and History. His grades again did not reflect his abilities since he had many other interests. On December 3, 1966, He received his first semester grades: "Got our grades today—I got 4 C's and 1D. The D being in Latin of course."

This era in the United States was a time of upheaval and protesting. Washington D.C. was a focal point as was the Catholic University. Father Charles Curran was an instructor at Catholic University and one of the sparks in some of the protests: "Boys at CU are upset because a Father Curran, who is apparently a young left-wing radical, has been told that his contract will not be renewed this coming June."[86]

---

[83] 8/5/1966 diary
[84] 8/15/1966 diary
[85] Xaverian college (Philosophy) is closed per Father Seraphin. See phone call of 3/22/2018
[86] 4/18/1967 diary

In the following days, there was more mayhem: "Again, much action because of the selfish young (kid) priest across the Street at CU. There was much hooting, noise, marching, etc. Beatnicks and others are arriving from outside [the area] to lend support to the rebellion. There is absolutely no respect for Church authority or law and order. CU is being turned into a savage bitter camp of young thugs. I hope the administration can hold out against such outrageous action." Shortly after, the University capitulated and reinstated Father Curran. [N.B. In 1986, the Vatican declared that Father Curran could no longer teach theology at the Catholic University of America schools, and he was neither suitable nor eligible to be a professor of Catholic theology.][87]

At a seminary, there is a rule which all seminarians are to follow. In Washington, the rule was adhered to more diligently than at St. Procopious. There were retreats on which Hector commented often that he was advancing spiritually. The Provincial for this area visited at least monthly and talked to each seminarian to ensure they were progressing in the spiritual life. The diary does not mention Mass and Holy Communion although it was most likely that they were a daily event. Occasionally, a mention is made of having a Latin Mass or a Polish Mass.

The effects of Vatican II were just starting to be felt in churches and seminaries worldwide. On November 17, 1966, Hector commented that not all the changes were to his liking: "I went to the Bishops' Conference at Caldwell Hall at the Catholic University today. I spoke with the New Hampshire Bishop and the Massachusetts Bishop. The Bishops' Council announced that as of December 2, 1966, Catholics in America will not be obliged to abstain from meat on Friday. This [abstinence] rule has been in effect for 1100 years. That's quite a record. What a time to live in the Church. Bishop X was gleaming with joy."

With all the controversy, it was difficult to get an answer to questions about the faith. Different priests gave different answers, because the Vatican II documents were ambiguous at

---

[87] Wikipedia on Father Curran

times. After a discussion on whether there can be multiple intentions at a concelebrated Mass, Hector writes that his motto will be: "Follow the Holy Father."[88]

On December 8, 1966, Hector renewed his vows and pleaded: "Blessed Mary, watch over me again for the coming year." He also implores the help of Jesus: "Jesus, please keep me constantly under your care during the coming year."

His health was good this year. However, an entry on December 21, 1966, related some issues: "Had a bad pain in my chest and arm while at the movie. Several times that has happened." There are many visits to the dentist, Hector had dental problems throughout his life.

Not all was happiness at the seminary as brothers and priests were leaving amid the confusion and turmoil. In later January of 1967, this entry was made: "Brother X has been told to leave and lured three boys away with him—it certainly is ungrateful of him to say the least."

From February 6, 1967, through the eleventh, there were no entries in the diary. Then there was an entry describing his first day home from the hospital: "Arrived home from the hospital today. My arm (hand) and foot still feel somewhat numb, but I really feel quite well. Thank God all is in order." Treatment involved the pool and whirlpool at the Catholic University.

There did not appear to be any visits from family except on April 1, 1967, when Hector's sister and husband visited him and went to some local sites. Letters arrived from home describing events there like the one on January 1, 1967, describing a fall Hector's mother had. On May 2, 1967, Hector received a big box of his mother's favorite May flowers.

Hector finished the school year on May 25, 1967, and headed to Stockbridge for the celebration of the Provincial's twenty-fifth anniversary and some work preparing for camp. On June third, Hector left for a visit to Gilford for a little over two weeks. Besides much visiting, Hector worked on his collections, gave a talk on glassware, and saw a few plays.

---

[88] 1/11/1967 diary

When Hector returned to Stockbridge for summer camps, he noted that the boys enjoyed all the events and recreation that was provided. As can be expected, not all boys were delightful: "Sorry to see some of the boys go, although others could not have left soon enough."[89]

On July 31, 1967, the boys and seminarians left for EXPO 67. The 1967 International and Universal Exposition was held in Montreal, Quebec, Canada. There were sixty countries exhibiting and the boys enjoyed many of the pavilions: "Up early and left for the Expo right after Mass. We arrived at Notre Dame and the pastor got us settled. We visited the oratory of St. Joseph, and the museum across the street. Visited the fair afterwards and saw the Magic Lantern. Very good."[90]

Hector returned to Stockbridge for a weeklong retreat with Father X—a Passionist Priest: "Father X talked on the importance of remaining recollected in a world of materialism." Hector made a plea for a good retreat: "Oh Jesus, help me to make this retreat a fruitful one so that I may obtain the grace so necessary for the attainment of your kingdom."[91] On August twenty-fifth, Hector appealed to the Blessed Mother: "I have nothing to offer you dear mother, I have no talents, no great skill for learning. But I love you and I desire to serve your Son, therefore, I offer up to you all that I lack, knowing that in doing so I offer you much."

On the feast of the Assumption, Hector and others renewed their vows in Brookeville, Maryland. On September 14, 1967, Hector left for Washington to start his fourth year of studies at the age of thirty-one.

---

[89] 7/29/1967 diary
[90] 7/31/1967 diary
[91] 8/18/1967 diary

Hector Bolduc as a Marianite seminarian with one of the boys at the summer camps. Magazine was the *INFO* sent out to present and previous campers.

Chapter Nine
Catholic University (1967-1968)

Hector was enrolled in the Catholic University School of Philosophy [now called School of Theology] from August 1, 1967, to May 1, 1969. He did not get a degree from the university since he transferred before he finished.

I talked with a Father Seraphin on March 22, 2018. Father Seraphin was at Catholic University as a teacher when Hector was a student there. He said that Hector Bolduc wrote a letter to the Cardinal complaining about Father Seraphin's teachings. Father Seraphin said that "Hector Bolduc was an ultra-conservative." If you think about all the rioting and Vatican II teachings at this time, I can see Hector being portrayed as a very traditional person.[92]

Hector did not spend much discussion on classes in the diaries. He did mention the following classes: History of Philosophy; Philosophy, Ontology [philosophical study of being], French, Metaphysics, Cosmology [study of the origin and development of the Universe], Logic, and Epistemology [theory of knowledge]. On December 11, 1967, he commented: "All I can say is BUSY!"

There were a few unique activities this school year. One was on January 12, 1968, when he displayed his jewelry collection in the music building where many attended. Another was a songfest by a very popular trio that Hector attended on February 12, 1968: "Brother Paul got special tickets to Constitution Hall to see Peter, Paul, and Mary. We sat on the stage and spent most of the evening backstage with the singers. Got to meet and speak with them. Met also a large group of U.S. Marines and Navy men all of whom were wounded. They recently returned from Vietnam. they were from the Bethesda Naval Hospital."

---

[92] see source 102 and 118

Hector, besides writing many letters home and elsewhere, had responsibilities in the garage maintaining vehicles, cleaning certain floors, and kitchen duty.

On New Year's Eve, 1967, Hector prepared for serving a Mass: "Preparing for the New Year's Mass. We had three con-celebrating—Father Provincial, Father Ernest, Father Martin. Very Lovely." Starting on January 8, 1968, the Forty Hours devotion became available to all the seminarians.

His diaries outlined activities like the last year with one addition: that he is teaching Catholic Christian Doctrine (CCD) classes at a local school on Sundays. Some of the topics were Parental Authority, Christianity, Buddhism, and Hinduism.

Much happened during these times in the political arena. The Riots of 1967 were among the most violent and destructive in U.S. history.[93] One hundred and fifty-nine race riots erupted across the United States. Various reasons given for the riots were high levels of frustration, resentment, and anger among African Americans, that were created by unemployment, poverty, racism, police brutality, and lack of opportunities. The diary entries start out on October 16, 1967: "Any [number of] peace demonstrations and draft dodger riots—a disgrace to the country." In typical Hector fashion, he did not just read about it in the papers, he infiltrated the rioters' meetings to get firsthand information: "Went to a "Peace" meeting which planned the strategy for tomorrow. The more I see these people in action, the more I come to see that they are hardcore communists."[94]

Classes were held but the riots continue for several days: "Regular classes. Much news on the riot downtown. Looks like the police have things well in hand, thank God. Many Communists involved. Horrible disgrace to those who have fought to make America what it is."

Simultaneously, turmoil continued in the Church, and this disturbed Hector: "Much distressing news about priests who are abandoning their faith because of their refusal to obey

---

[93] Google "Riots of 1967"
[94] 10/19/1967 diary

their bishops. They want out so they now have found a way out [Vatican II] which they use as a whipping boy. The Big Boy upstairs may have something to say about it."[95]

Hector recorded one of his many diary entries on October 10, 1967: "Worked on Renewal. Lord, give me the grace to know your will."

When I was in my early twenties, I can remember the big banners in church saying RENEW. I did not know what it was about, but it was 1967 and Vatican II was implementing some changes, so I figured that must be what it was about.

Hector made another comment about this year: "Went to the Shrine to see the "year of Faith" Mass celebrated by Cardinal X and the Apostolic Delegate. About fifty to sixty thousand at the Mass."

There were many changes to the faith happening during this time, although the major changes to the Liturgy made in 1969 were yet to come. On November 30, 1967, Hector described one of the lectures he attended: "Went to a lecture at CU by Brand Blanshard. Quite excellent. Met him personally afterwards. He leaves room for revelation where there is no contradiction with the Bible."

Father Provincial visited Hector on January 6, 1968, and they spent five and one-half hours talking. Hector records that it was "most informative." On May 21, 1968, he had another meeting with Father Provincial: "Had a long and informative talk with Father Provincial. St. Joseph, look down on this congregation and help it through stormy days ahead." The monthly retreats continued but they were not cloistered, as in the past. Movies, sports and other events happened on the same days.

Hector was an avid admirer of President Lyndon Johnson. On January 17, 1968, he was invited to the State of the Union Address: "Received an invitation from Senator McIntyre to attend the President's State of the Union Message this evening. It was a memorable occasion. Mr. Johnson will certainly be a hard man to defeat in the coming elections. On March 12, 1968, this entry: "The best news of the day is that President

---

[95] 9/25/1967 diary

Johnson won in New Hampshire. My Prayers were answered. Nixon was the Republican winner."

The real surprise to Hector came on March 31, 1968. His diary relates the event: "President Johnson has said he will not seek or accept the nomination for President of the United States. He also announced a bombing halt over North Vietnam. In doing so, he has proved to me and to the rest of the world what many of us had known right along; that he is the greatest president this nation has ever had, and that he is the greatest leader that any nation has ever had. Without the slightest bit of hesitation, he placed his nation, his people, the cause for world peace, above himself, politics, and other selfish matters. How great I feel tonight, having lived to know and see such a man as this. God has given us so few of them. He [President Johnson] referred to God many times during his address and concluded it by asking God's blessing on our nation and its people. To-night we have seen men, such greats of the past as Washington, Lincoln, Wilson, FDR, and Harry Truman dwarfed to mere in-significant has-beens."

Another event in 1968 that had a major impact on ev-erybody was the death of Martin Luther King, Jr. The best way to summarize the impact will be to quote Hector's words from April 4, 1968 through April 7, 1968: "A news bulletin has just announced that Dr. Martin Luther King Jr. has been killed in Memphis Tennessee. Ironic that he should die in this city so soon after a demonstration which he recently led caused the death of a young man. God is just. I have mixed emotions as I once admired Mr. King as being one of America's leading Negro promoters for peace and freedom. However, in recent years with his so called "peace marches" turning into riots and death and destruction and with his continued association with men such as Rap Brown, Stokely Carmichael, and with many famous (infamous) and influential Communists, I had to desert him. He ceased to be non-violent. I only hope that his death will not be the excuse needed to light our cities."

The next day's entry: "Went to school. There are reports of violence growing every minute. We went to the top of the building and watched the skies red with flames on three sides. The buildings across from the soldiers' home were silhouetted in flames and pinkish red glow. All day long, we saw heavy columns of smoke rising from many areas. Sirens filled the air all day and helicopters and planes flew over the city almost continuously. Ron, Paul, Roy, and I went to volunteer to fight fires and ran into looters on 12th street. We were nearly jumped on several occasions. One of the priests from St. Anthony's finally drove us home. This is a night to remember."

The next day's entry: "While we played ball on the Marist lot yesterday, bits of burned paper and ashes showered down on us. We had a game with the O.M.I. [Order of Mary Immaculate] and lost. The boys went home, all except John S. and Tom S. We watched the riots and looting all day. Troops are being called in. It seems incredible that these things are happening. Chicago, Baltimore, Memphis, Detroit, and other cities are also being hit. The worst seems to be Washington, followed by Pittsburg. Even Boston has its share. School was cancelled today until after Easter Vacation. We pray that law and order will soon prevail."

The last day's entry: "Tom S. and I went for a long walk today down in the heart of Washington. We covered ten to twelve miles. From 12th St. NE to the Capitol, Georgia Ave, H St., Florida Ave, E St. and other areas. We saw the fires, the looting and destruction firsthand. We also saw the victims and heard the comments of the people. Many people are frightened. We saw thousands of soldiers and witnessed a large gathering of people being broken up by tear gas. SafeWay stores seem to be hardest hit, as well as liquor stores, jewelry stores and clothing stores. Gutted buildings and debris were everywhere. The negro people have written a tribute to Dr. King in destruction and devastation."

Hector loved his country and the people in it. He was shaken by the lawlessness and the loss of life. I find it astounding that while the riots were in full fire, he and his friend were walking through the "war" zone.

On the last day of May, 1968, Hector finished school and left for his religious home—Stockbridge. He assisted at an ordination Mass: "Sunday—Alexei's ordination today. We drove up and were followed by the Teixiera family. The Mass lasted three hours. I helped in the sacristy with the lights, and incense. It was a lovely ceremony. We then drove back to Laconia. Everyone was at the house except Barb, Maurice, and Theresa. We had Mom's birthday party."

On the fifth of June, 1968, Hector heard of an assassination attempt: "Lauretta and Ray informed me of the attempted assassination of Senator Kennedy. I offered up my Mass for his recovery. They have the assassin—another Communist Jordanian. Oh God, what more are we to suffer at the hands of the Communists. God give strength to Mrs. Kennedy and her family especially Mrs. Rose Kennedy!" Bobby Kennedy died the next day: "Senator Kennedy has passed away—it is too tragic to comment." There are seven coded capital letters in the diary—MGHMOHS [May God have Mercy on His Soul].

Sometimes, Hector used up to thirty coded capital letters. These seven (above) I was able to decipher. I think most of the time, when he wanted to put something in his diary that he did not want readers to understand, he used coded capital letters.

During the summer, Hector worked with multiple vocation camps as he had the past two years. He authored the camp *INFO* magazine and received letters from old and new campers. During the camp, they traveled to Monument Mountain and "finished putting the initials (with a chisel and hammer) in the rock at the top—MVC—Marian Vocational Camp. And then chiseled 68."[96]

His friendship with Norman Rockwell continued: "Visited Norman Rockwell today with Bob K. Mr. Rockwell signed a stamp block for Bob and gave each a signed copy of his Stockbridge painting autographed personally for us."[97]

One of the trips after the camps was a visit to the famed (Sound of Music) Von Trapp's in Stowe, Vermont.

---

[96] 7/16/1968 diary
[97] 6/30/1968 diary

In mid-August, 1968, Hector returned to Stockbridge to have a long interview with Father Provincial and then on the feast of the Assumption, renewed his vows followed by a ten-day retreat. From there, he returned to Washington for his next year of school.

Father Bolduc at Von Trapp chapel in Stowe, Vt
10/1/2008

Chapter Ten
Catholic University (1968-1969)

During this school year, Hector began definitively moving more in the direction of Traditional Catholicism. He formed a "conservative" group at Catholic University. He had some discussions with the John Birch Society during this election year.

Hector began to express his conservative views more than before, both in words and actions. On September 22, 1968: "This evening, I called a meeting of several University students who are interested in supporting a conservative attitude at CU. We are forming a club which will be recognized by the University. Those in attendance were Pat, Daniel, Jim, Joe, Clarence, and me. We have things started." I had heard that Hector and Clarence Kelly had started an "underground newspaper" but upon reading the diary, it wasn't hidden: "Finished printing two thousand copies of the TSUNAMI newsletter."[98] I never found why they adopted the title Tsunami; it could just have been the word that means a tidal wave movement. More than likely, however, knowing Hector's penchant for acronyms, each letter could mean something.

On October 26, 1968, the first meeting was held: "Attended our first official meeting of the TSUNAMI club. Daniel was elected President. Mary Ellen was elected Vice-president and Treasurer. I was elected Secretary and Editor of the Newsletter. Nine of our charter members were present." Throughout the year, mention is made of meetings of the TSUNAMI where "much progress was made."

The newsletter was far ranging in topics as seen on the January 9, 1969, diary entry: "Met with Guatemala ambassador. Had a long talk with the "chargé d'affaires" who confirmed the Melville bus incident mentioned in TSUNAMI." And on February 8, 1969: "Clarence and I went to Arlington

---

[98] 12/12/1968 diary

to visit Mr. Thompson who was a former advisor to President Diem in Vietnam."

Hector was continually watching the liturgy and if he saw too many irregularities, he contacted his superiors: "Talked at a house meeting about the Beatnik Mass that is now being held here on Sundays by a floating parish. I am very opposed to it and volunteered to see Cardinal O'Boyle about it. Father Martin said he favored it strongly but would look into it more???"[99]

On November 3, 1968: "Had two very long talks with Father Martin concerning the irregularities at Mass." Hector favored the Latin Rite Mass, as can be seen on December 4, 1968: "We had another Byzantine Rite Mass today in place of the Latin Mass. No effort is being made to supply the Latin Rite members of this house with a Mass in their rite." At the back of the 1968 diary, Hector kept a log of which rite has been offered certain days to support his case that the Latin rite was not being offered. On the few days that the Latin rite was offered, Hector made a comment such as March 19, 1969: "Feast of St. Joseph. We had a beautiful Latin Mass."

When searching for Hector's records at Catholic University of America, I found no graduation records as may be explained in this Boston Herald paper article[100]: "Bolduc attended Catholic University in the late 1960's but 'I was removed from the degree program because they were not happy with my pronounced conservative position. I was frequently at odds with teachers.'"

Father Provincial had his scheduled visits with each seminarian and retreats were held monthly. Hector was still teaching the Sunday CCD classes at a local High School—he seemed to enjoy them. On October 13, 1969, he wrote: "Went to CCD and gave a talk on authority." In the diary on this day, there was a green typewritten note of introduction of the topic in the diary—"Brother Hector of the Marian Order will present the topic 'By What Authority Does the State Speak to Me.' During his years of Military Duty, Brother has worked with conscien-

---

[99] 9/3/1968 diary
[100] *Boston Herald*, July 12, 1987. Maverick Priest Carves Out Safe Niche For Latin Mass (source 3)

tious objectors, has been an interrogator of refugees from East Berlin, and is currently teaching and counseling at the D.C. Detention home." This mention of the Detention home is often in the diary. It appears up to four seminarians would go over and talk to the boys in the center.

The house where the seminarians live had, up to this point, been a thorn in Hector's side. He wanted a quiet, prayerful home and it had not been that way since his early seminary years: "at a long house meeting concerning the house schedule. Freedom for all—let everyone go his own way—each answers to his own conscience—HA!! The day will quickly come when I will say 'I told you so.'"[101] It helps to remember that Hector is in his thirty-fourth year and therefore is much older than most of the other young men in the house.

It was a sad year also, due to the death of Padre Pio on September 24, 1969: "Today, I heard that Padre Pio, the wonderful Italian Priest who led me to my religious life in this Congregation, had died in Italy close to his eighty-first birthday. He is perhaps the only man whom I have ever met who will one day be declared a saint by the Church. I know that I should rejoice over the fact that he is now in God's kingdom, however, I can't help but feel sad over the loss of a saintly man who was a comfort to millions during his life. I shall always treasure my visits with him. They were some of the happiest of my life." On June 16, 2002, Padre Pio was proclaimed a saint by Pope John Paul II.

Besides the seminarians, Hector had friends outside the house. Quite often, at least every few weeks, he visited with a Msgr. Ryan, a retired priest who was very knowledgeable about Catholic University. He was a great conversationalist and someone that Hector discussed his thoughts with: "Went with Clarence to visit Msgr. Ryan—we had a wonderful talk. [We discussed the] H Bomb on Hiroshima, surrender of Japan and peace feelers prior to the official surrender, the CU problem, and the Moral question."[102].

---

[101] 9/10/1969 diary
[102] 5/17/1969 diary

Miss Jamison is an older lady, I think, who Hector visited. He enjoyed her company: "Visited dear Miss Jamison—had a delightful visit. Watched the Democratic convention."[103]

Others that Hector kept in frequent touch with were Sophie, the seventy-seven year old cook, and Miss Bargin, the French teacher. Sophie was a very unusual older lady, as seen by this entry on April 7, 1969: "We [Sophie and Hector] went to the wrestling matches in Washington and Sophie had quite a time. She met [her friend] Bruno again. Haystack Calhoun won the twelve-man free for all. We had a party for Bruno's victory."

I have noticed that Hector enjoyed the company of older people throughout his life. The more opinionated they were, the better he seemed to enjoy their company.

Hector was still visiting meetings of the "enemy" to see what they were up to: "Went to a meeting of the F.O.R. which was a real commie front thing. They had a real dilly of a priest there who encouraged students to break laws, burn draft cards and files, etc."[104]

The most unusual event in this school year was Hector's taking on the cataloguing and evaluation of the total art and antiques collection at Catholic University. It all started with Hector's own initiative on January 7, 1969: "Went to see Mr. Rooney and Ross at the art center about having action taken on the art objects at the University." This involved dozens of buildings and vaults, uniquely identifying each item, cataloguing it, get an evaluation for higher value items, and in some cases helping in the sale of certain items. Here is a sample of the activities:

> January 28, 1969: Spent most of the day cataloguing the engraving collections at CU. Also got some work done in the vault.

> January 31, 1969: Went to the Administrative building and worked on the print collection. Have Nearly one hundred completed.

---

[103] 8/29/1968 diary
[104] 10/9/1968 diary

February 7, 1969: Had a meeting with the museum committee and we toured the vault, Curley Hall, the library, etc.

February 12, 1969: Went to see Dr. Peebles in the Greek-Latin department to catalogue a coin collection.

March 1, 1969: Took a man from the national Gallery to the vault at CU to see the stone statue of St. Peter and the wooden one of the Madonna.

Hector would spend at least parts of a couple of days each week on this task. He so loved great art and treasures that he wanted to make sure none were lost. This work continued into the next school year. It is interesting that he never had time to practice this diligence with regard to his own collection.

There were other activities as in the previous years: visits to museums, antique stores, and the opera. There were also many athletic activities such as football, basketball, swimming, pinball, wrestling, and weekly movies. I was surprised to see one TV program that Hector watched was the Miss America Pageant. I guess beauty is beauty.

There was one interesting trip to the library in Washington for research, where Hector had to use his calf wrestling skills: "Went to the library to work on my bibliography. Walking home, I was jumped by two colored men, one of whom came up behind me and put an arm around my neck and a knife in my back. I elbowed him in the stomach then kicked him in the face. I kicked him two or three times while he was down and he lost his knife, a switchblade with an eight" blade. They both got away. I called [the] police and we recovered the knife."[105]

On May 28, 1969, Hector left for Stockbridge, with a short stop in New Hampshire to visit his family. While home, he had an opportunity to give a lecture on June 3, 1969: "I presented my lecture to the Merideth Historical society on the history of books and printing. Forty-five members present."

Most of the summer was spent on four vocation camps for approximately twenty-five boys each. On July twentieth, during

---

[105] 4/7/1969 diary

the boy's camp, a momentous event occurred which stirred Hector's patriotic feelings: "Late into Monday morning—we watched the landing of Apollo 11 on the moon and later the first walk on the moon by Captain Armstrong. God is good. How wonderful to see our flag flying on the moon." And on July twenty-fourth: "We watched the astronauts land and be recovered by the Hornet. What a great day for America."

On July twenty-eighth, Hector received some welcome news: "Received word from Rome that Father Joseph Sielski has been elected our Superior General of the Marian Fathers congregation. He is the first American elected to that post. He is a strong, sensible man—thanks be to God."

From August ninth through the fourteenth, Hector was privileged to be included in discussions about the Stockbridge Marian chapter: "I spent most of the day in discussions with the delegates to the chapter. This may well be the most important chapter in years. I hope that the Holy Spirit is prepared to work overtime." On the last day, Hector had an opportunity to present some of the remedies he believed needed to be implemented: "I had a two-and-a-half-hour session with the provincial and his council today. I am very happy to have been given a chance to clear up some points. The council was very interested, responsive and I feel much was accomplished."

On August fifteenth, the feast of the Assumption: "I took my vows today. I renewed them for the fourth time. I trust our Blessed Mother will be with me and protect me during the coming year." This was followed on August eighteenth by a five-day retreat which finished with Benediction and the Papal blessing.

Chapter Eleven
Oblates of Mary Immaculate College (OMI) (1969-1970)

Most people return to college after they have packed the car, said their goodbyes and driven to the dorm to start their school year. Hector and his friend Mike tuned up their bikes, had some twenty-mile practice trips, and then left on their bikes from Stockbridge for Washington.

This was Hector's sixth year in the seminary. He was now thirty-three years old. His classes for this year were Polish ("Went to Hobart Street where Mrs. Wesalowska taught the four of us Polish")[106], Education, Arts, Ancient History, Dogma, Morals, Acts, Introduction to Liturgy, and Virtue. As is typical, Hector did not spend much time in his diary describing his classes.

Hector had regular meetings with Father Provincial. At times, the whole house was invited to a talk by the provincial. On March 13, 1970: "Father Provincial closed the visitation with a house meeting. Significant in this meeting was the fact that he stressed that we should first see to it that our main objectives (spiritual and scholastic) are accomplished before taking on other work and that we should not let outside activities interfere with these normal functions. He also placed household duties third on this list of priorities." I think this is good advice and am intrigued that Hector did not see the many outside activities he had as interfering. It may just be that he did not put all the spiritual activities in his diary like daily Mass, Confessions, rosaries, Benediction and the like. You will see throughout this book that Hector always had many, many outside activities.

Hector did occasionally comment on spiritual matters, especially when he attended a "lovely" Mass:

---

[106] 9/19/1969 diary

"Sunday—Mass—a lovely high Mass. Earlier, Mike, Sophie and I attended Msgr. Ryan's Mass at the Shrine."[107] And again: "Sunday—Had a Mass at the Shrine honoring the 100th anniversary of Vatican Council I. A lovely and moving Mass."[108]

Hector was part of a seminary choir that sang at area churches. On March 29, 1970, he wrote: "We had a beautiful Easter service at the Church of the Annunciation near Wisconsin Avenue. After, we went to the Shrine where we sang a most beautiful Mass under the direction of Mr. Norman. It was absolutely beautiful."

July 14, 1970, was a very happy day for Hector: "Msgr. Curlin called to say that Cardinal O'Boyle had accepted me into his Archdiocese. This is a very great day for me. It will indeed be a great pleasure and honor to serve under so great a man." Hector now had an assignment for when he became a priest.

On August 15, 1970, as in past years, Hector was to renew his vows on the feast of the Assumption: "Assumption—great feast day. Although I did not renew my vows with the order, I renewed them personally with God and the Church. I sang the Te Deum in thanksgiving for all His graces." This last statement is very puzzling—why would he not take his vows? It could be that he had decided not to be ordained in the Marianist order.

Hector kept his political contacts current. On November 18, 1969 he wrote: "Had a long talk with Senator (Ted) Kennedy. Quite enlightening."

On May 5, 1970, when more rioting occurred in Ohio, he wrote: "Much excitement over the incident at Kent University. Four students were killed. There is no question in my mind that the students were fully responsible. The national Guardsmen had been under continued attack for hours. We must return to a principal of law and order."

And on May 12, 1970: "Much damage at CU by vandals. Some by students, outside agitators, black militants who have come on our campus to cause trouble."

---

[107] 11/2/1969 diary
[108] 12/7/1969 diary

The all-consuming activity this year was a continuation of cataloging and selling of the art and antiques at the Catholic University buildings. The amount of work had increased significantly. There were weeks when four out of five days were spent working on this project. Here are some sample entries:

> November 12, 1969: "Mr. B. from the Smithsonian came to see the guns and weapons collection. They were very pleased. They also said many of the shells stored in the vault were very dangerous. I got a bomb squad to remove them immediately."

> November 13, 1969: "Mr. R from the National Gallery came to make sketches of the Quintin Massy painting. He is very optimistic."

> December 3, 1969: "The Spanish Ambassador arrived at 3:50 pm with his culture minister. It was my first meeting with the Marquise de Merry del Val. He was very excited about the 'great' Melillo Painting and extolled it to no end. He was also pleased to see the letter from Queen Isabella to Columbus. He was quite concerned that the painting (17th century) that we have was by the great artist Z."

> March 4, 1970: "Working on rock collection at the University. Two men were here and appraised the collection at $16,000."

> March 12, 1970: "Met with Mr. Webb and we discussed the fine arts insurance policy. Much has to be done to get things on the up and up."

> May 21, 1970: "The Eakins portrait was removed from sale today after getting the highest price for a painting in its class ($130,000)."

> May 22, 1970: "I found an important Eakins letter in the CU archives today where he refers to his painting of Cardinal Martinelli as 'My best work.'"

All during the summer vacation Hector worked on this project. There was an article about the May 22, 1970 diary entry in the *Laconia Citizen* edition of July 14, 1970. Below is the essence of the article:

Gilford Man is Credited with Washington Art Find
7/14/1970

"The painting by Thomas Eakins of Cardinal Martinelli, neglected and unknown for many years, was found by Hector Bolduc two years ago on the wall of a university building. Hector was cited as an alumnus of Catholic University of America—School of Philosophy.

"Undaunted by a lack of funds, Hector Bolduc arranged to have the painting restored free of charge by the National Gallery in return for allowing it to be hung there for one year. Conducting further research, Hector established that the painting had been a gift to the university by the artist in 1963. The original letter sent by Mr. Eakins referred to the painting as 'my greatest work.' When the painting was sold for $130,000, it was reported that the letter helped get this high bid.

"Besides the Eakins portrait, Hector has succeeded in authenticating several other unsigned works by other noted artists. Hector receives no compensation for his time and talents, except for the satisfaction of seeing great works of art bought to light.

"At a time when militant students came to the university campus defacing property, Hector organized a cleanup committee. Hector received a letter of recognition from the University president. In an article in the CUA school of Philosophy newsletter, it was noted that the preservation of University works of art proceeds almost entirely because of Hector Bolduc, an alumnus of the School of Philosophy, who is now pursuing his studies at Oblate College.

"Hector has single-handedly catalogued most of the art treasures on campus and completed many other works to ensure the safety and preservation of the works on campus.

"Besides his work in the art community, he has taught for two years at a Washington home for delinquents and helped in the rehabilitation of young drug addicts. He is a member of the CUA chorus and recently accompanied that group on their very successful trip to New York City, where they performed at Carnegie Hall. He also sings with the choir of the National Shrine of the Immaculate Conception. Hector sings in the baritone section.

"Hector Bolduc was the founder and Editor of the TSUNAMI (great wave) Newsletter, a monthly publication formed two years ago. His article concerning the Melville missionaries and their difficulties with the Guatemalan Government received nationwide attention.

"Hector Bolduc is a member of the French and German Clubs, he frequently lectures in the Washington area on subjects such as the history of glass, books, and manuscripts, antique jewelry, and famous gems." [End of article]

The effort above seemed to be a full-time job, but Hector continued his other activities (nonacademic) such as intramural football, choir, art viewings, concerts, and movies. He continued visiting his friends and confidants. That he was a very thoughtful person is seen in this May 10, 1970, entry: "Sunday—Mother's Day—Sophie was glowing with her double orchid corsage. Took her for a drive and we ended up in Brookeville where we visited with Father Fidelis and the boys."

As every other year, Hector was still working on his own antique collection and this year he accomplished two major finds. One on December 13, 1969: "Received my copy of the *Tres Riches Heures of Jean, Duke of Berry*, a magnificent work."

On July 14, 1970, Hector wrote: "I brought the two documents (one of the Declaration of Independence—100th anniversary—and the other commemorating the 400th anniversary of the discovery of America) to the National Archives. Both were authenticated by Mr. Burke and his staff. They claimed that they were the only two such documents in American History that contain the signatures of the entire government."

There was an article about this great find in the *Laconia Evening Citizen* on April 13, 1971, abstracted below:

Gilford Resident discovers rare historical documents

"The fabulous discovery of two rare historical documents was revealed this week by historian Hector Bolduc.

Outside of the Declaration of Independence, the Bill of Rights, and Constitution, these two discovered documents are the most important. They are the 'Administration of the U.S. Government at the Beginning of the Second Century, Washington D.C. July 4, 1876, U.S. Grant, President' and the other 'the Beginning of the 400th Anniversary of the Discovery of America—1492-1892.' Benjamin Harrison was President. Each is valued at over $100,000.

"Mr. Bolduc had done research on Civil War Colonel James D. McBride. The Colonel owned several printing companies. He had printed both scrolls and taken them to Washington where the various signatures were affixed. It seems his son sold at auction several scrolls including the two mentioned above for a couple of dollars. The purchaser traded them in Washington for an old Civil War gun. Knowing of Bolduc's interest in Civil War articles, the new owner then offered them for sale to Mr. Bolduc. Although not sure of their value at that time, Bolduc had a 'premonition' and after the purchase, took them to the National Archives last May where they remained for several months while undergoing intensive scrutiny and examination.

"Hector was offered $100,000 each but would not consider it. The documents have been loaned out for displays at the National Bicentennial Commission and at the National Archives." [End of article]

On May 28, 1970, Hector left Washington for Stockbridge with a U-Haul. After dropping off camping materials, he headed for Laconia for a birthday party for his mother. In the Laconia Citizen, there was an article about this visit: "Hector Bolduc has been visiting his parents. Seeing New Hampshire for the first time are colleagues of his at CU who are house guests of his parents: Professor Germain Bargin of Paris, professor of French at several Washington Universities; Brother Alphie Gagne MIC, of Stockbridge Mass, director of receiving at Stockbridge; Ann Wagner of Oconomowoc, Wisconsin, Student at the University; Tim Jurgensen of Savanah, Georgia, and Diane Diaz of Baltimore, both of whom graduated Sunday.

All belong to the chorus and several area organizations. This summer, Hector will be cataloguing the art collection at CUA."[109] [End of article]

On August 29, 1970, Hector left for the seminary.

---

[109] Date unknown

Chapter Twelve

St. Mary's Seminary and Consortium,Emmitsburg,
MD (1970-1971)

I talked to a Father Seraphin on March 22, 2018. He said that this seminary was very liberal and not very well liked and is now gone. It was in Bethesda, Maryland. There were one hundred nineteen students at the seminary when Hector arrived and shortly thereafter, they were down to one hundred seventeen. Hector wrote: "Ironic as it may sound, eleven St. Mary's College students were arrested on drug charges, as well as two girls from St. Josephs."[110]

Hector had six classes and an apostolate work. The apostolate work is mentioned on September 14, 1970: "Left for Mount Alto in the afternoon where a doctor and nurse briefed us on the hospital and its goals." There is a Mount Alto Veterans hospital in Washington, D.C. This may be where Hector was doing his work. On October 4, 1970, he wrote: "Went to Mount Alto on the monthly visiting program. George and I got in a Pinochle game with two old timers up there."

This year's courses were Dogma, Church History, Scripture, Homiletics [art of giving a sermon] History, and Morals. He commented on September 24, 1970, that with all his work, he could use thirty hours a day. Msgr. M taught both Homiletics and History: "After regular classes, Msgr. M. took all those in his Local History class for a field trip. We visited small churches and Mass houses in various small towns. The highlight of the trip was the visit to the Conewango where we saw the famous basilica there and the famous old Mass house [prior to 1741]."[111]

On the "giving sermons," those who have heard Hector's sermons after he became a priest know that he gave inspirational and thought-provoking sermons. It did not start out that way. On October sixth Hector wrote: "Very bad cold, sore

---

[110] 9/3/1970 diary
[111] 11/6/1970 diary

throat, headache, chest pains, etc. Have exams. However, I gave my sermon. Msgr. M. really tore it up. Now I know what he means by brutal charity."

There was also choir/music activity although it was not officially a course. The choir was very good and successful, but the music was far from Hector's favorite: "Had music practice. It is clear that the music director only wants guitar music—no Gregorian chant or serious music here."[112]

The Dogma class was the most demanding as seen from the following comments on December 13, 1970: "Tomorrow is the Dogma exam day. Pass or fail, it will be nice to get this wretched exam out of the way. Three solid weeks of studying." On the following day after the test: "What they said about Msgr. S.'s exam certainly was true. It was impossible to get all that material down in two hours. Everyone was stunned and is sure he flunked it." The class did not get easier as the year went on as seen by this comment on May 15, 1971: "Have over 420 pages of Dogma notes (for the exam)."

Hector was now classified as a second year Theology student. He was still active in the conservative group called the TSUNAMI as well as monthly meetings of the Legion of Mary.

In his journal there were comments about beautiful ceremonies and some about the problems of the times. This year, he continued to write letters to the Superior General, Father Sielski[113]. From the comments about the abuses in other diary entries, it would appear that he attempted to have Father Sielski fix the problems: "Left Emmitsburg at seven am and went to the Marian house.[114] Had a conference with Father Sielski , although not very fruitful, certainly served to clear the air. He was certainly made aware of how I feel about the entire situation, and I put down today a deadline for any further action. Father Bruno was called in on my behalf to act as a witness to this."[115]

---

[112] 9/28/1970 diary
[113] 2/16/1971 diary
[114] 3885 Harewood Road , NE
[115] 4/28/1971 diary

On October 25, 1970, Hector wrote in his journal: "Sunday—we had Benediction—it was optional, and it was encouraging to see how many attended. Had a penance service this evening. Several former Mount St. Mary's priests came." Another encouraging note on November 2: "We commemorated All Souls Day with special services at Lauds, Vespers, Compline and at Mass."

There were many remarks about craziness going on in the seminary: "Today, some of the less intelligent in the house decorated the chapel for Mass with streamers and balloons. It looked hideous and the vast majority of the house were repulsed by it. No one was consulted."[116] But through all of this, Hector kept his devotions and prayers: "St. Joseph, as we approach your feast day, help and protect me." He does have some good priests helping him through the rough times as seen on November 30, 1970: "Had a fine talk with Msgr. M. He pointed out many interesting facts about how art and history may be used in one's priestly formation and in parishes."

Hector made an interesting comment on February 11, 1971: "A sister came to speak to us today on the role of women in the Church. What she had to say was okay, but she was such a crybaby! 'We are poor unappreciated, downtrodden women.'"

On April 10, 1971, while on a short visit home, Hector made this interesting comment: "Participated as deacon in the Easter Services. Baptized Scott James St. Louis. I had to read and sing some of the prayers." I'm a little confused about Hector acting as deacon, as this diary entry of May nineteenth shows that he had not yet received the diaconate: "We were tonsured today. I am now officially a cleric. Cardinal Sheen of Baltimore performed the ordinations." Elsewhere, it says that he received the minor orders in 1972. So he must have "performed as" without "being" a deacon. Sometimes seminarians can perform as subdeacon or deacon provided that they do not do what is specifically bound with the order (reading epistle, gospel, putting the drop of water in the wine, cleaning the chalice, etc.) but from

---

[116] 2/23/1971 diary

what Hector wrote, it seems that he performed much of what should be reserved to a deacon (e.g. preaching, baptising).[117]

The monthly retreats were not always good, but on May 23, 1971, he was happy about this retreat: "Sunday—retreat Master is excellent. Finally, a retreat that has prayer and spirituality in it. So tired of having retreats where only social, racial, or military subjects are discussed. Went to grotto for my daily visit."

On April twenty-fifth: "Sunday—spent most of the morning and afternoon at Harrisburg attending rites for Msgr. M. Spent a good part of the evening up at the cemetery at the Mount, guarding the newly dug grave against possible vandalism. Jim Tucker accompanied me. I finished writing my paper today—Thanks, Msgr. M."

On April twenty-sixth: "We left for Harrisburg early. We had a considerable amount of practicing to do for the music. The Mass was splendid—five bishops officiated with Bishop L. as the main celebrant. Cardinal Sheen was there. Also concelebrating, were one hundred twenty-five priests. The Cathedral was full. A luncheon was held after the funeral. Then we had a procession back to Emmitsburg for the burial. I stayed for the entire affair until the last shovel of soil had been put in place. I stood guard over the grave all night." There is a reason for this guard duty. In other parts of the diary around this time, there are comments about drinking parties in the cemetery by local students. Both boys and girls participated with the number being sometimes as high as forty revelers. Hector had chased them out of the cemetery before on many occasions.

A major project besides the University art collection was undertaken this year. Hector, being interested in history, investigated many significant events, documented their significance with information and medals, and gave talks to groups on the background of the events. He made several medals to commemorate significant local events. There was a mail service on Lake Winnipesaukee near Gilford, New Hampshire, that had operated close to eighty years. Hector designed and had made

---

[117] This sentence is from Father Laisney's comments on the above functions that Father Bolduc performed without being a deacon.

a medal, cachets and news items about the boat. There was also a Statute at Large of the United States of America specifically approving the boat service as an official mail delivery solution for the Lake residents. The boat also carried passengers to the various islands.[118] The envelopes were postmarked on the floating Post Office and then, with the medal, sold for a nominal fee.

On May 31, 1971, Hector left for a vacation at home where he helped with the farming, painting, and gardening much of the summer. Hector's apostolate for the summer was in Lakeport at Our Lady of the Lakes parish. There were some side trips like the one on August 12, 1971: "Were up early and drove to Plymouth, Vermont, where we visited the Calvin Coolidge birthplace and cemetery. We also called on Mr. and Mrs. John Coolidge, son of the President. We visited the La Salette Shrine at Attleboro, Massachusetts and went to Mass there. We also visited abandoned houses by the roadside and then visited Gilmantown and houses of Grace Metalions. Went to drive in movie—two horror movies."

On August 21, 1971, Hector purchased a car: "Went to Meredith and put a down payment on the car [1929 Rolls Royce]." On the last day before leaving for the Seminary, he bought some jewelry: "Up early. Helped Pop pick corn, cukes, and tomatoes. I paid Mrs. W. $570 for the jewelry. Reserved a large lot of Linages plates [twelve], Boston and New England coin silver and a signed Hawkes bowl of cut glass."

Hector left for the Seminary on August 31, 1971.

---

[118] Lake Winnipesaukee Floating P.O. - Ernest Bolduc (1/1/1971, 1/1/2019), *Laconia Evening Citizen* (11/1/1970, 4/1/1971), Library of Congress (4/20/1971), *Brockton Daily Enterprise* (4-15-1972) (sources 53-60)

Chapter Thirteen

Mount Saint Mary's Seminary and Consortium (1971-1972)

Hector was now a third year Theology student. This period proved interesting and unusual as he vacationed for a month during Christmas time and then apparently left school before the term ended. Hector seemed to have become interested in the Society of St. Pius X [SSPX] since his good friend Clarence Kelly had been attending there in Écône. His first day back to school, on August 31, 1971, he visited an old friend: "My first stop on campus was to go to the cemetery on the hill and visit the grave of Msgr. M."

The classes this year were Eastern Christianity, American History, Dogma, Scripture, Canon Law, Morals, and the Bible. Not much mention was made about the classes except that he wishes there were "just more hours in the day".[119]

Hector's spiritual life included many of the devotions and practices of previous years: days of recollection; monthly Legion of Mary meetings; forty hours devotion followed by Benediction; monthly retreats; daily visits to the cemetery and grotto; and of course, daily Mass.

The Masses were of various rites and customs, and most were unacceptable to Hector. He wrote on September twenty-fourth: "A group from Washington came to offer Mass in the Maronite Rite. The Mass left much to be desired but the celebrant was especially gross using his sermon and talk before Mass as a means of attacking the 'Western Church,' 'Latin Rite,' and 'Rome.'" On November thirtieth he wrote: "Had a hideous Mass today celebrated by G. G." On December second and eighth, he recorded that there were good Masses, although he did not comment on the reason they were good: "Father D. L. was here and celebrated Mass for us today. He said a beautiful Mass and gave a most moving sermon. Hope he returns soon."

---

[119]   9/17/1971 diary

The people lecturing on spiritual matters were not given good reviews by Hector. Three examples of the comments in the diary follow. On October twenty-first: "Had a Lutheran speaker come over this evening for a talk on Vatican II. He was a good speaker and a good deal more 'Catholic' than some of our priests and many of our seminarians."

On November sixth he wrote: "Started our day of renewal this afternoon. Was not impressed by the speaker and even less by his sermon in which he completely ignored the readings and gospels and went on a rampage (very subtly of course) about war and peace, Vietnam, and the US government. There is no question but that he is a radical liberal."

On December twenty-fifth: "Had a pastoral day. Three negro ministers came to speak to us on black issues. Two had something to say. The third turned out to be just another black militant whose only purpose was to cause contention and disrupt what little balance exists between blacks and whites. He stated clearly that the only answer to the black–white problem was total violence meaning guns, revolution, and bloodshed."

Hector received a letter on 11/9 from his fellow TSUNAMI member who was now in Écône, Switzerland, with the SSPX.[120] In Hector's seminarian life he was not happy with the Catholic Church's teachings and liturgy since Vatican II. He now started listening to what the SSPX was teaching and practicing.

On December 16, 1971, Hector left for Germany to visit his relatives and old Army camps, and to make his first visit to the SSPX seminary in Écône. Below are the diary entries as summarized from this period:

> December 21, 1971: "Train to Basel, Switzerland. From Basel, I went to Berne and then to Beige and then off to Écône. I stopped in Sion and called Clarence who brought me to the Seminary. The trip through the mountains including the Matterhorn was fabulous. There were clouds on many of the high peaks and occasionally sunlight would filter through. I had a beautiful evening at the Fraternity of Pius X.

---

[120] I believe this would have been from Clarence Kelly

Had Benediction, Compline, and prayers. Got to meet and speak with some of the boys. Most are French. Clarence and I had a brief talk with Archbishop Lefebvre. He struck me as an extremely humble, pious, and dedicated man."

December 22, 1971: "Spent a beautiful night in a warm bed under thick blankets. This morning was clear, and I got a magnificent view of the mountains from my bedroom window. The mountains tower more than two miles high. When the sun rose and hit them, the view was spectacular. There are wine fields (vineyards) all around. Very delicious bread is served here along with butter and water at all meals. Clarence and I went for a walk across the river this afternoon to Sion, which is a quaint town with the ruins of an old castle. We had a long talk on many matters. I wrote and mailed some cards out. Got some reading done also. Attended a spiritual conference and all other liturgical functions, wanting to take full advantage of this unique situation."

December 23, 1971: "Was up early again and had Mass after morning prayers and Lauds. I spent most of the day speaking on Padre Pio and on getting information about the theological and canonical aspects of the old and new Mass. There were some interesting points made. I also had a long conference with the rector—Archbishop Lefebvre. He is a fascinating individual. There are preparations being made for Christmas. I wrote many letters and postcards. Turned out to be a lovely day. I got to explore some of the underground passages and cellars in this old place. Wish I could stay longer but I must get to those Mosaics.

After visiting the SSPX seminary and making no entry in his diary of a decision about attending the seminary, Hector left on December twenty-fourth for the secondary purpose of his trip, which was viewing mosaic displays throughout Europe. Below are summarized some of the interesting diary entries:

> December 24, 1971: "Was up early and attended Mass in the Chapel of St. Pius X. Then to Sion to catch a train to Milan to Bologna and then to Ravenna. Here I am at last. I took a well needed shower and had a good dinner then went for a walking tour of the city. My first stop was St. Vitale, the Orthodox Baptistry. I walked all over the city until Midnight when I went to the Cathedral and attended Mass. While traveling, I have just begun to realize how much we really lost when the Church discontinued the use of Latin."

> December 27, 1971: "Went to St. Apollinaire Nuovo and climbed the ladder and scaffolding to examine the mosaics. Got a close look at the cross and head of Christ. Visited, examined, and photographed five other churches. Arranged with the director of St. Vitale to have men with ladders there at four pm to examine and photograph Justinian and Theodora. They are beautiful. The Cornelian in Justinian's broach is fabulous. The face and headpiece of Theodora is simply outstanding. Visited and photographed many other locations."

> December 31, 1971: "In Athens, Greece, I climbed to the Acropolis. What a lovely place. We could see the whole of Athens. I stayed till midnight on the Acropolis with some people I met there, an Arab named Mohamad and an English couple named Mr. and Mrs. Bates. We watched the new Year enter from way up among the ruins."

January 5, 1972: "Arrived in Istanbul, Turkey, tired and dirty and went to the hotel. I visited the director of the Hagia Sophia and made arrangements to photograph the mosaics tomorrow. I visited the Topkapi museum. Someone tried to pickpocket me today. I walked around the city tonight—a dangerous thing to do."

January 6, 1972: "Met with the Director of the Hagia Sophia museum and he got me a revered old guard to conduct me through the labyrinths of the old church. We went through passageways, tunnels, and over domes and cupolas of Hagia Sophia. It was unbelievable. We went to the very base of the dome, and I was allowed to examine and photograph the mosaics there. We also examined the mosaics on the second landing by use of a two foot wide catwalk. I must admit I was at times frightened, but everything held together, and we returned safely. I acquired a small piece of mosaic from the former floor and an iron lamp bracket from the very dome. It was really thrilling. I walked over the bridge to the Asian side of Constantinople and examined all the walls of the city. I watched the fish boats come in and walked the dock section. Visited the open bazaars."

January 8, 1972: "Got a cab in Istanbul and went to the outskirts of the city to call on the Patriarch Athenagoras. He was pleasant and we spoke in French. The visit was short, but I felt I would like to meet this man simply for history's sake."

January 11, 1972: "Arrived in Vienna at seven am. Went first to the hotel and then to the Cathedral of St. Steven where I met an Austrian who spent the re-

mainder of the day taking me on foot for a walk
of Vienna visiting many places; a dozen churches;
the treasury where the jewel collection is kept, the
library of rare books, the two palaces which included a tour of the rooms of the former Emperor. The
table setting was exquisite. I also visited the opera
house."

January 13, 1972: "A DAY TO REMEMBER. Up early and went to the Hungarian Seminary. At 9:30,
I had a private audience with Cardinal Mindszen-
ty that lasted about fifteen minutes. He told me of
his devotion to the Blessed Virgin Mary. I asked for
and received his blessing for my future priesthood.
Before leaving, the Cardinal gave me his personal
card with his autograph. Visited the tombs of the
Hapsburgs at the Capuchin church.

On January fourteenth, Hector visited in Germany and on
the twenty-second, he flew back to Washington, D.C. for a retreat and school, which started on January thirty-first. From
Hector's notes on his visit to Écône, it appears that Hector had
fallen in love with the Tridentine Mass. In fact, the opposite
seemed to happen when he returned to Maryland where he
receives two minor orders on January 26, 1972: "I went to
the Shrine and in the Crypt church, I received the two minor
orders of Lector and Acolyte. Bishop H. was the celebrant."[121]
And on January twenty-nineth: "The ceremonies officiated by
Bishop G. and directed by Father T. S. began at nine am. We
received the order of sub deacon in a very moving ceremony. It
was the largest class in history. We had a class picture and went
to a banquet."

On February sixth, Hector began attending weekly Tridentine Masses: "Sunday—Mr. N. and family picked me up
and we drove to St. Athanasius church in Virginia where we

---

[121] His diaries don't mention Hector getting the minor orders of Porter
and Exorcist

attended a Tridentine Mass. I spoke with some of the parishioners about my trip to Switzerland. Afterwards, we went to the home of Mr. Bill Collins where we spent the day. I met Tom Collins (Deacon—St. Mary's in Baltimore) and Joe, Chris, and Ken."

Hector commenced teaching Catechism classes at St. Athanasius. On February twenty-fourth, Hector sent a note to Cardinal B. about his recent diaconate order. It appears that at this point Hector was still planning to be a priest under Cardinal B. On March nineteenth, Hector commented on attending Mass: "Mr. Collins came later, and I went later with him to attend Mass in Vienna. It was a beautiful Tridentine Mass."

In the 1972 diary, there were two pieces of scrap paper with addresses: one with Reverend Frederick Nelson at Our Lady of Prairies at Powers Lake, North Dakota. Father Nelson had one of the few Traditional parishes in the United States at this time. The other address was of Father Anthony Ward in Écône. This most assuredly showed a movement toward Tradition.

Hector was continually working on letters, either receiving or sending. On November fourteenth: "Got twenty letters off today".

There was fun to be had at the Seminary: it may be football or cards or a good fight. On December 7, 1971, "Decorated most of the day. The class of third Theology was in charge of all arrangements. We arranged for the Mass, then a champagne party, then dinner and a reception following with beer and homemade goodies. We sang and had a great time."

He notes on February 19, 1972: "We had a rip-roaring snowball fight, third theology against the remainder of the house. We were greatly outnumbered as many didn't come out, but we put up a good fight and had fun getting pushed and rolled up and down the snowbanks. One window in the priests' lounge was broken."

From seeing all the films he watches, either on TV or at the theater, his clear favorite, as you might expect, was John Wayne movies. Here is a diary entry from February 26, 1972:

"Watched John Wayne movies from nine pm to two am. Mc-
Clintock and Operation Pacific. The entire fan club was there."

There was still work this year with the Catholic University
Arts collection as seen on November fourth: "Went to CU and
spoke to Mr. A. and Mr. M. regarding the 17th century animal
hunting Persian rug. Had some offers on the jewelry but didn't
accept them." Concerning his own collection, he stopped by
antique shops frequently and on November twelfth, he noted
the authenticity of items: "Went to Smithsonian where Drs.
Vladimir and Elvira who authenticated my 2-ducat gold piece
of Julius II."

For his apostolate, Hector worked at the Montrose girl's
reformatory counseling the girls. On February 29, 1972: "After
a full morning of classes, we went as usual to Rosemont to
counsel girls. I had a very fruitful day with Melba who really
opened up."

The journals show that Hector still had his interest in politics. In 1972 there was a presidential election during which
the independent candidate, George Wallace [Hector's choice
for President] was shot.[122] Richard Nixon was reelected President. Hector commented on a previous president, Harry
Truman, who died on December 28, 1972: "Harry Truman, the
greatest president this nation has ever had was buried today."
Other items of interest noted were a riot in Attica prison, and
an Apollo moon landing.

It appears that Clarence Kelly was sympathetic to the John
Birch Society: "Went walking around the board walk. After
dinner, we took a fishing boat and caught over one hundred
mackerel. Ed and Clarence tried converting a lady in one of the
cabins to the true Church. They also introduced her to the John
Birch Society [JBS] and the 'Great Conspiracy.'"[123]

On April 15, 1972, Hector left for a month's vacation in
Florida where his brother Sam lived along with his parents. On
May sixteenth, he returned to Gilford to visit, bale hay, tend to
the huge gardens, and celebrate Mom and Pops fiftieth anni-

[122] 5/15/1972 diary
[123] 9/17/1972 diary

versary on June 24, 1972. Doing all this work on the farm may have led to an operation in late July on his right elbow.

On the first of August, Hector gave a talk: "Worked on my lecture—Sam helped me. Had the lecture on 'History of Jewelry' at the Meredith Township Historical Society."

Hector had a talk in early October with his "pop" about Hector buying the farm: "Pop and I discussed the purchase of the farm. Looks like he really wants to sell it and I will be happy to own it."

On October sixteenth, Hector left for a vacation in Florida for three weeks and then a hunting trip in Indiana for a week. Upon returning to Gilford, he traveled to Boston to have a meeting which is somewhat secret: "See Vol III p 610 for notes on meeting in Boston with the members of the F.C.M. (old A-66). Some good material but still hung up on the P.Q.A.T.L of C. [six capital coded letters]. Will look into it close before committing my sell." The above sounds like it came from a spy thriller but the last sentence suggests it might have something to do with selling antiques?

At the back of the 1972 diary is a list of songs which brought back memories or had special meaning to Hector: "Canadian Sunset, Moonlight in Vermont, Red Sails in the Sunset, Pomp and Circumstance (graduation), Jack the Knife (basic training), Wheels, Walk don't run, Midnight in Moscow, Patricia, Ramona, Auf Wiedersehen (German), Release Me, La Mer, To Dream the Impossible Dream, George Patton."

Chapter Fourteen
Mount Saint Mary's Seminary (1973)

A highlight of this year was the winding up of "the case of the missing coins" which is too interesting to be left out:

In September of 1971, Hector asked Ernest to send him three gold coins as part of a class assignment. When the package was opened in Maryland by Hector, the three gold coins worth over $6000 were missing. The rest of the story, as Paul Harvey would say, was a testament to the Bolducs' perseverance and ingenuity. Claims for lost property were made at both ends of the delivery [i.e., Maryland and New Hampshire] by Hector and Ernest.

Soon, investigators were questioning Hector and Ernest separately. The written texts of these interviews were not what the two brothers had said in answer to the questions. From then on, all communications were done in a written fashion to reduce Post Office and FBI investigators distortions. Polygraph tests were requested but Ernest asked that all the Post Office people also be checked. This was refused. Several code systems for communications were set up between Hector and Ernest as they felt their telephones were being bugged. Physical threats were made against Ernest by the post office employees.

At some point, Hector decided that working with the post office and FBI wasn't getting anywhere so all the written communications were bundled up and mailed to President Nixon with a request for an answer within seven days. Even though the President was sick, the answer came with a check on July 24, 1973.

At the end of 1973, the newspaper reported that some of the people (from Manchester and Boston) investigating the case were found to be part of a ring that took items from the mail.[124]

The year 1973 was Hector's last semester in Washington. He spent it at a Miss Jameson's house rather than the seminary. He worked around the house doing repairs and updating. Miss Jameson and Hector had many talks and enjoyed each other's company: "Miss Jameson and I really had some laughs. When I told her that the best way for a woman to catch a man was to keep her mouth shut, she answered 'Now you tell me.'"[125]

Hector's classes were somewhat unusual: Sex Ed; Abnormal Psych; Mariology; Pastoral; and Religious Existence. Certain of his teachers were not to his liking: "Had class with Father D. where we discussed King's book 'the Church.' Father D. is a real modernist and a heretic. He openly teaches that Christ didn't found the Church and had no intention of doing so. If this continues, I shall have to be forced to drop his class. The other students go right along with him. They have no concept of Catholic doctrine or traditions."[126]

Msgr. R was still a confidant and friend of Hector's. They talked about the situation in the Church during these times: "Mgr. R. is home from the hospital. He is very much disgusted with the present attitude of the Church especially over the silence of the American Bishops over the recent Supreme Court ruling on abortion. They spent thousands attacking the American stand on Vietnam and now sit silent when a real moral question arises. It shows how horribly decadent the hierarchy in this country have become and how very tied to politics they are."[127]

Hector continued to go to Virginia for the Traditional Latin Mass where he gave sermons and taught Catechism class. On April seventh, Hector was driven by Mr. Collins to Monroe, Connecticut, to Our Lady of the Rosary Chapel: "We were in-

---

[124] Ernest on 10/20/17. Also, more than 2 inches of backup material in Gilford. (source 1)
[125] 2/6/1973 diary
[126] 2/9/1973 diary
[127] 2/5/1973 diary

troduced to Father Francis Fenton.[128] He seems to be very dynamic and well-ordered person. After a most wonderful Mass, we had a long private meeting with Father Fenton and met a considerable number of his parishioners. We drove back to Washington later. I wrote to Archbishop Lefebvre. It was nice seeing Miss Jameson again."[129]

On April seventeenth, Hector received a statement from Father Fidelis and sent it off to Switzerland. It seems the wheels were now turning for Hector to attend the seminary in Écône.

On May 3, 1973, Hector left for Monroe, Connecticut for the first Mass of Father Clarence Kelly and three days later, the ceremony occurred: "The Mass was by far the most beautiful I have ever witnessed. It was without a doubt the first Solemn High Mass celebrated in the U.S. in five to ten years. Father Fenton and I assisted Clarence. We stayed up late and had a wonderful time. I was so fortunate that I was able to participate in this truly historical and gracious event."

Hector was back in Washington for a full day of classes on May 16, 1973: "A Sister Jeanine G from Notre Dame academy in Baltimore spoke to us on Homosexuality today at Father H.'s class. She was a full-fledged proponent of it and stated that the Church's teachings on this matter were wrong. A priest supported her views. Both are associated with a group called Dignity."

On May 25, 1973, Hector left Washington for the last time as a student at the seminary. He had to leave the seminaries that were teaching errors and go to a seminary that taught the true faith. He fought the novelties and abuses with the TSUNAMI newsletter and in the classroom. He wrote letters to the Superior General of the Marianites. He was a pioneer with only a

---

[128] Founder of the Orthodox Roman Catholic Movement. See fr.fenton. wordpress.com

[129] From Wikipedia about Father Francis Fenton. The Orthodox Roman Catholic Movement (ORCM) is a group of priests founded by Fr. Francis E. Fenton acting on the suggestions of Fr. Joaquin Sáenz y Arriaga, S.J., and was the U.S. organization parallel to the Mexican organization Unión Catolica Trento, founded by Fr. Saenz along with Frs. Moises Carmona and Adolfo Zamora. Fr. Fenton was a founding member of the "conservative" John Birch Society, and was on its American Opinion Speakers Bureau

few others in the United States to take up the battle against all the novelties of Vatican II.

Hector arrived home for summer vacation on May twenty-sixth and worked most of the summer on the farm with many side trips antiquing. The farm was overrun with slugs and chipmunks and on Jun sixteenth he wrote: "Have killed about fifty chipmunks."

There was enjoyment on the farm as Pop would tell stories for the enjoyment of his sons such as: "The hay was a good six feet tall and lay on the ground a good foot high after cutting." Pop talked of some amusing story—"In the early 30's or late 20's where Pop owned a corn cutting machine, he used to go the various farms and cut the corn. At the D. farms on Ladd Hill, Mr. Valore D. owned a fine team of grays. One had a habit of picking a foot up and resting the other foot while standing between loads of corn. Pop teased Mr. D. about his lazy horse and pop used to prop a two-by-four plank from the ground to the horse's side as if it were too weak to stand by itself. One day, two well-dressed grain salesmen came to see Mr. D. while they were working and noticing the two-by-four, asked what was wrong with the horse. Mr. D. was really disgusted with them noticing this and gave a kick to the piece of wood knocking it away whereby the horse fell to the ground. Everyone laughed except Mr. D. who had some choice words to say to my father."[130]

As I have noted before, when it came to farm work, even though the family members were on their own, they always seemed to be up to "the farm" when work needed to be done: "Anita and Norman up to help with the hay. Baled three hundred two bales. Budd came up to help as did Armand."[131]

At last, Hector sent his trunk air mail to Switzerland on August 2, 1973. Four days later, Hector said goodbye to Mom and Pop: "Mom cried."

---

[130] 7/7/1973 diary
[131] 7/11/1973 diary

The Sacrament of Holy Orders
will be conferred upon
Hector Ludger Bolduc
of the Society of Saint Pius X
June twenty-ninth
Nineteen hundred and seventy-four
nine o'clock in the morning
at the International Seminary of Saint Pius X
Econe, Switzerland
by the Most Reverend Marcel Lefebvre
Titular Archbishop of Synnada
Superior General of the Society of Saint Pius X
Introibo ad altare Dei
Ad Deum qui laetificat juventutem meam

Chapter Fifteen
SSPX—Écône (1973-1974)

Before traveling to Écône, Hector took a tour. As with most of Hector's trips, they end up at their destination eventually but visit some interesting sites first. He first visited his family in Mulheim and went then to see his old barracks in Friedberg.

On the feast of the Assumption, he was in a church in France: "Went to observe Mass as celebrated in several churches large and small. Same errors as seen before including consecrations that were devoid of meaning and incorrectly given. Really no true Mass. Horrible profanations everywhere."

Hector traveled through Germany where he visited relatives and then on to London, Holland,[132] and finally, a train to Basel Switzerland on October 5, 1973: "Train to Riddes and called the seminary and they sent a car to pick me up. The mountains are lovely. Saw the Archbishop and was shown to my room which is #6. Was in the house only a few minutes when I felt right at home. Don Sanborn came to say hello".

It is clear that Hector had reached his spiritual home and was at peace. The clearest way to show this is by way of some of the diary entries during this period in early October:

> October sixth: "Started classes in chant. Really fantastic being in a real seminary."
>
> October seventh: "Sunday—Left for Augustus Italy for our retreat. 'Jesus, thank you for not taking my life while in the state of sin.'"
>
> October eighth: "Retreat. The spiritual directors are excellent. Father Snyder is one of them. A very wise

---

[132] In Holland, S- Hertogenbousch. Netherlands. Confirmed the town was first named bois le duc. Later shortened to Bolduc. I have a copy of the coat of arms. (source 98)

and holy man. This has the start of being one of the very best retreats I have ever had."

October tenth: "Father Snyder talked on simplicity—there is nothing so difficult or complex as simplicity. A beautiful atmosphere here with the retreatants."

October eleventh: "Continue to explore the mountains and rock formations. The surrounding castles are most interesting structures. My soul really has been lightened by these few days of retreat. I can see now more clearly how far from God I had strayed because of the modernistic and satanic influences in the 'new' seminaries. Thank heaven I am now free of the corrupting influences of Mount St. Mary's and Father X. He truly was a devil."

October fourteenth: "Sunday—took a ride to the mountain behind the seminary. Wonderful views. The changing colors of the leaves was not nearly as lovely as in New Hampshire. Walked on the ridge."

October fifteenth: "Eagerly awaiting the return of Fathers Clarence [Kelly] and Anthony [Ward]. Had a meeting with M Le Chanoine Berthod today to review all my courses and it was discovered that I was only missing some work on indulgences and the practical application of the Sacraments according to the Roman Ritual. I am now close to ordination. I received many spiritual books to read. I will start a very active deep spiritual renewal from this day forth."

October sixteenth: "How beautiful it is to hear the Salve Regina sung nightly. There is a lovely statue of the BVM right outside my door with a votive candle lit. I have pledged to say my rosary before it every night for all those who are looking for the Tridentine Mass, and for my parents."

The tone of his diary has changed from one who was un-happy to one who is delighted and excited to be where he is. He is also still in very fine physical shape as the seminarians are taking long hikes into the mountains beyond the seminary and vineyard: "Left for the mountain walk at 7:15 am. Our group of seven was led by Denny R. We tried a very strenuous endurance route and succeeded. We climbed to the Rambert cabin (2594 meters or 1.6 miles) and down again and then up through the Collin pass and down the other side. We got back at six pm. The views were magnificent. Coming down was almost perpendicular and quite spectacular." On February 5, 1974: "Went on a hike to Finhaut. Steve K, Jerry H, Warren K, Terrance Finnegan, Father Post, and I. We had a great time. Had lunch at a restaurant on top—it started snowing hard. It was beautiful to see. We sang songs all the way up and back. We said the Angelus at the small chapel on top and the rosary on the way down. We played baby foot when we got back.[133] There is much enjoyment on these hikes among the seminarians. The views and companionship are pleasurable."

On November thirteenth, he had a talk with the Arch-bishop: "Had a most interesting conference with Archbishop Lefebvre this afternoon. Subject: the Spirit of Poverty." The SSPX priests take the vows of chastity and obedience but not the vow of poverty. I wondered how the Archbishop would view Hector's collection of "treasures" and their value. I think the key word used in the diary was "spirit." You can have trea-sures but just cannot be attached to them too much.

Hector was still working on world political issues and working with certain clandestine organizations. There are many diary entries that just have many capital coded letters with periods after each letter. Capital coded letters means Hector doesn't want anybody reading the diary to capture his private thoughts.

On November nineteenth, he was communicating with the President of Greece: "Received a call from the Greek represen-

---

[133] Baby foot is a table game with handles on each side with a ball in play and each player tries to have his players on the table kick the ball into the opponent's goal.

tative from Germany who informed me that President Papado-poulos had received and read my report and was pleased." This quote was followed by twenty capital coded letters.

On December thirteenth: "Finally got all the material concerning the Israeli's plan to forge old texts and documents to try to discredit the Catholic church and Christ. The letter from Frankfurt absolutely confirms that the Jews are buying all blank pieces of parchment. They are truly diabolic—see Book 66, p 78."

On December nineteenth: "Received a letter from Msgr. Ryan. He had some very excellent and fatherly advice to give me. Had a long talk with Father Snyder—I thought he ought to be informed. Heard from G today. Much going on in the African countries and Spain. Anarchy and assassinations are feared. The communists will use the weakened state of Europe and America to further their dirty work. They hope that other nations will not want to interfere for fear of upsetting the peace talks between the Arabs and Israel. How right they are!"

On December twenty-nineth: "Went by train to Frankfurt to meet I.A. and exchange information. He says we can expect attacks on oil storage areas all over Europe conducted by Israeli agents, who want to keep the price of oil up and assure fantastic profits of their Israeli owned oil companies. I translated the six reports he gave me, but I have not had time to copy or code them."

The above entries don't leave much to the imagination about Hector's political activities.

I received a letter from Ernest (Bolduc) that included a poem Hector wrote and sent to the *Herald of Freedom* newspaper while he was at Écône in 1974. I thought about including it since it represented Hector's thoughts about his country at this time. I concluded that it was very appropriate especially as I am writing this paragraph in late October 2020 just before the U.S. election of a President and the poem is more pertinent almost fifty years later:

An Answer from "Uncle Sam"

You wonder what happened to "Uncle Sam."
Well then let me tell you for that is who I am,
A nation of people that once was so great,
That seems to have stumbled and slipped as of late,
My Armor was God and you cast him away,
And in the schools, you forbid His children to pray,
The laws of my land you threw careless aside,
And you burned my flag in your arrogant pride.
You run riotous and wild in my city streets,
Your blasphemies have shackled my feet.
With fetters of sin, you have bound both my hands,
And the sins of your flesh have laid waste to my lands.
You have sullied my heroes and defiled their names,
And brought forth false Gods and adored the profane.
You lay down your arms on the field of battle,
But my unborn you slaughter like diseased cattle.
The cancer of Communism gnaws at my bones,
While divorce and adultery decimate my homes.
The just are defied while criminals brag,
For over the mouth of Justice you have placed a gag.
Turn back to your God, source of power and might,
Only He can deliver you from your wretched plight.
For He is our strength, our one and our all,
At His Word the chains which bind me shall fall;
And you'll see a change come over our nation,
When you offer to God a fitting oblation.
Of prayer and sacrifice, honor and love,
He'll be pleased and send His grace from above.
For when you have purged yourself of your sin,
God will once more give you that will to win.
The righteous will triumph, and justice prevail,
With God as your leader, you cannot fail.
But remember my people, the hour grows late,
You know not the hour, the day, or the date.
If you want to remain the world's greatest nation,
Then fall on your knees without hesitation,

And raise up your voices to God up on high,
And take up the motto, "LIVE FREE OR DIE."

There were still happenings in Rome with the implementation of various parts of Vatican II. Hector had strong feelings about the changes as he had seen throughout his life: "Wrote to Father Fenton. There is a lot going on in Rome. I am a Roman Catholic, a member of the One, Holy, Catholic, and Apostolic Church. I can accept no compromise on items of faith no matter how small."[134]

Archbishop Lefebvre gave talks frequently to the seminarians on many subjects. On December third: "Archbishop gave a conference on charity today. Towards one another and on the importance of the more advanced students giving a good example to the younger or newly arrived students." Again, on December eleventh: "Archbishop gave a talk on Modernism. This evening, I encountered him kneeling in front of the statue of our Lady on the first floor, praying with head bowed." Finally, Hector was receiving true and traditional teachings at this seminary. No heretical talks there.

The liturgy was especially pleasing to Hector as this note testifies on December twenty-fourth: "Practiced singing almost all day. Had solemn Vespers this evening celebrated by Archbishop Lefebvre—beautiful! Started services at ten with Matins and then had Midnight Mass followed by Lauds. Finished at 1:35 and then had a nice banquet. The services were magnificent, especially the *Te Deum*." Hector had a splendid privilege on March 10, 1974: "High Mass with the Archbishop and I was sub-deacon."

On January 9, 1974, Hector had a talk with the Archbishop: "Had a long talk with Archbishop Lefebvre before he left for Rome and Paris. He asked me to go to Fribourg to be with Father Jean Yves Cottard, who is alone in our house, and possibly take courses at University of Fribourg. I will go about the fifteenth, as the Archbishop left it up to me."

---

[134] 11/26/1973 diary

On January tenth, Hector had a talk with Father Snyder: "We both agreed with the Archbishop's policy of not associating with any of the many small factions in the Tridentine movement. We serve all who are in need of the true Mass and the Sacraments but are not involved in any of the politics." On January twentieth: "Had an interesting talk with Father J. Y. C. (in Fribourg) today. Got a lot of interesting insights into SSPX. We discussed aspects of the Society, and both agreed on the need of strict obedience to the Archbishop. When one enters the fraternity, he owes that to the Archbishop." This is an important statement about obedience to the Archbishop, especially as it relates to the difficulty Hector had in 1984 by not obeying the Archbishop.

Hector was happy to be in Fribourg: "I am so pleased with my stay here. I really have profited by it. Father Jean is a fine person to be with."[135]

The area where Hector was now staying has many museums, libraries, churches, and antique shops. He had more time to make visits to all these. He purchased antiques like gold coins, books, and jewels to send home. As of April 18, 1974, he had sent twenty boxes of books home. People have asked me where did all of Hector's collection in Gilford come from? After only seven months in Fribourg, he had collected those twenty boxes of books alone. Écône's libraries were very deficient in the quantity and variety of books and so Hector was quite pleased to be able to stay in Fribourg. On January thirtieth there is this comment: "Did some research on the Ritual and the Mass. Found several most interesting volumes. There is a fine set of works on the Greek and Latin Fathers of the Church at the library."

On March 30, 1974, great news for Hector: "forty-five boys received minor orders. We had a grand Mass and ceremony. Msgr. Lefebvre met me in the corridor today and asked me to come to see him before leaving so he could talk to me about ordination. I was so happy I could have floated."

---

[135] 1/23/1973 diary

On the following day, Hector and the Archbishop had the talk: "Archbishop Lefebvre spoke to me this evening and informed me that I would be ordained to the Diaconate on June 29, 1974, and to the priesthood when he comes to the states soon after. This is the happiest day of my life. Weatherwise, it was a magnificent day."

There was a small change of plans on April third: "Archbishop Lefebvre arrived today and informed me that I would become a Deacon at Pentecost and a Priest on June twenty-nineth. I will write home at once."

On April eleventh, Hector commented on the services: "Lovely services today. I was subdeacon for the Vesperal Mass. The epistle which I sang went very well. We had adoration this evening until midnight. Anyone who has ever witnessed the awesome beauty of the rituals of the Roman Catholic Church could not help but be moved by them and I am sure could never accept the cold, emptiness of the *Novus Ordo* with ever feeling deep in the soul, a longing for that which was lost; and without living with the knowledge that he was spiritually poorer for the loss of it."

On May second, Hector left for Rome with others to tour the churches and receive his Pius X chalice. There were no notes on where or how he got this chalice. In a sermon in 1974, Father Bolduc related the story of how he obtained the St. Pius X chalice. What follows is a summary of his talk:

> Some years ago, a bishop in Italy decided to divest his churches of old antiquated things in his churches. He offered for sale these items [statues, crosses, chalices, ciboriums, and other items]. He came under fire from the local Catholics of the area for selling their heritage. The bishop, to avoid criticism, sold the remaining items privately. The buyers had to sign a document assuring the seller that they would not disclose the bishop's name or the price of the item. In 1973, he sold more items and among them was the chalice that was presented to Father Giuseppe Sarto [the future St. Pius X] when he became a bishop. This was the chalice he used and liked as a priest and when he became a

bishop, the chalice was given to him. The man in charge of selling the items for the bishop was a good friend of Father Bolduc's and knowing that Father was traditionally minded, he contacted him.

Father traveled to Italy and authenticated the chalice over several months. The paten is inscribed with his date of Pius X's ordination, consecration as a bishop and cardinal, and the date he became the Vicar of Christ. After Father acquired the chalice and paten, he had inscribed on it the date of Pope Pius X's canonization as a saint.

It was very providential that Father got the chalice of St. Pius X since many of the precious sacramental objects were gone when Father went back to get another item. He learned that a Jewish man had taken them, removed the precious stones and melted the items down to make jewelry.

The chalice is now in the Immaculate Conception church in Gilford, New Hampshire, being used by SSPX priests that offer Mass there. It is one of the highlights when a priest visits Gilford to be able to say Mass with the St. Pius X chalice.

Father's older brother Ernest relates that it has over three hundred precious gems that are two different colors of red.

Source: Father Bolduc (25 minutes into the sermon) and Dave Melechinsky. who was present at Father's 1974 sermon.

Hector wrote on May twenty-third: "Had a long talk with Mgr. Lefebvre. He was much pleased with the chalice of St. Pius X."

On May sixteenth: "Had a great discussion with Fathers C. and S. about our 'cabin' in Canada. We have a number of things in common." Hector will dream his whole life about the "Cabin in the Wilderness." Fortunately for all of us, he saw his vocation of saving souls as more important than his solitude in the Canadian wilderness.

After a week-long retreat, on June 2, 1974, came the day Hector has been waiting for: "This certainly was a great day in my life. At a magnificent Pontifical High Mass, I was ordained to the Diaconate. Others in the house received the sub-diaconate [one of which was Bernard Tissier de Mallerais]. It was a lovely and very moving ceremony. The chapel was full, and it was a lovely day. I signed the necessary papers and took the oath of Faith and the oath against modernism. I also sat at the head table with the Archbishop and other priests of the house. We sang Vespers and Compline and the Litany to the Sacred Heart at the grotto. I remembered Mom and Pop at the Mass and all the family. Our Blessed Mother has answered my prayers."

Hector left for Paris where on June seventh, a Mrs. Orsini took him to her storehouse of vestments and Mass items to allow him to pick out what he would need as a priest.

On Sunday, June twenty-third: "Sunday—a great day. Father Barrielle celebrated his fiftieth anniversary as a priest and we used the new chapel for the first time. At a special Mass this evening, I was formally received into the Fraternity of SSPX. Archbishop Lefebvre gave me a medal and a nice crucifix."

On June twenty-sixth: "Had a complete Mass practice with Gerry and Terry. Bernard Waltz[136] and Pierre practiced for the sub deaconate." On June twenty-eighth: "The new chapel is finished and decorated and is magnificent. St. Peter's couldn't look nicer to me. Pierre Blin, Bernard Tissier de Mallerais, and I took the oath against Modernism. Will make my general confession tomorrow. I am tired but don't feel like sleeping. Father Snyder has been most kind."

On June twenty-nineth: "Saturday—*Tu es sacerdo in aeternum secundum ordinem melchisedech*. Today, on the feast of Sts. Peter and Paul, at a Solemn High Mass which began at 9:30, **I was ordained to the Sacred Priesthood**. Mom and Pop were both very nice. Another Mass practice with Father Snyder. It rained all day."

---

[136] In the diary, it was Bernard Fellay but Father Finnegan said that was not possible and it had to be Bernard Waltz.

Then on June thirtieth: "Sunday—my first Mass at nine am. This morning Father Snyder assisted me at nine am Mass. Michael Hand and Gerry Hogan served. Mom and Pop received Communion from me first. We then drove to the Great St. Bernard with Domenick and had a great time. The mountains and snow were lovely as were the St. Bernard dogs. We ate at the Restaurant Napoleon Bivouac. Thank you, Mary, for this day."

Returning to the States on July 7, 1974, Father Bolduc stopped in New York to say Mass at Clarence Kelly's chapel. On the same day, he left for New Hampshire and arrived home at three a.m. and spent the week relaxing and getting the hay in.

Father had his Mass in his hometown on July twenty-first: "Sunday—a very wonderful day for me, I celebrated my first Solemn High Mass at a private chapel we built at the Moose Hall in Laconia. Father Ward was my deacon, Father Post—Subdeacon, Father Kelly—preached, Charlie—MC. Michael and Terry were Acolytes. Roger Bolduc and Donnie were cross bearer and thurifer. The Mass was lovely. Reception at the KC hall."

On July twenty-sixth, Father Bolduc flew to Washington to have a reunion with Miss Jameson and the Little Sisters and Mass at St. Athanasius where eighty-one parishioners attended. He returned home and gave a talk to the Meredith Historical Society on the "History of America in Medalic Art."

On August 13, 1974, Father left for his first assignment as a SSPX priest: "This is the first time I have ever been concerned about leaving the folks. Pop does not seem well. Father (Anthony) Ward met me, and we went to a house at 3838 Ravenna Avenue [Detroit, Michigan]. We talked late in the evening about our plans."

**Father's first blessing as a priest   with parents kissing his
hands in Écône, Switzerland**

Consecration of Queen of Angels Church - Dickinson
Archbishop, Fathers Bolduc and Dolan

Archbishop with Fr Hector Bolduc in Dickinson TX

Chapter Sixteen
St. Joseph's Seminary (8/1974-12/1975)

Father Bolduc's first assignment was around the Detroit area and more specifically Armada, Michigan. Within a few days of his arrival, the priests moved their home from Ravenna Ave in Detroit to Armada, Mi. which was the SSPX's first seminary in the United States. There was much work to do on the rectory house and chapel. In the lower level of the church was the dormitory for the seminarians. The good news was that the parishioners in the Detroit area were thrilled that they had been selected for the seminary site since that included daily Masses and Sacraments. There was great enthusiasm from the men and women of the parish in helping with the move and then fixing the plumbing, electrical, walls, and exterior. On September twenty-first: "Lot of men working here today. Work on my room, sacristy, office, dryers, cement floor on the chapel. It was really encouraging."

Some of the names of the workers are familiar to many traditional Catholics such as the Perry's, Bartnik's, Gayner's, and Uncle Joe. Uncle Joe was eighty-seven in 1974 and was an accomplished builder and carpenter. (I have a portable altar he made which is simplistically beautiful.) With all his skills, Father worked right with the men whenever he could. He enjoyed manual labor and was quite often right in the "mix" as on October nineteenth: "Worked hard with the men on the basement and sacristy. Poured the footing for the garage."

Father Anthony Ward, the rector, asked Father Bolduc to be the administrator of the house and procurator for the Society in the U.S.[137] Father Ward traveled to Houston with successful results. In time Dickinson, Texas, was to become a large traditional parish.[138]

---

[137] 9/18/1974 diary
[138] 9/16/1974 diary

On September twenty-nineth, St. Joseph's parish and seminary had their first Mass in the new chapel. Father Bolduc was serving the two Detroit parishes. One was named Immaculate Conception Chapel and was situated on Six Mile Road.[139] The other was just referred to as "The Hall."[140] There were also Masses at home chapels mentioned on October 4, 1974: "I went to the K. chapel for First Friday devotions. Brought Holy Communion to Mr. Moor."

On October sixth, a retreat started for thirty to forty people. Father L. gave the retreat and Father Bolduc assisted with some lectures: "I gave the conference this afternoon speaking on the crucifixion and justification."

Father received some complaints from his older brother in Gilford about his lack of communication: "Ernest called and wanted to know why I hadn't written. I am just too busy."[141] Those of us who knew Father are familiar with the long hours and busy schedule he kept.

The seminarians arrived in late September and immediately began to help with the sacristy assignments, traveled to the Detroit chapels with the priest, and pitched in on many work assignments. Some of the names of the young men attending the seminary were Mark and John Violette, Rick Allouse, and Chris Ahearn.

On October twenty-first, Fathers Ward and Bolduc left for meetings in Switzerland. Father Post covered the Detroit and Armada parishes while they were gone. Father Bolduc found it great to be back at Écône: "Wonderful meeting friends again and meeting the new arrivals. Had a long talk with Father Snyder. It was lovely singing Compline this evening, the chapel was darkened, all but for a spotlight which was turned on to the statue of the BVM while we were singing the Salve Regina."

Father had "long talks" with Jerry Hogan, Terry Finnegan, and Dan Sanborn. After four days, he left for Paris and worked with a parishioner on obtaining some vestments and doing some bartering: "After Mass, we drove to Mrs. Orsini's and I

[139] 2/7/1975 diary
[140] 4/27/1975 diary
[141] 10/11/1974 diary

Archbishop with Fr Hector Bolduc and Other Priests
at *The Angelus Press* in Dickinson TX

helped fix some collapsed shelves. Mrs. Orsini gave me a lovely, boxed chalice to bring back to the States." This is just one of many examples of how Father collected so many religious items.

Upon returning to the U.S., Father Bolduc visited Father Kelly in New York, where: "Father Kelly and I had a long talk about the Society and the John Birch Society."[142]It appears Father Kelly was in favor of the John Birch Society whereas Father Bolduc was not, based on comments throughout his diaries.

After the renovation work at St. Joseph's was completed, the dedication was held on November tenth: "Sunday—went to Detroit for the two Masses at eight and nine. Rushed back to Armada for the dedication of the chapel and house. We had fifty-eight guests in our little chapel plus nine of us. After the dedication, we all went to the VFW hall in Mt. Clemens and had a banquet. two hundred forty-four attended. Uncle Joe sat at the head table with us, and he was just beaming. When we returned to Armada, Father Ward opened a bottle of champagne which his father had given him to celebrate the investiture of the cassock for Richard Aluise, Gerald Generalli, and Mark Violette. St. Joseph must have been pleased."

Father Bolduc had not given up his love of history and antiques. He had not been at Detroit more than three days when we see this entry: "Had a call from a Dr. Darrell C. from Washington about the discovery of a Gold Taft (Presidential) Inaugural medal. We will try to raise the $15,000 to purchase it."[143]

On October fourteenth, the first day of classes for the seminarians was held. The only class Father Bolduc mentioned being responsible for is a history class: "Spent the morning giving classes in History—the period of Justinian."[144] It is a little confusing in the diary as to how Father can be teaching classes. He will have many long periods, as you will see, away from Michigan.

---

[142] 11/4/1974 diary
[143] 8/16/1974 diary
[144] 12/12/1974 diary

On December fourteenth, Father made his first of many trips down to the Southwest, specifically Houston, Texas. He spent three weeks in Houston. On Sunday: "Went to Marriot Hotel where we had Mass for about two hundred and fifty. Several men came over and we discussed plans for the next two weeks."

Father was thirty-eight years old and at this point had a fun comment on December eighteenth: "Noticed a lot of grey hair this evening while combing. With what I have been through, it is a wonder I have any hair at all. Thank God for favors."

Father Ward was covering a parish in Colorado Springs, Colorado, at the end of January 1975.[145] There were tensions between the Catholic Detroit diocese and St. Joseph's as seen on February 10, 1975: "I wrote to Bishop Dearden (Detroit diocese) asking that he correct the false statements which he has made concerning SSPX."

On February fourteenth, Father Bolduc again flew to Houston for a ten day stay. He then proceeded to San Antonio to say Mass for forty-five people. During this trip, the Houston Catholics Traditional Movement had a meeting at which Father was present. On returning to Detroit, Father prepared a report to the Society on the state of the finances and property holdings. It is not clear what geography this report covers. Father also made hospital calls as part of his duties and specifically mentions one to Kitty Haf of the Haf sisters.[146] Father mentions on March twenty-third, Palm Sunday: "I went to Detroit for the two Masses. We had five hundred total parishioners at both Masses. Gave marriage instructions."

On March twenty-fourth, Father left for a weeklong trip to Houston where the parish was growing at a fast pace: "Had a total of over five hundred (at both Masses) with sixty-five to seventy-five new families registering over the Holy Week. Flew to San Antonio this afternoon for Mass. More than one hundred thirty attended."

---

[145] I believe this is the area that Father Ward went to when he left the SSPX.
[146] 3/19/1975 diary

On returning to Detroit, Father worked with Father Ward, his rector, on plans for the SSPX and the house in Armada.

Father's apostolate continued to grow. His travels started on April eleventh with a trip to Oklahoma City for Mass for eighty people. The next day, there was another Mass in Oklahoma: "Had Mass for eighty plus including a group of nineteen from Springfield, Missouri, who drove five hundred miles one way for the Mass. I flew to Houston in the afternoon. Eventually, Springfield will get on the Mass circuit and not have to make this drive."

Imagine the Traditional "pioneers" and the sacrifices they made to attend Mass. During this trip to the southwest, which lasted eleven days, Baton Rouge, Louisiana, was added to the Mass circuit. In typical Father Bolduc detailed fashion, he commented on April twenty-second: "I have had a very full two weeks. Total communions this trip—one thousand, three hundred and eighty. Total confessions—five hundred fifty." Added to the circuits in the Southwest were St. Louis and Kansas City, Missouri, and Dallas, Texas.

In mid-June, Father had a brief three-day visit home to see his family. He then flew to New York where he talked on many subjects with Father Clarence Kelly. During the rest of the summer, he covered the Southwest circuit and made calls to Father Ward in Armada.

There was progress in Houston as regards purchasing a church: "Got a total of eighty thousand dollars in pledges towards the purchase of the church and school."[147]

Father was involved in some litigation in Washington, D.C., that pertained to the St. Athanasius Traditional chapel that he attended before leaving for Écône. It was an ownership issue. The controversy ended in a joint custody of the church with each group saying Mass there every other weekend.

On July 21, 1975, Father contacted a Mr. Beemster. This was the first time he was mentioned in the diary. Mr. Beemster became a benefactor and friend of Father's from 1975 forward, especially in the Green Bay, Wisconsin, area.

---

[147] 6/4/1975 diary

Father had his first Mass in Green Bay on July 26, 1975. The next day, a Sunday: "Mass—two hundred attended. Twenty-seven confessions. The Mass was broadcast over the radio. Breakfast at the rectory. Went to lunch at the country club to which the Beemsters belong, and then had an evening Mass. Met a lot of people who were very grateful for the Mass. Toured the town and Green Bay Packers stadium and training area. Eighty-six communions." One of Mr. Beemster's companies was responsible for installing the artificial turf at the stadium. Mr. Beemster's main revenues were from hydroelectric power plants in the Green Bay area.

On September 10, 1975, Father flew back to Detroit for a two-day visit and was not especially happy with the progress there: "Worked around the house—lots of neglect. The cars are in terrible shape. Paid a bill at Wicks for thirteen thousand plus dollars." There was not much more involvement for Father at St. Joseph's in Armada and the rest of the calendar year was spent in the southwestern United States.

The good news in Houston was that arrangements had been made to buy the church and school. On November twenty-second, the parishioners were working on getting everything ready: "A large crew is working. It certainly is edifying to see all these people working together for their church and so happy."

Eight days later, a comment appears in the diary telling of elation about the new purchase: "Regular Sunday Masses—new faces. All are grateful that the church has been saved and that the True Mass is once more available. We all worked late at the church. Everyone who passes by or visits is impressed by the cheerfulness and vigor with which the people are devoting themselves to this project."

On December eighth, enough work had been done in the Houston school auditorium to have Mass there: "Morning Mass at the auditorium and two more in the evening for well over four hundred. [We had] Benediction. Men and women worked on the church all day."

Shortly after, on December twelfth, Father flew to Oklahoma City where: "We discussed with S. and Ken B. about the incorporation of the Oklahoma City group under the SSPX. Then we had a men's meeting to discuss incorporation. All in favor. Mr. W. is to be Treasurer, Mr. Tom C. is my assistant working with Mr. Ken B. All are very happy."

From December twelfth to December twentieth, Father Bolduc flew on fifteen flights to the various chapels to say Mass. He wrote on December twentieth: "All the groups are growing; we just need more priests." This need for vocations continued throughout Father's life.

On Christmas Eve, last minute work was going on: "Worked all day at the church. Everyone was exuberant with the results. Msgr. Connally was present for the Mass. He distributed Communion and heard confessions and sat in the sanctuary. Sister Regina played the organ and we had carols for one hour before Midnight Mass. We all took a minute to thank God for making all this possible." Then on Christmas day, this entry: "I celebrated Midnight Mass this evening. First, I exorcised the Church and read the Propers of blessing and dedicating of a church. We had four hundred fifty to five hundred at the midnight Mass. The chapel is without doubt one of the most beautiful in all of Texas and perhaps in the U.S. Had the two Christmas Masses this morning with one hundred fifty to two hundred in attendance. I flew to Oklahoma City for evening Mass there and returned to Houston."

In closing out the year of 1975, Father had visited a new mission in El Paso, Texas. On December 29, 1975, Father commented on how nice it was to have a real Church to go to: "Mass at the Tovar home (El Paso) and then flew to Houston. It is nice to have a permanent place to say Mass. Communions and confessions have gone way up here and there has been an increase almost everywhere I go. I keep communion and confession accounts in my smaller volume."

Chapter Seventeen
Southwest Circuit (1976)

Father was continuing his ministry with the chapels and churches in the southwest during 1976. On January 29, 1976, a new priest enters the picture: "In St. Louis, I met with the Beemsters and Father Lucien[148] Pulvermacher of Minnesota who is a Capuchin traditional priest. He hopes to help me in the South West district.[149] I met with the [Dickinson] board of directors and then met with the group in general. I hope I am able to settle the differences that have arisen here. There are some groups that are vying for power." Father Carl Pulvermacher proved to be a strong ally for Father Bolduc, especially in Dickinson, Texas.

Father Bolduc found time to visit his parents and other family members in Florida on February 4, 1976: "Get-together at Pop's place. We spent the evening singing songs—French songs. Pop was at his best and sang songs I hadn't heard for a long time."

With all the traveling, Father contracted a cold and when he returned to Kansas City, he went to Dr. Ackley's house for a shot of B vitamin, and he got a "bone cracking." There were rumors going around about his illness: "Spent all day trying to handle the upset yesterday.[150] I still have a cold. Called Father Ward to see if he had heard anything about the rumors that I was on my deathbed or that I had suffered a nervous breakdown. I called Father Kelly in New York and spoke to Father Post."

On February sixteenth, Father Bolduc flew to El Paso, Texas, to say Mass in Juarez: "Mass at the home of a lawyer in Juarez. It is very moving to see the simple but deep faith of the

---

[148] I think Father Bolduc meant Father Carl Pulvermacher
[149] There is not an official SW district until 1977. At this point in time, Father Ward was the U.S. District superior—from Father Laisney's comments.
[150] The upset on 2/12/1976 in Houston was due to a men's meeting where there was mention of a reorganization of the lady's guild and the men's club.

Mexicans. Many of them were moved to tears at having the true Mass again. This evening we had Mass at the Church of the Immaculate Conception. Father John said it would be the last time we could use his church."

On February 22, 1976, which was a typical Sunday, Father said three Masses in Houston, took a flight to New Orleans for Mass for seventy people and then flew back to Houston for a finance meeting. This is amazing if you stop to think about it. Four Masses, travel to/from the airport twice, confessions, a flight of three hundred fifty miles, and then a meeting with parishioners. Somewhere in there we hope he had time to eat. Seven days later we see a comment about Father's meal schedule: "Regular Sunday Masses, flew to Tulsa for an evening Mass. I had supper at the B. family and realized that the supper I had was the first meal I had in two days. It didn't seem to bother me at all. Meeting after Mass to discuss finances."

Father Carl Pulvermacher assisted Father Bolduc on the circuits in the Southwest. There seemed to be no fixed rotation. There were some disagreements at certain parishes as seen on April 8, 1976: "Flew to St. Louis for Mass. There was much discussion concerning Father Pulvermacher's visit there. I think that things are cleared up. When fence walkers leave, it is rarely a loss." There are other mentions of issues with Father Pulvermacher but in the end, Father Bolduc decided that he was doing the job and he needed his help.[151] On April nineteenth, Father had to fly back to Gilford: "Flew to New Hampshire and Ernest and Barbara picked me up. Arrived at midnight early this morning. Attended Theresa's (Budd's wife) funeral. I said the rosary at the funeral home. The Mass was at Sacred Heart and was dreadful. Father B had the service and was "overjoyed" at her death. I did not stay in the church for the Mass. I said my own funeral Mass for Theresa in keeping with the traditions of Holy Mother Church."

While in Houston, there was discussion of a school for the children.[152] This issue became more important as the year pro-

---

[151] 4/28/1976 diary. In the end, not any mention of making a decision to keep or not keep Father Pulvermacher. Also see 4/30/1976.
[152] 3/28/1976 diary

gressed. In fact, this may be the issue that caused a breakup in the relationship between the lay board and Father Bolduc.

On May 6, 1976, Father flew to St. Louis where a momentous announcement was made: "After Mass, I met with the board of directors about a change in the bylaws. This ensured that the priest and only the priest will have full and complete and final say in all matters and relegated the board to an advisory position." It is not clear on how the bylaws were changed, but in other entries in the diary, there was some contention between the lay board and the priest. In mid-May, everyone was working around the clock to prepare the Houston chapel for the Archbishop's visit. Mr. Brown picked up the Archbishop on May twentieth: "Four morning Masses. Also had a large confirmation class. A large delegation is here from Mexico and other areas. The Archbishop has had several meetings with the Mexican priests. The D. family (9 children) from Florida arrived via airplane and were all confirmed. The dinner went off very well. I have had several Baptisms and conversions."

The very next day: "Sunday—four morning Masses to accommodate crowds and a late afternoon Mass. The confirmation ceremony was another large one. After the ceremony, we had a meeting between the Archbishop and the priests and the lay board and school board members. It was not very fruitful with the lay board being defiant against the establishment of the school."

On May twenty-fourth, Fathers Ward, Bolduc, and the Archbishop flew to New York where they were met by Fathers Kelly, Post, and Sanborn. There was a dinner reception for the Archbishop with more than six hundred persons attending: "The Crosier presented to the Bishop is magnificent." On May twenty-sixth, there was a meeting: "with the lay board which was geared to force the Archbishop into throwing in with the John Birch Society and the O.R.C.M. [Orthodox Roman Catholic Movement] The Archbishop made it clear that under no condition would we have anything to do with either. We can no longer staff their chapels. The Archbishop was emphatic on this point. He was just as rigid with Msgr. M. and his attempt to force two rejected seminarians on the Archbishop. I have never seen him so inflexible."

There was a Mr. K that arrived from Houston to advise Father Bolduc that two men in Houston were attacking him and had called a meeting to denounce him.[153] Flying back to Detroit for a four-day convention, Father Bolduc and others gave instruction to the attendees. During the convention, Father Bolduc met with some Houston parishioners along with Father Ward and Mr. Beemster: "Father Ward and Mr. Beemster were most upset and openly accused the malcontents with breaking confidences and twisting things others said."[154] Father flew back to Houston on May thirty-first where the issues came to a head:

> June 1, 1976: "I called [a member of the lay board] and asked to meet with him. He came over with R. and stated that they would not budge on their position that the shrine and all donations made there belonged exclusively to the three lay board members and not to the people. 'This is our private chapel' I was informed 'and all of you (including the people) are here at our invitation. Anyone who doesn't like it can get the hell out!' They agreed to pay me for the money they had borrowed from me and for all the other expenses they had made at my expense. I informed them that I had bought and paid for the baptismal font and would therefore keep it. A member of the lay board admitted breaking into my file cabinet and stealing my file cards."
>
> June 2, 1976: "I started moving my things out of the apartment last night and concluded today. I also went to the Shrine and took whatever possessions I had there. They admitted that they had taken my vestments and cassocks and other material. There must be something mentally wrong with those peo-

[153] 9/27/1976 diary
[154] 5/29/1976 diary

ple to stoop to outright theft. Father Carl decided to leave and announced this from the pulpit. He told the board who tried to force him to stay that he would only stay if the lay board apologized to me. They arrogantly refused to do so."

June 3, 1976: "We met again with many people of the chapel. Meetings are being planned for tomorrow night. I flew to St. Louis and had Mass. Father Carl Pulvermacher will assist me in my work. I called Father Ward who is showing very little patience and a short temper. He must make a firm stand. [More information in the diary but it was confidential.]

June 4, 1976: "This evening, two meetings were held at the rented hall, one in support of the board and one in support of me and the SSPX. There was a total of eight present at the Shrine (where the board supporters were) and two hundred adults, representing ninety percent of the people, at the hall. Many came by the Brown's home to see me afterwards. I really felt good."

June 5, 1976: "Flew back to Houston. We drove by St. Joseph's Shrine and saw the two-armed guards there with shotguns, etc. It is a real scandal to the people."

This was a hard time for Father Bolduc. He had been friends with the lay board members. It was never clearly pointed out what the disagreement was about but there was the "school" issue mentioned above. Another potential issue was the lay board trying to tell Father Bolduc how to run the spiritual side of the parish. We recently saw how Father Bolduc set up the St. Louis parish.[155] Father pursued legal means to retrieve the parish buildings, but these efforts failed.

On June 29, 1976, Father made a few calls: "I called Father Ward this morning and had a long talk with him about the problem in Houston. He informed me that he will no longer accept calls from the members of the [Houston] board. I hope

---

[155] See 5/6/1976 diary

this is an indication that he is catching on to what has been going on. I called Écône and spoke to Father Snyder and Father Dan Dolan who is newly ordained today. This day will go down in the history of the Church as a great occasion. Archbishop Lefebvre disregarded Vatican Officials and it appears even Pope Paul VI by ordaining thirteen new priests and thirteen sub deacons. The Catholic Church will not be destroyed. Excommunications may come but it will be empty in the face of justice, truth, and tradition."

Father spent some time at the end of July in Green Bay, Wisconsin: "It is nice to be up north where you can open a window and where there is a breeze and fresh air."

From Green Bay, Father flew into Houston for a meeting of the board of directors of the Legion of St. Michael, the traditional group that was looking for a new church. At the meeting, they discussed that there had been no Latin services at the previous church for over two weeks.

On July twenty-eighth, Father Bolduc flew to Paris and traveled to Écône by all night train for a two-month stay. The Archbishop was waiting for Father Bolduc's arrival. There was much going on at Écône due to the condemnation of the Archbishop by Rome: "A large number of journalists and reporters have descended on Écône to write about the affair. Msgr. Lefebvre is busy trying to take care of everything. He is calm and confident—one can feel a certain grace flowing from him.[156] There are six to eight reporters per hour who call or come. All want five to ten minutes, which turns out to be one to two hours. All of Europe is aflame with indignation concerning the ill treatment of the Archbishop by the Vatican. This will not die nor will the Archbishop relent in his determination to save Holy Mother Church. They have not been able to buy him out. He will not be corrupted."[157]

Father had a long talk with the Archbishop on August third: "Found out much of the deceit and lies told him by the lay board [from Houston]. He gave me full permission to say

[156] 7/30/1976 diary
[157] 8/2/1976 diary

Mass in Houston and all other places and made it clear that I represent the Society in all places where I go and that the Society does not in any way represent the previous lay board, neither will they assist them in any way. Msgr. also gave me permission to purchase the property I want. Msgr. gave me three frames containing the relics of saints which I will bring home with me."

Father made a trip to Rome to say Masses on two graves: "Said Mass over the grave of St. Peter. It was a great moment for me, I have always dreamed of celebrating Mass at St. Peter's tomb, the prince of the apostles. Nevertheless, because of all that has transpired at the Vatican, I could not help but read the prayers of exorcism and sprinkle holy water. It was a moving experience for me and one I will never forget."[158]

Before leaving Écône, there was a situation that Archbishop Lefebvre asked Father Bolduc to address: "I had a long talk with the Archbishop and Father Roch today. The Archbishop is concerned about the relationship and unity between his priests in the U.S. He has asked me to work on this when I return. He is much concerned about [a certain priest's] refusal to cooperate with the priests in America."[159]

On August twenty-second, Father began a weeklong retreat: "Feast of the Immaculate heart of Mary. Msgr. Lefebvre celebrated the community Mass and gave an inspirational sermon. Just hearing him makes you want to go out and do great things for the Church. I celebrated Mass at the chapel of Saint Pius X. Took the train to Weisbad, Suisse, where I joined Franz Schmidberger. I will be assisting him with a retreat this week."

After the retreat, on August twenty-nineth, he wrote: "I arrived in Lille early this morning and went immediately to the sports arena. The crowds were already starting to arrive, thousands and thousands of them. There were over one hundred fifty newspaper, TV, and pressmen there. The Archbishop gave a tremendous sermon[160] which was interrupted several times

---

[158] 8/12 and 8/13/1976 diaries
[159] 8/15/1976 diary
[160] Search internet for archbishop lefebvre address at lille france

by bursts of applause. The police told me they estimated the crowd at ten thousand and that over two thousand had been turned away from the door as the arena was full. I helped give Communion."

There was a repeat of this in another city on September fifth: "Sunday—Mass went beautifully. We were able to control the greedy and almost inhuman newsmen. There were three thousand five hundred forty-four persons present for the Mass. I counted them personally. The sermon of the Archbishop Lefebvre was excellent. He spoke on the priesthood. He said that he is ready to go to Rome and kneel at the feet of the Holy Father and obey him. But 'if he (Pope) asks me to become Protestant, I will not obey him, never.'" He was excellent. After the Mass, I drove back to Écône with Denis Roch and Timothy Dowling. There is talk that the Papal Nuncio from Paris has visited the Archbishop to arrange a meeting with the pope. The Archbishop has agreed as long as there are no conditions and as long as the invitation comes directly in writing from the pope."

On September twelfth: "Sunday—Archbishop returned at 4:15 pm today. He had Mass and then assembled us in the conference room where he told us of his visit with the pope. Fathers Kelly, Morgan and I got together afterwards and wrote down all his impressions and comments as accurately as we could remember them. This is certainly an important and historical moment in the Church. The pope has made a tremendous blunder. He has given an audience to an Archbishop who was supposed to be suspended *a Divinis* and gave this audience on the conditions set by the Archbishop. The Pope said he would reflect on what Archbishop told him."

After this, there was a general chapter meeting of the SPPX where elections were held. Father Kelly was appointed Superior of the U.S and the Archbishop told Father Bolduc to return to Houston and purchase the house there.[161]

Upon returning to Houston, a thousand letters were waiting for Father's response. In addition, Father received an

---

[161] 9/14/1976 diary

update on the lawsuit with the Houston lay board: "The men briefed me on the condition of the lawsuit. It seems fifty-fifty with our side having the most support from the people but less legal footing because of the board which changed the laws and constitution to suit itself. I had a press conference at the Lodge, which was well attended, and which got much publicity. Later this evening, I went for a live TV appearance."[162]

The Mass circuits had been serviced by Father Pulvermacher and possibly others, but now Father Bolduc returned to his work on the circuits and searched for a church in the Houston area. Father Bolduc had found two priests in Summers, Arkansas, that would possibly help him out with some of the chapels.[163]

On October seventh, Father Bolduc flew to St. Louis and again laid down the rules: "I had a meeting with the board and explained that I am forming a group under the Society [SSPX] in St. Louis and the priest here (me at this time) will be absolutely and completely in charge. This seemed to be well received by the majority. I also came down hard on the visionaries and those who are trying to play both sides."

Amidst this, he arranged an adoption as seen on October eighteenth: "Picked up the adopted baby and then flew to Kansas City where I gave her to her new mother." Father operated an adoption agency. He saved many babies from abortion, paid for the care, and often helped educate the children. He started this agency after a family tried to sue him because the child was found to have a medical condition and they wanted a child that was "normal."[164]

Father made a trip on October 16, 1976, to Green Bay to offer Masses there. I have received a copy of the sermon that Father gave and have summarized it. Father had just returned from two months with Archbishop Lefebvre in Écône, during which Father explained that some very important decisions were made, and the future of the Catholic church will be

---

[162] 9/17/1976 diary
[163] 10/4/1976 diary
[164] Ernest Bolduc interview 12/15/2017 (source 26)

changed as a result of this meeting. Some of the highlights of the sermon were:

- The Archbishop was suspended but this is based on an unjust reason and therefore it is an unjustified suspension.
- Remember obedience is mandatory only with true teachings.

The Archbishop is having Masses in Europe with ten thousand people attending. European Catholics are supporting the Archbishop at the forty-eight percent level. Something is happening to the Mass and Church. The Archbishop's statement is one of the most important documents in the Catholic Church [June 29, 1976, statement].[165]

- They talk about the Conciliar Church now—not the Catholic Church. It is the Schismatic Church, new doctrines which have been condemned by the Catholic Church throughout the ages. The new doctrine of everybody's right to religious freedom/conscience is not Catholic.
- This is why twenty-four million American Catholics have left the Church and, in the world, one half of the Catholics have left the Church. A new church has been formed dedicated to the Conciliar, dedicated to the destruction of the Catholic Church. The Conciliar Church authorities say that if those that were at the Council of Trent were alive today, they would not say what they said at the Council of Trent.
- No one has the right to say what Christ said was wrong, we must remain with the Roman Catholic Church—only this way can we save our souls. The Conciliar church doesn't care what you believe as long as you keep sending in your checks.
- The Archbishop visited with Pope Paul VI who asked him "What am I to do?—the Archbishop told him to correct errors of Vatican II. The Pope said he'd talk with

---

[165] See *Apologia Pro Marcel Lefebvre* Part one – pages 205-214

those in the Church who authored Vatican II.

- We need to pray to the Holy Ghost to right these wrongs, change peoples' hearts to return to the true Church teachings. The Archbishop suggested that one church in each diocese be turned over to Tradition.

The purchase of a church in Houston was pursued by the parishioners: "I am planning our course of action for the purchase of our property. We are all offering very special prayers for this intention. I am making a special novena for our efforts."

Father traveled to New Hampshire to apply for a loan of five thousand dollars for earnest money for the transaction. He also investigated borrowing money using his coins as collateral. On November seventeenth: "Today we continued working for the purchase of the property in Dickinson from the Diocese to the Society. There is no question that the Bishop knows he is selling it to a church group. He wants a stipulation made in the deed calling for the demolition of the main building to begin within twenty-four hours of the transfer. We will not agree with this. Our lawyer is doing a great job."

"Mr. Beemster wired the remainder of the funds—God bless him." On November eighteenth: "Paperwork is all in order and we may see it completed by tomorrow. Praise be to God. After considering many names, I have decided to call the new church 'Queen of Angels Traditional Roman Catholic Chapel.'"

On December fourth, Father wrote: "Many people at the chapel are getting it ready for the Mass tomorrow, including the sisters who painted and scrubbed: Mrs. Brown, Mrs. Green, Mr. Edenberg, Hugh Dawson, the Boddy's, Mrs. Kennedy, the Kunkel's. We got all the church cleaned out and removed the bell from the tower." The above diary entries by Father Bolduc about the purchase of the Queen of Angels church are recalled somewhat differently if you would like to read Father Finnegan's entry in the Pioneer Testimonials (see Appendix C). It is not unusual to have different perceptions of an event from two different people who have different viewpoints, background, and experiences.

Father was active in Mexico, working to establish the Traditional movement there as seen on December eighth and December nineth: "Flew to Mexico. Mr. Gonzales met me at the airport. We drove to the town of Atlatalureun for Mass in a lovely old Augustinian monastery. It is fascinating. There were seven hundred people present and gave me a welcome like an Archbishop. Flew to Acapulco. A large crowd was there to greet us. I met Father C.R. and several other priests. The entire day was spent talking to various groups of people. I spoke to forty young men who came from all parts of Mexico, who do various works for the Tridentine Movements. We had Mass of the Immaculate Conception with somewhere between twelve hundred and fifteen hundred persons present, and with many more outside the church. The crowning of the Blessed Virgin Mary preceded the Mass. There was a large firework display and a band playing music. The name Lefebvre was emblazed in one of the fireworks displays."

On December sixteenth, Father flew to New York to work with the other U.S. priests [Frs. Kelly, Sanborn, and Post]: "Mass early with the sisters then took a flight to New York. Fathers Kelly and Post picked me up. We had a long and fruitful meeting which proved quite helpful. Those things which were implemented were in substance the things which we discussed in Switzerland and which I had been trying to initiate the past two years, especially as regards local inventories and regular financial reports. Father Ward was not present."

August 1979 Angelus sponsored conference and Marian Pilgrimage to St. Mary's. His Grace is autographing copies of the *Apologia Pro Marcel Lefebvre,* volume I.

Back row, left to right: Fr. Carl Pulvermacher, O.F.M., Cap.; Fr. Philip Stark, S. J., Dr. Malcolm Brennan, Fr. Bolduc, Michael Davies, Msgr. Hodgson.

Front row: Unknown man, Midge Hanrahan, Phyllis Graham, Mary X, Carlita Brown.

Chapter Eighteen
Southwest Circuit (1977)

The past year had been tumultuous in Écône, Houston, and Detroit. The Archbishop made Father Kelly District Superior of the United States in place of Father Ward. Father Ward was at the seminary in Armada, and all was not well there. Father Ward had packed many of the liturgical items and was leaving Armada: "Some of the women are in today and going over the linens in the sacristy. Everything is gone. Fortunately, some of the faithful had some things at their houses and have agreed to finish repairing and laundering them. I am teaching the catechism classes."[166]

The situation in Armada was complicated with lawsuits, hidden bank accounts, and parishioners that were confused: "Father Kelly, Joe Collins and I drove to Detroit where we had Mass. We had a question and answer session—there was silence from those that Father Ward cultivated. It will be a long time before we discover just what he has told them in order to turn them so vehemently against the Archbishop and the Society."[167]

On January 24, 1977, Father flew to Florida to be with his parents and brothers—Sam and Budd. He had purchased land and a house in Port Richey and spent a few days there visiting with family. Father said Mass in Fort Lauderdale and Tampa during this four-day visit.

During this year, there were many chapels that Father tried to visit and say Mass, flying every day or every other day. Besides the two in Florida, he visited Tulsa, Dallas, San Antonio, Houston, Kansas City, Springfield, St. Louis, El Paso, Juarez, Green Bay, New Orleans, Oklahoma City, Birmingham and Mobile in Alabama; Beaumont, Texas, and Little Rock, Arkansas. A few of these Mass centers were just opening and had

---

[166] 1/11/1977 diary.
[167] 1/9/1977 diary

infrequent Masses, the rest had Mass weekly or every other week. Only one, Houston, had its own Church. Fathers Carl Pulvermacher and Bolduc shared the work in these numerous locations. Father Post covered California.

Throughout Father Bolduc's priestly years, he searched for good priests to help take care of the Mass centers and when he found such a priest, he had great difficulty in retaining him. On February 8, 1977, there was a Father V that came to help and on the next day: "Father Carl has been showing Father V. around—he is working in the garden and is a real worker and should be of great assistance." On April eighteenth, upon returning to Houston, Father Bolduc commented: "Father V. and his aunt left in my absence—they gave no reason."

Father talked to many other priests. On September 27, 1976: "Drove to Summers, Arkansas, where I visited Holy Redeemer Monastery and spoke with Fathers Thomas and Charles. They seem to be simple, devoted, and holy priests. The four priests and one brother would like to come under the protection of the Society. I have tentatively accepted them." The next mention of these priests is on July 25, 1977: "Early this morning, I drove to Summers and visited with Father Charles and Father Tom. They agreed to come to Houston and commence work with us as soon as they are able to sell their chicken farm." These priests were mentioned into 1978 but they never arrived in Houston to help. Father Bolduc was considered a good judge of character but the task of recruiting priests for the parishes was not often successful.

The work on the church and property at Dickinson, Texas, had been going on in earnest. The improvements included the church, rectory, dining room, classrooms, and grounds. Father was impressed with the parishioners and the work they accomplished. There were some issues, though, as seen on March twelfth: "Worked on property today. It is being done by the same old standbys. There are a couple of malcontents trying to destroy the group here. They spend too much time on the telephone and not enough time on their knees." There is some unexpected help that shows up on April sixth: "A man arrived today—his car broke down and he was broke. He worked several days catching up some of the jobs around here—at ten dollars per day—it was providential." The payments for the mortgage were due every month and Father was thankful for Mr. Beemster's [Green Bay] help: "I got a letter from Mr. Beemster with another fifteen thousand dollar check for the payment of the mortgage."

There was a garden being planted in Dickinson. [What is that saying – "you can take the boy out of the farm…"] On March eighteenth: "I finished planting the garden—three dozen tomato plants, a dozen of pepper, onion, okra, peas, beans, corn, carrots, beets, radishes, and a number of kinds of flowers including a lot of gladiola bulbs."

And of course, there was the never-ending search for church items. On March twenty-third: "Went antiquing in Austin with Mr. Brown. I bought an altar for two thousand seven hundred fifty dollars. I bought a baptismal fount for five hundred dollars."

A year had elapsed since Father's sister-in-law [Budd's wife] had died, so he flew to New Hampshire to say Mass and visit the family. Father was never one to shy away from a possible encounter as seen on April thirteenth when he visited the local Catholic school: "I went down to the school to speak with the 'nuns' about the CCD program they are teaching. They are obviously teaching heresy and anti-Catholicism. They openly say that the consecrated host is not the body and blood of Christ. I wrote a letter to the local Bishop, not that it will do any good."

Father had bought a main altar, two side altars, statues, and a communion rail in an old church in Kansas City for use at the new church in Dickinson. On May thirteenth: "We started dismantling the side altars and then worked on the main altar. Each piece is numbered and tagged. I bought many other things while I was there." On May twentieth, the altars were to be installed: "I arranged with R&R marble company to install everything—it will take two weeks. I used the jack-hammer again."

There was some news about the Archbishop coming to Dickinson for the dedication of the new Church. As a result, on May twenty-fourth: "There are threats being hurled at every side against the Archbishop. They think they can frighten us. They forget that it is in persecution that we obtain our strength. It is in their hatred for our defense of Holy Mother Church that God showers his graces on us."

On June 21, 1977, Mr. Beemster informed Father that the publisher of *The Voice*, Mr. McGovern, was not well. He proposed that Father Bolduc publish it. Father weighed the offer. On July nineteenth: "We have decided to publish a Catholic newspaper with the first issue on September first. I think this will be a very important factor towards the success of our work." In August, Father started working on the plans for the paper. On September sixteenth: "We decided to put the printing press in one of the back classrooms." On October fourteenth: "Printing press has been delivered. I think it will take an expert to set this up for printing." On October twenty-first: "Printed some materials on the press". On December fifteenth: "Father Carl is going to print five hundred more calendars tomorrow." And at last, in the diaries, the first mention of the name of this paper on December 30, 1977: "[worked on] articles for *The Angelus*."

The dedication of the "Queen of Angels" church in Dickinson was scheduled for July 10, 1977. The Archbishop was scheduled to be there. The preparations for this glorious day had been proceeding for three months. Time was short and on June twenty-eighth Fr. Bolduc wrote: "Working around the Clock." On July second: "Saturday—work day—it is edifying to see the dedication of the laymen here. They work tirelessly day after day and all because they want the Mass. There is no turning away from the truth. The Bishop's chair was delivered today—it is magnificent. It was built for a Cardinal in the 16th century." On July seventh: "Pews being finished. People working day and night. Ernest [Bolduc] and family are helping." Finally, the dedication day, July 10, 1977: "Sunday—More than one hundred newsmen showed up for the press conferences.

After that, we had the dedication of the Church and then the Pontifical High Mass. Six hundred people inside the Church and two hundred outside.[168] The priests celebrated Mass at the three altars simultaneously. This evening, we had Confirmations and Benediction and Vespers. It was a glorious day."

The plan was that Archbishop Lefebvre would go to Mexico for confirmations the next day: "Went for a tour of Galveston by car. We were tired but wanted to get out of the house and dodge the newsmen. The Communist Bishops from Mexico asked the government to prevent the Archbishop from traveling to Mexico. The government capitulated to their demands."

On the following Sunday, July seventeenth: "First full day of Masses [at Queen of Angels]. Six to seven hundred attended Mass. Masses at 7:30, 9:30, 11:00. Flew to New Orleans. Had one hundred eighty attend."

The day after the feast of the Assumption, Father flew back home to Gilford for five days with his family and friends. While there, he had several calls about the death of Elvis who had died on August 16, 1977. He was interviewed by several reporters by phone. He went through some of his Elvis souvenirs. After a visit to Ernest's home on the ocean, he left for Houston.

In Houston, preparations were being made for the very first day of school at Queen of Angels.[169]

On September fourth, there was a major problem in Oklahoma City: "The Spaeth's met me and took me to the Mass center. I informed the congregation that since the board had decided to have nothing to do with the SSPX, I would not be returning."

On November fourth, Father left for New York: "A family took me to the house in Oyster Bay. The house is beautiful and should be quite suitable as a headquarters of the Society. Archbishop [Lefebvre] arrived this evening. The court here has decided in our favor, and we expect a good crowd." On November sixth: "Sunday—dedication of the chapel and the property. The

---

[168] Carlita Brown, who was present, said the number outside was somewhere between 100 and 200.
[169] 8/29/1977 diary

services were beautiful. We went later to the Huntington town house where we had a banquet for the Archbishop."

On November eighteenth, while in Beaumont, Texas: "We worked all day getting things ready for the banquet this evening. We had a tremendous amount of cooperation from all our people as usual. Friday night devotions followed by a High Mass by Father Carl. I helped with the choir. The banquet was a great success. Two hundred fifty to three hundred attended. Mrs. M. talked about the traditional movement all over the world."

For Christmas Eve Mass, Father was sick but continued his circuit and Masses: "Flew to New Orleans for Christmas Mass at the motel. Over one hundred fifty Communions. Flew back to Houston. I have a bad cold. Got everything ready for the midnight Mass. We celebrated Midnight Mass to a full and overflowing Church. The choir was beautiful. The ciborium of hosts was forgotten during Mass, and I had to give communion to over four hundred with only ten small hosts and one part of a large host. I couldn't help but think of the multiplication of the loaves."

Early days of St. Marys. Father and Archbishop

Chapter Nineteen
Southwest Circuit/St. Mary's (1978)

It would be a momentous year for Father Bolduc and the Society in the United States with the founding of St. Mary's in St. Mary's, Kansas. Father was also to have help with his enormous workload with the ordination of Father Finnegan [June of 1978] and a priest from New Caledonia named Father DeGallier.

There was much work on *The Angelus* with the first issue to be sent on January 15, 1978. This was thanks to Mrs. Brown, who oversaw layout, and Father Pulvermacher who was the operations manager, i.e., the one that tried to cajole the old printing press to keep printing. Father Bolduc did not mention that he was the main contributor of articles at this point. On January 6, 1978, he wrote: "We are all busy trying to get *The Angelus* together for its first real issue." By the middle of February, subscriptions were up to five hundred.

On May twentieth, on a visit to New Orleans, Archbishop Lefebvre made an announcement: "Angelus press was appointed publisher of books for the Society." On June twenty-eighth, Father Bolduc wrote: "He [the Archbishop] is pleased with *The Angelus* and he wants us to continue with it and enlarge it and also to print booklets and publications for the Society."

On June thirtieth, while at ordinations in Écône, Father Bolduc talked to various editors about publishing their books or magazines at Angelus Press. With Father Pulvermacher and Mrs. Brown, Father Bolduc was writing articles. It was a huge undertaking, as seen by the August twenty-second diary entry: "Worked until 1 a.m. [on articles for *The Angelus*]. Thank goodness God gives me the strength to accomplish all that has to be done here for the Church." In the July 1978 edition of *The Angelus*, there is a notice that Angelus Press is the English language publisher and editor for Archbishop Lefebvre and the International SSPX.

The first visit to St. Mary's is recorded on January 31, 1978: "We went to the old seminary at St. Mary's, really just what the seminary needs."[170] On February eighth: "Mr. Tony A. of Denver, Colorado, wanted to discuss the sale of St. Mary's Kansas property to the Society. We discussed this for a long time, and I stated my terms to him. He said he would poll those involved and get back to me. I felt that Fathers S and K had handled the matter badly on their visit to Kansas. They just were taken aback because they are not in their proper environments and because of the size of the place which overwhelms them. I have started a Novena to our Lady, Queen of Angels, in hope we can expect a suitable purchase." It was only two days and Father got his answer: "Mr. Tony A. from Denver called and informed me that he had agreed to accept my offer for the property in St. Mary's Kansas. It came as a pleasant surprise. I called both Fathers Sanborn and Kelly. They do not feel that they want the Seminary to be in Kansas. I will arrange for the property and the $200,000 mortgage[171] to be given free of charge to the Society. Father Kelly and I had a conference call with Mr. Tony A. and we agreed to meet in Phoenix on the twenty-third of February to finalize the agreement. It was difficult to convince Father Kelly."

Father arranged to have a lawyer, Mr. Skidmore, with him at the Phoenix meeting on February twenty-third: "This morning, after breakfast, we held a meeting with the St. Mary's Corporation. We have agreed on a price of two hundred seventy-five thousand dollars. No announcement is to be made until June. We agreed to bind the deal by means of our personal verbal agreements and by letters exchanged between Mr. Skidmore and one of the partners, Mr. M. All went quite well. I was certainly glad Mr. Skidmore was with me. The only two changes from our original agreement were that they want to keep about 15 acres. We agreed on 100 feet from the farthest corner of the building, and we must have access to the road which leads to the back of the building."

---

[170] The we are Mrs. Hanrahan and Mrs. Shay
[171] According to 11/2/2020 email of Father Laisney, this mortgage that existed on the property was paid off by Mr. Beemster

On March twenty-seventh, Archbishop Lefebvre had sent Father Roch to view the property: "Mr. Gayner met us at the airport, and we went directly to the College at St. Mary's where our friend showed us all through the property. We both celebrated Mass at the Gayner's chapel for a small group of friends. Everyone is anxious to be able to announce the good news."

There was some difficulty, so Father Roch flew to New York on the next day: "Flew back to Houston and Father Roch back to New York. Difficulty with Confirmations at Mr. Beemster's chapel in Green Bay. Father Kelly refused the Archbishop to visit there or to have Confirmations. The Archbishop called Father Kelly and ordered him to schedule the visit." A very telling entry on April 20, 1978: "Father Kelly tells me that all public appearances of the Archbishop are cancelled in New York. There must be more here than meets the eye."

On April twenty-eighth, Father Bolduc flew to Green Bay to arrange financing for the St. Mary's properties. On April twentieth, Archbishop Lefebvre was in New Orleans: "Held meetings with the Archbishop and other priests. Present were the Archbishop, Fathers Roch, Kelly, Sanborn, Cekada, Bolduc. Discussed the search for a seminary in America. Father Cekada gave a report (sponsored by Fathers Kelly and Sanborn). Father Cekada violated the agreement we had with the company who owns the property in Kansas by informing the local bishop that the seminary was going to be in Connecticut. The Archbishop nixed the property in Connecticut." The Archbishop then flew to Kansas: "Visited St. Mary's. The Bishop was much impressed and again gave me the authority to proceed. Went to Topeka where several groups welcomed the Archbishop." The Archbishop then went to Los Angeles, Armada, and finally to Green Bay for Confirmations.

There was an interesting note on May 26, 1978, while Fr. Bolduc was in Armada: "Tonsure for the seminarians. Father Roch and I drove to Miss Cook's in the Irish Hills with Mr. Perry to see her. She certainly is a remarkable woman." Father Bolduc would establish a loving relationship with Miss Cook until her death in 1993. Miss Cook had a small sparsely built house that she had incorporated into a small chapel. Father loved her as his own mother and had monthly Masses at her house for a small parish there until her death. Over many years, Father would sacrifice his health and his time for so many souls like Miss Cook.

On June seventeenth, there was a note that a check from Mr. Beemster had arrived for eighty-eight thousand dollars. On June nineteenth, plans were made: "Went to St. Mary's and said Mass. Met Jim R. and went through all the property. Decided to put a temporary chapel in the Library and Priests quarters in Infirmary. Carl is arriving with a load of Mass materials from Arkansas. Celebrated Mass with the group and told them of our plans." On June twenty-third, the deal is done: "Mr. Skidmore and I went to the title company and St. Mary's is now ours. I will do something for our Lady as promised. There were a few surprises. They wanted to reserve a small tract of land near the powerhouse, but we vigorously objected, and they consented. We also asked for a stricter application of the "blanket clause" for an easement and they granted this." The worldwide announcement of the purchase of the St. Mary's College was made in the July 1978 edition of *The Angelus*.[172] The above-mentioned promise to Our Lady was documented in that article:[173]

"The matter was quickly placed in the hands of our Blessed Mother. Novenas and prayers were offered at chapels all over the country asking that if our Lady deemed it desirable, she should remove whatever obstacles were present and through her intercession allow us to find the means by which the property could be obtained and returned to God's service. A solemn promise was made to the Mother of God that if the property were obtained, a jeweled crown would be made in her honor which would grace the statue at St. Mary's. The obstacles were many, but they quickly vanished! No matter how serious, each difficulty was disposed of as if by miracle. Only those who were intimate with the purchase could realize just

---

[172] *The Angelus* page 21
[173] See *The Angelus* October 1978 page 18 – A Crown for Our Lady.

how great a part our Blessed Mother played in the acquisition of this famous property which bears her name.

"We ask devout Catholics throughout the world to assist us in fulfilling this vow. Those interested may send contributions of gold, silver, old jewelry, precious stones, or cash to *The Angelus*."

On June twenty-fifth, Father left for Écône for ordinations. Father discussed with the Archbishop the plans for the Society in America: "The Archbishop announced the purchase of the property in Kansas and that he expected great things. He wants pilgrimages there in honor of our Lady."

Help arrived in Dickinson when Father Finnegan came on July thirteenth. Now four priests resided there, including Father D.G. and Father Carl. On the same day, in St. Mary's, Father Bolduc was building support for the work at the new grounds: "I held a meeting with the town manager and other town officials. Afterward, I had a press conference. Everybody wants to help." On July twenty-seventh: "Drove to DeWeese Nebraska to look at three altars. Bought all three for twelve hundred dollars." Two of the side altars were plaster and the large central altar was carved wood.

Father flew to Boston and then on to Gilford to visit the family. On August tenth, he and Pop agreed on the sale of the farm: "I decided I would buy it in two phases: Phase I—part on side of road with house and front field up to State owned land. The rest after the death of Mom and Pop."

On returning to St. Mary's before August fifteenth he wrote: "First pilgrimage here—sixty people. We had a candlelight procession, sang hymns, said the rosary, recited the Litany of the Saints, made the consecration to Mary. The evening was beautiful." On August twenty-eighth, the commencement of school was mentioned: "First day of school."

The massive extent of needed repairs and maintenance was noted on September sixth: "Bought two hundred ten gallons of paint for the interior of the Church. Set up scaffolding."

During this period, Father was not working solely on issues at St. Mary's. The four days from September second through the sixth, Father flew in and out of Dallas, San Antonio, El Paso, Juarez, and Denver. To accomplish all this work, there were many entries such as the one on August twenty-third: "Worked to two a.m."

On September eighth, he purchased the famed bishop's chair: "Worked on the church all day. Brother Anthony and I drove to a small town not far away to see the Bishop's chair. I bought it for two thousand dollars giving a two hundred dollar downpayment. It is a chair formerly used at St. Mary's and was used by Father Damian the Leper." Father was having trouble containing rumors in St. Mary's as many people claimed to know what was going on: "Two parishioners came to me with some alarmist matters. I informed them that should they be approached by anyone wanting information about anything concerning any activity at St. Mary's, they should contact me."

On September 18, 1978, Father went to St. Louis for an auction at a church, and he said: "the main altar is magnificent." On the next day: "Went to the auctions in disguise this morning. We bought all the main items except the 'presents' table which was once part of the main altar. The pulpit and baptismal font are magnificent. We started taking down everything as soon as the auction ended. We got the stations, three altars, altar rail. Many people were weeping at the auction. The church is gorgeous. We worked until dark and slept overnight in the church. We paid a total of ten thousand dollars for all items. Misters Boddy, Stromberg, and Killian plus many others were there helping. Over the next eleven days, altars were dismantled, packed, labeled for reassembly, and shipped back to St. Mary's for storage. Mass was held at this old church—Sacred Heart Church—with candles and Coleman lanterns. The dismantling lasted until the thirtieth. It is quite a story of people working for the Church. Tons of material and lots of work."

Father Bolduc took sixteen pilgrims to view the Shroud of Turin from October third through the eleventh. Brother Augustine and Father drove to Wichita to visit Father Charles and Tom [there may be hope still that they will join Father Bolduc]. Father had breakfast with Mr. Beemster on October twenty-second to arrange for additional financing "for the cost of our new heating system." On October twenty-fifth, representatives from KATO company from Denver were in St. Mary's for the dedication of the plaque given by KATO noting the gift of the property to SSPX.[174]

On November 8, 1978, Father received a dreadful call while he was in Houston: "Got a call that the Immaculata at St. Mary's was on fire. It appears to be serious. I made reservations and have taken a plane to St. Mary's and got to get there right away. I called New York and informed Father Kelly. His reaction surprised me. I arrived in St. Mary's late this evening and saw the destruction of our beautiful Church. The firemen are on duty all night and there is still a lot of flame and burning at the center of the church."

Betty Pappas described her sentiments in a report in a local paper[175]: "The flames ate at the interior and then we could see them in the choir loft behind the rose stained glass window that always was the jewel in the center of the crown of the chapel. I watched as the intense heat melted the lead and the colors melted away; one by one the windows popped, a sickening, stomach-sinking sound. They were all gone. To me, the chapel died today, and I mourn its loss along with the many who loved it for its beauty, its religious significance and its historical memories. It will never be the same. But, life goes on, we have our memories, and the chapel will be rebuilt. I can accept all that, but today our chapel died and I cried."

On the next day in the diary: "This morning we had Mass on the portico or entrance of the ruined Church. We had forty to fifty people attend. The townspeople here have been wonderful as have the firemen and police. Only the shell is left. A few windows remain but the magnificent rose window is gone. The stone walls that are left seem to be sound and hopefully will be able to build on to them. People come all day to offer condolences and offered assistance. It is sad. I have announced

---

[174] KATO company donated St. Mary's to the SSPX
[175] St. Mary's College History, 1980 (Source 11)

Archbishop and Fr Bolduc at Pontifical Mass in St. Marys

August 15, 1980: Assumption Pilgrimage. Banquet in west gym. Left to right: Mr. Limieux (Canadian seminarian), Gene Berry (ordained in Écône in 1981; left the SSXP in 1983 with the "Nine"), Fr. Kathrein (Redemptorist from California), Michael Davies, Fr. Hector Bolduc, Fr. Joseph Collins (left the SSPX in 1983 with the "Nine"), Fr. Yves Normandin (Canadian priest, forever allied with SSPX, died Dec. 30, 2020), Fr. Hugh McGovern again today that we will rebuild. This will certainly bind us more closely together."

There was renovation work going on in the Immaculata when the fire started, and one possible cause was a shorted wire. On the tenth of November: "Went through the ruins with the fire Marshall and the insurance agent and a representative from the engineering company. I was pleased to find that the entire three and one half million [from the insurance company] will be applied to the church."[176]

Father had a wedding on November eleventh near Pittsburgh and then went to New Hampshire to establish his corporation: "Explained to Maurice my plan for a non-profit organization called Traditional Catholics of New Hampshire (TCNH) and got his, Doris', and Ernest's agreement to serve on the board." It is not clear what motivated Father to initiate this corporation at this time, but I think it was prudent as he had many treasures and properties worth millions that should have oversight in case of Father's death. Article two of the Articles of Agreement for TCNH states the object of this corporation: "to promote and foster the truths, doctrines, and traditions of the One, Holy, Roman, Catholic and Apostolic Church according to the decrees of the Council of Trent and as expressed in the Bull *Quo Primum Tempore* by St. Pius V and to promote and defend the use of the Latin Tridentine Mass."

On November 20, 1978: "Flew to Topeka where Brother Augustine took me to St. Mary's. Working on the restoration [of the Immaculata] with Dave Gayner, Jerome Gayner, Mr. Killian, and Dr. McKenzie. Have an engineering firm involved." On December twenty-eighth: "Went to Topeka to meet with Mr. Gayner, representatives of Black and Veatch and the men from Casson company as well as lawyers—we are trying to get contracts together for reconstruction of the chapel. There is great hope that the chapel can be rebuilt."

There was work to be done campus wide. Heat was now in some buildings, but they had been neglected for many years.

---

[176] It turned out to be one and a half million dollars as seen later in the diary

On November twenty-fifth: "We worked in Bellarmine clearing junk out of all the rooms and sweeping them out. Then we cleaned the entire top floor of Loyola Hall. Boy, what a mess. There were heaps of dead pigeons, dung, debris and trash."

The circuit of Mass centers continued as last year with the addition of Raleigh, Wichita, and Charleston (South Carolina). In New Orleans, an offer was made on a church and school.[177] On February second, there were more difficulties in St. Louis: "Flew on to St. Louis, where there were issues and confrontations among the members. Offered Mass." This chapel was mentioned a few more times during the year as on November 26, 1978: "Flew to St. Louis and had Mass. The sermon was directed at a dissident group that was being very divisive and slandering me."

On Easter Sunday, Father set a record with four flights and four Masses on the same day.[178]

On June seventh, there was a problem in Springfield: "Some trouble there with a Mrs. X who is trying to take over the chapel and get Father D. to service the chapel."

---

[177] 2/26/1978 diary—offer was rejected.
[178] Flew from Kansas City to Oklahoma City, then Tulsa, then Dallas, Houston (last Mass).

Chapter Twenty
Southwest District/St. Mary's (1979)

Kansas, a flat land with few trees, can be a harsh environment. The wind can blow loud, fast and steadily and take an already cold day and make it much colder. On the first day of 1979, St. Mary's received one foot of snow, without counting the drifts, and the temperature was minus sixteen Fahrenheit. On the thirteenth of January: "Lots of snow—got old faithful out [1933 Chevy]. Mr. and Mrs. Hannah and Mr. Gayner made a communion rail." Eight days later, Father flew to Juarez, Mexico, to say Mass. What a difference in climates for Father's body to adjust to.

There is a note in the diary on January fifteenth: "Name selected for school—St. Mary's Academy." A new chapel was added to the circuit with the addition of Rapid City, North Dakota.[179] There was a new helper for the circuits by the name of Father Jean Michael Faure, who was to handle San Antonio, El Paso, and Juarez.[180]

While at Green Bay on the fourth of February, Father received a call: "This morning I had confessions and early Mass. I then blessed throats and had breakfast with the Beemsters. During breakfast, Brother Augustine called to inform me that Archbishop Lefebvre had called and wanted me to return his call. I called immediately and found out that he wanted to inform me of his decision to put the seminary of St. Pius X from Armada to St. Mary's. He wanted to make sure that the buildings were available as he knew of plans to open a college there. He said that he had not informed Father Sanborn or Kelly but would speak to them about this soon. I was most happy, although I know there will be great opposition. He confided other information as well, including his approval of having the five lower seminarian years at St. Mary's."

---

[179] 2/2/1979 diary.
[180] 2/24/1979 diary

Father left for a meeting in Écône on February 26, 1979, regarding the seminary in St. Mary's. On the way to Écône, Father Bolduc had researched the creators of the original stained glass in the Immaculata. Although the company had been bombed during World War II, the drawings for the Immaculata were in the basement of the factory and somewhat readable. This event is detailed in the March 6, 1979, diary entry: "This morning, I celebrated Mass early and then went for a meeting with Mayer Glass company representatives. I met the elder Mr. Franz Mayer (eighty-four years old) and another elderly man who is one of the last artists in the old style. They have succeeded in locating some of the original sketches of our windows [for the Immaculata church]. I hope to be able to return for one day later in March to take care of more business."

On March eighth through the thirteenth, 1979, meetings were held to establish the seminary at St. Mary's, Kansas: "I had an exceptionally long—three hour—conference with Archbishop Lefebvre. He insists that the Seminary at Armada will be closed and will be transferred to St. Mary's. He also said this was definite. He informed me that Father Richard Williamson would be sent to America to replace Father Sanborn as seminary rector and to replace Father Kelly as district superior. This news will certainly be hard for these priests to take although I welcome it as a means of saving both the seminary and Society in America. Without some action at this time, there would be no seminary in the U.S. next year and the Society would be greatly endangered as well.

"I met again at length with the Archbishop. We went over all of the plans for St. Mary's, and he selected the rooms at the seminary which are to be used by the new seminary. He again reiterated his plans to have the seminary there and he said he hopes that this decision will be accepted by the other American priests. Thus far they have stated that they would go there only under obedience.

"I also met with Father Williamson who informed me of action he wants me to take upon my return to St. Mary's. I hope we can get everything together so that we can avoid difficulties."

Fathers Sanborn and Kelly arrived on March 12, 1979, and on the following day, there was another meeting: "This afternoon, we three Americans had a meeting with Archbishop Lefebvre, Father Roch, Father A., Father Tissier, and Father Williamson. Many points were bought up. Some points concerning actions and activities at the [new] seminary, which I consider quite important and serious, were handled in a noticeably light manner. The major decisions reached were: 1) The seminary at Armada will be moved to St. Mary's, Kansas; 2) I will remain in charge of rebuilding the chapel and preparing the faculty building for occupancy by this fall; 3) Father Kelly remains as superior of the Northeast District for his term; 4) Father Sanborn remains as the rector of the seminary; and 5) I was named as head of the Southwest District, which was just now formed, and which is to include Mexico. The seminary is placed in a zone surrounded by five states. Neither district will violate the zone of the other."[181]

Father Bolduc was back at St. Mary's on March twenty-seventh: "Fathers Sanborn and Cekada arrive. [Make] suggestions for costly improvements. They do not want to come here. They are going completely contrary to the directives given by Archbishop Lefebvre. We all went to Topeka for dinner with Mr. Gayner." There was a note on page nineteen of the April 1979 edition of *The Angelus* that the seminary move to St. Mary's has been cancelled as: "many families had sold their homes, terminated their employment, and moved to St. Mary's." The implication was that there could not be both a seminary and a school on the same campus.

In late March, Father traveled to New Orleans: "Meeting with the dissident group who was insisting that they are put in charge of the priest and the property. I of course informed them that they would never be allowed to control the church and that I would never allow a protestant organization to take over our group. The most important aspect was that all were put on notice that because of their boycott, they were in fact

---

[181] On 3/14/1979, Father Kelly, Bolduc, and the Archbishop met, and the Archbishop drew the line of division. Father Kelly has 24 states and Father Bolduc has 21.

not parishioners as they were not fulfilling their obligations to support the parish or the priest."

For the first time, on April 3, 1979, St. Vincent's in Kansas City, Missouri, was mentioned: "Visited churches for sale including St. Vincent's in Kansas City, Missouri. The church is beautiful but located in a bad area. I do not think the area is so bad and I think it could easily be taken care of, but many of the people feel it is dangerous. They panic at the mention of the word black or negro. Mrs. Shay drove me back to St. Mary's in a snowstorm." As expected, knowing Father Bolduc's project management capabilities, work continued at St. Mary's Academy: "Men have been working on plumbing and painting at Bellarmine Hall and on the kitchen equipment at St. Joseph's hospital. It is magnificent."[182] And a few days later: "Cleaning out of Immaculata—using a bobcat for the rubble."

The St. Louis parishioners purchased Grant school for a permanent home for their Mass. This was the third "real" permanent church in the Southwest district after Dickinson and St. Mary's.

The Angelus was being published regularly and on April 23, 1979, published a new book.[183]

On April twenty-fifth, in Houston, there was the Southwest District priests meeting: "Priest meeting with Fathers Carl Pulvermacher, Finnegan, Post, Hogan, and Khoot. Fathers de Mouliere, Pevada and Msgr. Donahue were absent. Mass had Father Post as celebrant, Fr. Carl as Subdeacon, Fr. Finnegan Deacon, Fr. Hogan was MC. Mass was well attended. There was coffee and cake at the hall afterwards so that the people could meet the priests."

At the end of April in St. Mary's, there was a meeting with the two managers reporting to Father Bolduc: "Meeting with Mr. Gayner and Mr. Belderok. Had a short business meeting with the work crew. We are zeroing in on the work in the sacristy of the church and in the finishing up of the Bellarmine Hall and starting Loyola Hall. We could do it, but it will take

---

[182]   4/4/1979 diary
[183]   Most likely one of the *Apologia Pro Marcel Lefebvre* by Michael Davis

a lot of work. The whole campus is in bloom with flowering trees, apple, cherry, and redbud."

On May 9, 1979, Father Bolduc mulled over purchasing the acreage behind the school at St. Mary's: "An all-office day. Paperwork has picked up and must be taken care of. I answered thirty-one letters today. I started putting material together on the development. I would like to go ahead but feel I need more information. We must be able to come up with the desired funds at the right time. No need starting it if we can't go through with it." Three days later, he decided to go ahead: "Spent the entire day cleaning up my desk and table and drawers. Worked on files. Much work was done in the lawn and flower beds. The men worked in Loyola Hall. Carl Boddy and Mark Schaefer worked in the gardens. I continued burning stumps. Mr. Gayner and I discussed the development in the back of the college. I have decided to go with it at their price. There is such an interest on the part of so many traditional Catholics." The price was agreed upon on May twenty-fourth: "I drove back to Topeka and had a meeting with our lawyer in Topeka, Mr. John Freiden, and our lawyer from New York, Mr. Alfred Skidmore. We discussed the fire insurance settlement. [Met with] Mr. Tony Batlagara of Denver and we went over the plans to buy the property."

To understand Father's thinking on the purchase of all that land, an article in the *Laconia Citizen* on June 12, 1979, sheds some light: "Another summer project is a four hundred acre farm. Father Bolduc, who grew up on the Gilford farm of his parents, notes proudly that all food for the [St. Mary's] campus will be raised on the premises, including pigs, milk, beef cattle, and fruit. Beehives are also being set up. 'Hopefully, in a year we will be completely self-sufficient.'"

On May fourteenth, a new chapel was established in Columbia, Missouri, with Mr. Taylor as contact person: "Flew to Columbia. Jim Taylor picked me up at the airport. Had Mass for the first time. We had twenty-four at Mass."

Father, throughout his life, would rather work with his hands rather than office work. On May 30, 1979, he had a chance to do just that: "I spent all day up in the barn with Tommy Shibler. We cleaned the remaining stalls, washed down the barn, unclogged the drains, and connected the water to the barn using a hose. It was nice getting out and working physically."

On June 12, 1979, the diary entry notes that Father flew to Detroit [Armada] and met the Archbishop there: "Had the tonsure ceremonies—for eleven boys. Four received the orders of lector and porter. Talked with the Archbishop about purchasing the remainder of the property at St. Mary's. We discussed the redistribution of the states covered by the seminary sector. I was assigned Colorado, Kansas, and Missouri. Father Kelly received Nebraska and Iowa. There will be no seminary district in the future."

While in Detroit, there was a dedication on June fourteenth: "Today we had the dedication of the Church at Redford—St. Anne's. There were two hundred ninety-three present—rather disappointing."

On June twenty-first, there was a surprise forty-third birthday party for Father. As always, there was a great amount of work being done at St. Mary's, all aiming at being ready for a retreat on July sixteenth. On July third he noted: "worked on restoration of the buildings. We are making great strides in the cement walk construction. Thus far, we are up to date on the work. We must keep ahead of it." There was much farm work going on at St. Mary's with the garden, pigs, and chickens: "Our one hundred fifty chickens are laying one hundred twenty to one hundred thirty eggs per day."[184]

Father detailed the scheduled retreat: "Retreatants are starting to arrive on July fourteenth. We have a larger number coming than expected. Worked all day on the rooms. The women are doing a super job, as are the men." A few days later: "I returned to St. Mary's. We have a total of twenty-nine men for retreat. This is nineteen more than the goal we had set. We are working on the last-minute preparations for the rooms in Loyola and the kitchen is getting in shape."

---

[184] 7/7/1979 diary

During all this frenzied work of getting ready for the Arch-bishop's visit on the Assumption, Father returned to one of his hobbies for some relaxation. On July 31, 1979, he notes: "Celebrated Mass early and then went down to the ANA[185] convention. The Inaugural medals from my collection were of-fered late this evening. The Taft-Schoolcraft gold broke records [$32,000]. The 1941 silver went for $25,000. The other two major medals went equally as well. The place was in bedlam after the auction. I couldn't be more pleased. Mr. S., the new owner, was happy, and I was elated. Mr. S. bought most of my pieces. I bought a proof 1877 cent for $1100."

The Archbishop flew into Houston on August 12, 1979: "We chartered a plane which flew us directly to Port Arthur [Texas]. Seventy-five cars full of Vietnamese met us at the airport. There were gongs and fireworks waiting for us when we arrived. We had the dedication, Confirmations and Mass. Then were entertained with dinner and Vietnamese dancing. We returned to Dickinson late. There was a large contingent waiting to greet us. The Archbishop viewed the print shop and offices [in Dickinson]."

On August thirteenth: "We flew on to Kansas City. We drove to St. Mary's. An exceptionally large crowd was there to greet us. We got the Archbishop settled and then toured the property. The choir is practicing. The crowd here already is tremendously large. The Archbishop celebrated Mass this af-ternoon to a full church." On August fourteenth: "We had Mass with the Archbishop as celebrant. The seminars and lectures are going well." On the feast of the Assumption: "This morning the Archbishop laid the cornerstone for the chapel.[186] A huge crowd was on hand. Over Two thousand people were here during the day. We celebrated a Pontifical High Mass with more than one thousand people in the chapel and many more outside. The Archbishop gave First Holy Communions. We had a banquet where we fed more than one thousand two hundred. In the evening, we had Vespers and Benediction as well as Compline.

---

[185] ANA – American Numismatics Association
[186] I believe the chapel referred to here was the burned Immaculata.

We had a candlelight procession to the statue of the Blessed Mother with the singing of Hymns. Michael Davies gave an excellent talk. He did much to bring unity. Praise be to God. We had a beautiful day, and the entire pilgrimage was a success."

Father traveled to Dickinson on August twenty-fourth: "Father Finnegan picked me up. I have not been here for some time." There was much work on *The Angelus* while Father was in Dickinson: "All day working on *The Angelus*. Talked about issues of circulation, new issues, new approaches. School opened today, our enrollment is small, but the quality is high."

Father flew to New Orleans on August 28, 1979, and spent some time on the books and the state of their finances: "Wrote several papers on recommendations." Father was trying to ensure that all efforts here were in accordance with his directions: "I met with Mrs. B. She assured me that all the teachers are Catholic and have agreed to teach all subjects including religion according to our specifications. Met with men's club and gave them specific instructions."

On September 2, 1979, while in St. Louis: "We had a meeting where we decided to go ahead with the school to beat the new laws being enacted the first of the year." It would include Kindergarten to Grade five. They accepted two teachers and planned to hire a third if the salary could be agreed upon.

On September 3, 1979, Father flew to Boston to finish the arrangements for buying the family farm at a price of one hundred thousand dollars. This would give Pop the necessary funds to live off the interest. On October 10, 1979, Father returned to complete the sale: "The farm became mine today. Thank goodness for that. It is saved from destruction or building companies. I gave Pop a check for fifty thousand dollars and will give him another tomorrow."

On September tenth, St. Mary's Academy had their first day of school with eighty-two children. Father visited all the classrooms and taught two classes in religion. After school was started, Father left for Paris on September nineteenth. He also spent time organizing the Southwest District: "Spent all day putting last minute preparations in order. Will travel light.

Have a hundred and one things to set in order prior to departure."

In Europe Masses were to be said by the Archbishop in large stadiums and exhibition halls. On September twenty-second: "Went to the hall again today to help. The phone at the house in Paris rings all day long, every two minutes. Book stands are set up today for the literature of the Society [SSPX]. I had a long meeting with the Archbishop today. I was able to present all the points which were necessary. We are at last ready for tomorrow. I have been assigned to assist at Benediction and Vespers." The next day, the Mass was held: "Sunday—a glorious day. The police estimated the crowd at twenty five thousand. There were certainly twenty thousand at Mass. One hundred and twenty-five seminarians were there from Écône, Zaitzkofen, and Albano. Over hundred priests are here. I shall have to write separately about the Mass. It was a glorious and moving day. Many people openly wept. How these people love Archbishop Lefebvre. They cheered him wildly but with reverence. They knelt for his blessing as he passed. It was clear that they view him as a savior of the faith and the Church. The entire ceremony went smoothly. I heard confessions from 8:30—11:00: thousands went to confession. At Communion time, more than two thousand received communion in less than fifteen minutes. The Archbishop introduced the "Crusade" element to his sermon. This had taken root because of questions I had asked him the previous day about his coat of arms."

Just before leaving for home, Father met with a sculptor on September twenty-sixth: "We left for Tennessus after Mass. The castle is lovely. Mr. Piecheud is a very talented man. We toured the property. After eating, I discussed the making of a statue for St. Mary's as well as a crown and crucifix. Mr. Piechaud agreed. I shall have him make a statue of the Blessed Virgin Mary and the child Jesus and a crown for each."[187]

It may appear that during this period, Father was taking care of St. Mary's and the rest of the district was being managed by other priests. However, until 1984, Father was flying from

---

[187] Mr Dominique Piechaud Tennessus Amoillox 79350 Chiche France."

chapel to chapel due to a shortage of priests or to "put out a fire" in one of the chapels. For example, on October 16, 1979: "Got a lot of letters off today. I called Mrs. X in Phoenix to determine the size of the house there so I could send a pastor. I discovered that the lay group there was trying to put the property in their own name. Also, that three men had been busy agitating the group. I called Mr. Skidmore and flew right away to Phoenix. On arrival I found Father R. was not there. I called Mrs. X to have several meet me at the rectory but found no one had a key (so they say). I am staying the night at the Royal 8 motel and arranged a meeting with some of the laymen here tomorrow morning." At the meeting, Father brought things under control but mentioned that his visit "was none too soon."

Father also helped with the Sacraments with "friendly" priests as on October twenty-second: "I got a call this morning that I had to go to Madison, Wisconsin, to give the last rites to Father Keys who suffered a heart attack. I went to Mr. Beemster's lawyer's office and signed papers for the mortgage of St. Mary's. We went over all the arrangements. Mr. Beemster gave me a check for fifty one thousand dollars plus securities for twenty four thousand dollars. I then flew on to Madison. When we got to the hospital, we discovered that Father C. was already there. I spoke briefly with Father K. and checked into a motel."

Father did not do all this work by himself. He had many people keeping track of his schedules, taking shorthand, arranging flights, and in some cases, actually piloting him: "Worked all day cleaning up letters. Mrs. Belderock is helping me. Mr. Belderock flew me to Wichita where I celebrated Mass and flew back to St. Mary's."[188]

There were more newly established chapels to service as seen on November fifth: "After breakfast, I took an early morning flight back to Denver and on to Aspen. The Cerise family picked me up and drove me to their house and on to the Taber home. I have decided to try and come here once a month to provide Mass for these people." On November fourteenth,

---

[188] 10/20/1979 diary

Father flew to the Raleigh Durham airport and had Mass and Communion for forty people.

Back at St. Mary's, Father had to spend time with the boys, especially on discipline throughout this school year: "Flew back to Kansas today and started work right off in the office. Had several boys in for a talk. We will have to effect a change of attitude in some boys or insist on their leaving. Some obviously resent being here because of the discipline which we insist be maintained."[189]

Father had a hectic schedule and kept long hours leaving little time for sleep. As a result, he was often sick with a congested chest, flu-like symptoms, headaches, colds, and general weariness. Fortunately, there were doctors available at most chapels to help him out as happened for four days around Thanksgiving, 1979: "Dr. Braun gave me a shot of penicillin. Still have a bad cold. Went to bed early as soon as Benediction was over." And: "Cold is somewhat better, and my voice is back." I would not say that Father was a sickly person, but he did push his body more than anybody I have known and thus succumbed to these maladies.

He did not stop performing his duties but did seem to rest more after these times. On the feast of the Immaculate Conception, he had an unusual accident that kept him on crutches for a few weeks: "Immaculate Conception—Mass at St. Mary's. Rented a plane with Mr. Belderok to go to Wichita. While moving the plane from the hanger, the wheel hit my foot and the brake drum gave me a bad cut. I had to go to the hospital and get thirty stitches taken. Luckily, the tendon was not cut. We had to cancel the trip to Wichita, and I was in the emergency room quite a while. However, I did go to Kansas City this evening with Brother Augustine and the sisters and others. We celebrated Mass for them and sang Compline. Returned to St. Mary's."

On December 21, 1979, there was a surprising entry: "We are still awaiting news on the contract for buying the Church in Kansas City. I flew to Monett and celebrated Mass there. We

---

[189] 11/27/1979 diary

flew back in heavy fog. Mr. Belderock had to come in on instrument control." This was to be the first diary entry on the purchase of St. Vincent's.

The Christmas period was terribly busy for priests then as it is now, but Father's schedule was typical for this year:

> "December twenty-second—drove to Wichita, Kansas, from St. Mary's (one hundred sixty-three miles) and drove back after Mass.
>
> December twenty-third—Mass at St. Mary's and drove to Kansas City (ninety miles) for Mass and then flew to St. Louis for Mass.
>
> December twenty-fourth—flight at 6:44 am out to Kansas City and then drove (ninety miles) to St. Mary's. Celebrated midnight Mass and then a party at Belderok's house.
>
> December twenty-fifth—Mass and then drove to Kansas City and flew to St. Louis for Mass.
>
> December twenty-sixth—Drove to Columbia for Mass there. Took Holy Communion to hospital.
>
> December twenty-seventh—Flew to Topeka and then on to St. Mary's for an evening Mass."

The next few days were some of the same schedules and the year finished on December thirty-first: "Returned to Kansas City. I went to the tailor and picked up my suits. Had copies of photos made. Celebrated Mass at the Ackley house. Flew to St. Mary's. I celebrated Mass at the Assumption chapel this evening. Afterwards, we went to the Belderok's home to usher in the New Year. We sang most of the evening. There was an array of delicious foods."

Archbishop Confirmations also included - Fr Bolduc
St. Marys

St. Mary's College staff and students

Chapter Twenty-one
Southwest District/St. Mary's (1980)

The year 1980 was a growth year across the Southwest District with the highlight being the acquisition of Saint Vincent's properties in Kansas City. The proposed seminary at St. Mary's had not been mentioned and the move of the seminary from Armada Michigan to Ridgefield, Connecticut had been accomplished: "Father Williamson called and wants me to go to the seminary in Ridgefield, Connecticut for a meeting."[190] Four days later Father was at Ridgefield for a meeting: "Fathers Williamson, Roch, Kelly, Sanborn, and I were present. The topics of discussion—Virginia, the loan to me, Father Dolan and his chapel in Missouri."

On the fourth of January, due to flight problem to Monett, Missouri, which did not allow Father to travel, St. Mary's held a first: "We had first all-night adoration, benediction and novena to Our Lady of Perpetual Help."

On the seventh of January, the SSPX acquired the church and property in Spokane, Washington: "Got up early and said my morning office and then Carl Boddy drove me to Manhattan where I took a plane to Spokane. I was met at the airport by Mr. M. and Mr. O. We had lunch and then went to visit Fr. DeBusscher. Went to church and had Mass. I am staying at the O.'s home. Went to the lawyers and registered the transfer of the property to the Society."

More than any person I have known, Father Bolduc, throughout his life, corresponded in writing to as many as forty-five people a day. He was very appreciative when he did not have to write out or type letters himself: "Worked all day in the office getting correspondence out. Mrs. Mary Gayner came and took down letters. She took some home with her to finish.

---

190 2/1/1980 diary

I really got ahead. Worked late tonight. Got several letters off to the circuit."[191]

Father was involved in the school even with his circuit schedule, Southwest District responsibilities, and *The Angelus*. Father continued to write articles for *The Angelus*. In November and December, he authored an article: "An Open Letter to the Bishops of the American Catholic Church."

Often his diary reflected counseling and discipline being administered when Father was in St. Mary's: "I gave out punishment this morning to the boys involved in the inking of the classroom."[192] And a few days later: "We had a teachers meeting this evening after school was out. The matter of the use of the paddle was brought up and I issued new directives in their use. Only Mr. Belderok, Mr. Taylor, and I will give swats."[193] There were several instances in the diary when Father performed as the role of infirmarian when one of the students was hurt: "Frank M. hurt his arm today where he fell while visiting at the Hunt house. I took him to the emergency room at St. Francis with Brother Augustine. He has a chip in the elbow. We got home late."[194]

Father had a pilot in the parish that could quickly get him to a sacramental emergency: "Got a call this morning that Mr. O. in Monnet was in the hospital with a heart attack. Mr. Belderok flew me there and I gave him the last rites and Holy Communion. Flew back to St. Mary's."[195]

There were several entries about Father selling off his "treasures" for the benefit of the Society. The question has been asked how often this happened and how much he contributed. He produced a goodly sum. Diary entries such as this one on February 17, 1980, record his generosity: "Sunday—Father F. celebrated Mass this morning [at St. Mary's] and I introduced him. I flew to Kansas City, celebrating Mass there, and on to St.

[191] 1/24/1980 diary
[192] 2/2/1980 diary
[193] 2/27/1980 diary
[194] 2/14/1980 diary
[195] 3/6/1980 diary

Louis for my second Mass of the day. I left two silver bars in St. Louis to be sold for St. Mary's."

On March 10, 1980, Father left for seventeen days in France. He met multiple times with the Archbishop to discuss many topics, one of which was the Archbishop's visit to the United States.[196] He was able to visit Mr. Piechaud to review the design of the Blessed Mother statue and corpus for the crucifix. Father flew back to New York to visit with Mr. Skidmore [his lawyer], and then flew on to his Sunday circuit. It was interesting that with all the work Father had in the States, that he was able to take the seventeen days for this trip. There was some relaxation time included on this trip but every day, he was visiting with nuns that might help with Father's schools, talking to parishioners about how St. Mary's worked and could work in France, and saying Solemn High Masses for Sister Marie Gabriel's fiftieth anniversary as a nun.[197]

Upon returning to the States, Father flew to a new chapel in Lake Tahoe, Nevada, to bless the chapel and perform two marriages: "We had the double couple wedding early this afternoon. Steve and Kathleen were married, and Bob and Marianne were married. I celebrated the Mass and Father Post was Deacon and Father Finnegan was sub-deacon. This evening, we had a grand time with Father Finnegan at the piano. Blessed the chapel this morning."[198]

During April Father attended to some of the chapels and schools that needed his attention as on April 21, 1980: "This morning I drove to San Antonio, and I celebrated Mass for the group. I then went to breakfast with the F. family. I flew to New Orleans. Brother B picked me up at the airport. I had a talk with Father Stark and another one with Mr. B. and with all the teachers. I met with both Mrs. B. and Father S. Little was accomplished in remedying their differences. However, I

---

[196] 3/14/1980 diary
[197] Founded in 1974 when the first Sister received the religious habit, the Congregation of Sisters of the Society of Saint Pius X was established to facilitate the apostolate of the priests of the Society of Saint Pius X. The founders, Archbishop Marcel Lefebvre and Mother Marie-Gabriel Lefebvre, his sister, were both missionaries in the Congregation of the Holy Ghost.
[198] 4/12/1980 diary

have a much clearer view of the situation and will send down directives to be followed." As with any organization of strong-minded individuals, the chapels and schools of the Society required much time and patience from Father Bolduc.

If you have had the chance to visit St. Vincent's Church in Kansas City, you would be spiritually uplifted by its beauty. By May 1, 1980, it was finally (almost) the property of SSPX: "The papers for our Church were prepared today. This is the feast of St. Joseph so it is appropriate that our church in Kansas City would have been secured on this day. I offered special devotions to Saint Joseph. We have petitioned our Blessed Mother for fourteen months for the purchase of Saint Vincent's Church. Three Hail Mary's have been offered at each Mass for all this time making over one thousand five hundred Hail Mary's." Then on the next day: "Today is the feast of St. Athanasius. It is appropriate that we should be notified today that the bishop of Kansas City has sold us the beautiful Saint Vincent's Church. We bought it through a third party. This is a glorious day as the church will be returned to use as a true Catholic church and that it will become Archbishop Lefebvre's cathedral. This ends fourteen months of intensive work. Joe Zubeck and Al Walters deserve a lot of credit for their untiring work in this matter. I offered a special prayer of thanksgiving this evening and offered the candle promised to our Lady. We had all night adoration and devotion this evening."

During these times, almost two decades after the start of Vatican II, more and more parishes were trying to return to the traditional ways. Father was contacted by a group in Fort Lauderdale, Florida, on May 8, 1980: "This evening, I had a meeting with the board of Our Lady of Fatima. I proposed that they turn the property over to the Society and that I in turn would send a Society priest there to take over. Most seemed in favor. They will think it over and contact me."

In the middle of May, 1980, Father met the Archbishop in California for a fifteen-day visit to the United States. The trip involved Confirmations, dedication of a church, and ordinations. The trip from California to Spokane, Washington, was exciting as they saw Mount St. Helens standing dark at the top in contrast to all the snow around the other mountain tops.

After the dedication of the Immaculate Conception Church and Confirmations for One hundred seventy-six persons, they celebrated a fiftieth priestly anniversary: "We went to a luncheon for Father Debusschere's fiftieth [priestly] anniversary. There were four hundred people there." On Sunday, May fifteenth, they left Spokane: "We were up early and went to Father *DeBusschere's* home chapel. He had forgotten the chalice, so we hurried to the chapel for Mass, and both received [speeding] tickets. After breakfast, we went to the airport and left for Los Angeles. We flew past Mount St. Helens as it was erupting. It was an awesome sight. A large black cloud over one hundred miles long quickly developed in the area. We were fortunate to leave as we heard later that the airport was closed."

In Los Angeles, the Archbishop confirmed two hundred persons and the church, St. Redero, was dedicated. The next day they flew to Phoenix where fifty were confirmed.

In Phoenix, the Archbishop became ill, and the liturgical services were curtailed. On May 22, 1980, they left for St. Mary's, Kansas: "We were up early this morning and left for home. In Texas, at our regular stop, we had the starter on the right engine worked on. The Archbishop rested. After we had it fixed (two and one half hours), we went to St. Mary's. As we passed over St. Mary's, the children were all assembled in the courtyard in the shape of a cross and everyone waved white handkerchiefs. We had the Mass and first Communions with the May crowning."

Then to Kansas City for the dedication: "Archbishop visited the new Church (St. Vincent's), his Cathedral chapel in this country. He was most pleased and said he would come next year to dedicate it. Quite a few people were on hand to meet him. We then flew on to St. Louis and had Mass and Confirmations. Afterwards, we had a banquet which was attended by more than one hundred fifty people."

The last leg of the visit was to the seminary in Ridgefield, Connecticut, for the ordination of one priest, and other seminarians received minor orders. Over one thousand people attended the ceremonies.

The good news from the Archbishop was that a seminarian would be ordained in June and assigned to St. Mary's. His name was Joe Collins. The Archbishop related to Father Bolduc that Joe had some personal views on the new Mass and the Pope but would give the Society viewpoint in public. The day after Father returned to St. Mary's on May thirtieth, he had another tragedy at the Immaculata chapel: "Father McGovern arrived today. We also had several tornados in the area. One passed within sight across the road, another to the back of the property. The high winds toppled the front wall of the Immaculata and part of the left wall. It is a terrible catastrophe. We also suffered much tree damage. The rain, thunder, and lightning were the worst I have ever seen. What a welcome for Father McGovern."

The parish celebrated Father's fortieth-fourth birthday on June twenty-first with a cake and singing. He had been preparing for an extended leave that would take him to Europe for almost a month. It started with a pilgrimage group that met in Paris and after some sightseeing, left for Écône to attend ordinations on June twenty-seventh: "The ceremonies were beautiful as usual. Almost one hundred priests attended with more than one hundred fifty seminarians and scores of nuns along with five to seven thousand laymen. What a glorious day for Joe [Collins]. I acted as his assistant priest. The Archbishop gave a moving sermon which was optimistic but cautious as usual."

After the ordinations, Father left to visit his relatives, the Hittles in Mannheim, Germany, and then onto visit the Piechaud family who showed Father the beautiful carved oak crucifix that he had commissioned. Before leaving for Boston, Father met with the Archbishop. They discussed a number of matters and agreed on a certain positive plan of action for the district of America.

Upon arriving in Boston on July thirteenth, Father discovered that his father had had a stroke. He spent five days visiting him at the hospital and doing work around the farm.

He then flew to Kansas City on July eighteenth and the next day, which was a Saturday: "We had the first Mass at St. Vincent's today. Two hundred people attended. The Church looks beautiful. We have a lot of work to do yet. I drove back to St. Mary's with Brother Augustine and a group of others who had come for Mass."

A retreat was being conducted on campus by Fathers Finnegan and Babinet. All the workmen on campus were preparing for the pilgrimage in August on St. Mary's campus. The heat in Kansas this summer was extreme: "More people are arriving, and it looks like we will have quite a crowd considering the fact that many canceled because of the heat." The start of the pilgrimage was on the feast of the Assumption. Well over five hundred people attended and Father was very happy with the three-day event. When Father had a busy schedule, such as the trip to Europe followed by the pilgrimage, his correspondence fell behind, but he had his ways of catching up: "Got caught up on back correspondence by working through the entire night. There were few interruptions with the phone, and I was able to get a lot done."[199]

The 1980-1981 school year started [in St. Mary's] with finances and administration needing to be addressed: "We are really zeroing on the finances here. Mr. Gayner and Mr. Belderok are making plans to get more out of what we have. We are operating under a deficit, and we must make that into a profit."[200] With the arrival of Father Collins, Mr. Belderok removed himself from the principal's position: "Had a number of meetings about the school. Met with Father Collins. I think the change is good, but I hope Father Collins is not too over-burdened as he must work his way into the position gradually. Mr. Belderok will stay on to help him for a time."

The Kansas City parish was growing and up to eight hundred people were attending Mass. The school in Kansas City started as well this year with challenges from the local diocese: "I drove to the school early with Mrs. Shay. We celebrated

---

[199] 8/21/1980 diary
[200] 8/29/1980 diary

Mass for the children. The two Catholic teachers went to Communion. I then spoke to the children. Looked over the school. It was our first day and we are proud of it. Forty children are enrolled. Spent a lot of time at the Church. Had an interview with a reporter. Checked over the work. Dave Shibler is here painting. The diocese is trying to give us trouble over opening the school. However, I am determined as they are. They sent the safety inspectors today to close us down."[201]

During the remainder of 1980, Father continued to travel to various missions. One visit was to Armada, Michigan, to visit the old seminary and the Perry family. Then he visited Albuquerque, New Mexico, and El Paso, Texas. El Paso had found a potential chapel site that Father thought an "ideal property for the SSPX." On October 7, 1980, others joined Father on a visit in Mexico: "I was up early. We went to the airport and Frs. Finnegan, Babinet and I flew on to Mexico with Mr. Belderok. The weather is fine. We had meetings most of the day. Celebrated Mass this evening. I gave a short talk to the people. More beautiful weather. We prepared to leave for California in the morning. The property is in very good condition. Attendance is up."

As Father Post was ill, Father Bolduc visited the chapels of Bakersfield, San Jose, Sacramento, Lake Tahoe, Seattle, Kennewick, Spokane, and Missoula [Montana]. He gave talks to the parishioners, offered Mass, inspected the finances, and made recommendations: "I celebrated Mass early and then we flew to San Jose. Mr. J. and Mr. S. picked me up. We had short meetings. Father Post is sick. He got up late this afternoon. We went over books and records. Had a talk with some of the laymen this evening. CCD classes are to be started. Better financial records need to be kept. I appointed Mr. J. as coordinator under the supervision of Mr. S. who will leave soon."[202]

After returning to St. Mary's for a few days to catch up on correspondence, Father flew to Guadalajara, Mexico, to look at

[201] 9/4/1980 diary
[202] 10/10/1980 diary

a potential chapel site. He found the asking price excessive and recommended against buying the property.

In typical fashion, Father commented on the elections. He was elated with the Reagan win: "The election is in and it looks like Reagan will win by a landslide, thank God. Getting rid of the Carters will be a great victory for the anti-abortion forces."[203] Father needed to get to Green Bay to get help on financing: "Worked all day in the office. Mr. Belderok and I flew to Green Bay later today. Had a good flight. I met with Mr. Beemster and arranged to get the property in New Orleans and Dickinson taken care of. We also discussed the new property in El Paso and the start of a college at St. Mary's this fall."[204]

Father often mentioned working on articles for *The Angelus* which was still being printed in Dickinson, Texas: "Worked late tonight on articles for *The Angelus*. I did most of my basic work on the plane flying back to St. Mary's."[205]

A few days later, Father was in Fort Lauderdale, Florida, where he finished the purchase of the chapel: "Very early this morning, I celebrated Mass and went to the airport where I took a flight to Fort Lauderdale, Florida. Mrs. O. picked me up at the airport. We went to Mr. Edwards' office and went over the deed and agreement for turning the property to the Society. We agreed on the changes. We then went out to eat and Mrs. O. brought me back to the rectory. Mr. P. was at the meeting also. I was quite tired."

After the legal changes were made, the board of the chapel met and unanimously agreed to turn the property over to the Society. After completing the transfer in Florida, Father left for Dickinson, Texas: "Celebrated Mass very early and then got right into work. Went over the financial records. Brought Communion to Sister Mary James. Had meetings with several members of the parish. I was up late taking care of business. I helped collate *The Angelus* for the month of December. Had a meeting with the men (work force) of the parish. We went over all the things which need to be done."

[203] 11/4/1980 diary
[204] 11/8/1980 diary
[205] 11/9/1980 diary

There was also further attention given to *The Angelus* as seen in these diary entries on November 19, 1980: "The four advanced copies of Michael Davies' book *Pope Paul's New Mass* arrived today. It should make quite an impact on Catholic writers and readers across the world. Packed and got things organized for the plans for work around the parish. We will renovate the back of the school building for a complete Angelus [Press] printing establishment. I suggest the boarding in of the walkway outside the building. I also gave the okay for buying a new system for addressing and labeling *The Angelus.*"

After a visit to Green Bay on November 22, 1980, Father went to visit his old friend in the Irish Hills, Michigan: "Miss Pat S. picked me up at the airport with Julie. We drove to Miss Elizabeth's home where we had Mass for about twenty people. We had lunch afterwards."

Upon returning to St. Mary's from a visit to El Paso and Mexico, Father was anxious for the first Young Adults Get Together (YAG). The motivation for the YAG was to allow young single adults to meet in a Catholic setting: "Had our first full day of conferences and meetings. The hayride and bonfire were most successful. All enjoyed the square dance. Father Collins has a cold. I shall have to take all the conferences." The conferences were successful: "Our conferences went well. There were lively questions and interest shown. The spiritual exercises, confessions, etc., all were well attended."[206]

Father flew to El Paso for a retreat with the other priests. However, he could not resist, even at a retreat, observing the physical condition of the buildings: "We are starting the retreat late today. I went through all the property. Very little has been done and much more needs to be done. I have set goals for the chapel, the convent, and possibly the novitiate house to accomplish prior to the Archbishop's visit. The chapel needs complete painting. The convent is filled with junk."[207]

On the next day of the retreat: "Another fine day of retreat. Picked up supplies at the Farm-Dry. There is little that

---

[206] 11/28/1980 diary
[207] 12/15/1980 diary

has been done. Dave Shibler, Dave Vogel, Fred Shibler, and Dennis Murphy arrived from St. Mary's. They brought many tools and supplies including the vestments and the organ. They have already begun on the chapel." [Father was in violation of the advice given to retreatants—"shut off the world and talk to God."]

On the nineteenth, the retreatants took advantage of the local religious sites: "We had a cold windy day. This afternoon we went to the mountain of Christ the King. We made stations on the way up and prayed at the crucifix on the summit. I held a conference in private with Father L. and went to confession. We had more conferences which were excellent. I really needed a retreat. This is the first real retreat I have had in this country since my ordination."

On Christmas Eve, Father celebrated Midnight Mass in Kansas City: "Got some work done this morning and met with Father Collins. I then drove to Kansas City and heard confessions in the afternoon and at night before the Midnight Mass. Celebrated the Mass. The church was beautifully decorated. This is our first big function at the St. Vincent's church since its purchase. The church was full, about eight hundred people. We had very cold weather. Several children made their First Communion and Confession while others made a solemn Communion."

St. Marys visit Archbishop, Father Bolduc procession
leading to Immaculata

Chapter Twenty-two
Southwest District/St. Mary's (1981)

Father's year started out with a visit to Mexico with Archbishop Lefebvre. The Archbishop flew into El Paso and was most pleased to visit the El Paso chapel and discover that the price was only two hundred thousand dollars.[208] On January fourth the new church was blessed: "Blessing of the chapel and Mass—chapel full to overflowing. Many came by to visit us and to praise the new church and school. The people have done an excellent job of fixing the houses and chapel. Father Babinet and I went today to the Holy Family Church to visit Fr. Getty and the Vicar General of the diocese. They were most worried and anxious over our presence here. I made it plain that while they do not want disunity in the diocese, we would be quick to answer any charges against us. There was a meeting of the Archbishop with the SSPX priests and those associated—Msgr. Phillipe de Mouliere, Fathers T. Fonkey, Pulvermacher, Post, Stark, Finnnegan, Collins, Bolduc, and McGovern. Archbishop spoke about the relations between the SSPX and himself. "

The trip through Mexico lasted eighteen days with stops at several cities. Security was tight with Mexican police and bodyguards for Archbishop Lefebvre, as seen in this entry on the nineteenth: "Fathers Alphonsus, Babinet, Archbishop, and I said Mass in our room. Drive to Mexico City. Stay at Mr. Florence's house—VIP treatment. Police agents assigned to guard the Archbishop." There was a three-page addendum to this diary page about Guadalajara, Mexico: "As we were getting out of the car, reporters were taking photos. One young man— maybe 20— was taken from the reporters and roughed up and taken to the terminal where he was roughed up more. Turns

---

[208] The asking price was $300,000 and Father Bolduc was having difficulty negotiating the right price due to SSPX priests wanting the church enough to pay the asking price.

out he was from Argentina and had a gun. I was glad I had been very careful to accompany the Archbishop on this trip acting as sort of a bodyguard. I was more than careful after that."

On the January seventh, a typical entry: "Drove to [San Lucas] Ojitlan, to the village of St. Luke's parish. Greeted by two thousand people. We walked along the street to the church amidst songs and garlands. Had one hundred fifty confirmations and nineteen baptisms. The people are so happy to see us. It is hard to get used to the different customs, such as the women nursing their children at the breast while they are being baptized and confirmed. Much work is needed here."

On the final day of the visit to Mexico, after visits from police pestering the Archbishop not to go into Mexico City due to diocesan pressure: "Drove to shrine of Our Lady of Guadalupe. Press conferences—quite positive except for Communist papers Unamarso and Trento. The Archbishop made it clear that the Pope is the Pope. Many traditional groups and Father Bolduc reminded all the priests and the Archbishop that they should stay neutral. They must come to our chapels—we will not celebrate Mass in their chapels. I feel this trip of the Archbishop will be the most important he has ever made. Mexico is a key country as regards the faith. We have here an untapped source of vocations. The faith and tradition are strong here. The Archbishop has made a tremendous impact."[209]

Back at St. Mary's, after an absence of over a month, Father found some parishioners with their own agenda: "Mr. X. has been doing a lot of damage to St. Mary's trying to sway parishioners to the John Birch Society. Lots of damage."[210] More bad news came on March tenth, when Father F. left the Society: "Father F. came over—he has left the Society but wants insurance from us, etc. He got a rude awakening in the application of brutal charity."

With the Archbishop due to arrive in May, Father Bolduc went to the bank on April 27, 1981: "To bank to see if I could

---

[209] 1/23/1981 diary
[210] 2/3/1981 diary

get a personal loan for the Archbishop's visit." It was approved four days later. Father did find the bank account low at times, and he worked with the banks or the antique dealers to come up with the cash needed. Mr. Beemster was also a great help in the Father's endeavors as seen on May 3, 1981: "Sunday—at St. Louis—Mass and then on to Green Bay. Mr. Belderok had a long meeting with Mr. Beemster about the purchase of four hundred acres for the college. Mr. Beemster has agreed to help us as he recognizes the importance of the land for the future of the college."

At the end of May, classes ended, and Father rewarded the students: "Took the students—first and second honors—into town for ice cream. Giving students more latitude to go into town on their own." On May 29, 1981: "Graduation. McCabe theater and ended in large gym this evening for the dance. Graduated six boys and two girls. Spring Waltz. How beautiful it was."

Now that the school year was over, Father wanted to get the farm going strong: "Now that students [are] gone, got two hundred more baby chicks and Kevin now will have time in the gardens. Karl Stromberg and Grandpa Gayner are working on the fence around the convent."[211]

There was another diary entry on October 27, 1981: "Kevin F. bought two pigs. I would like to start the farm up in earnest this year. Next year, I want to start raising some of our own grain and many more vegetables." There were another fourteen pigs added the next day and there was work on the new pig pen and hen house.

On November 2, 1981, more plans for the farm: "I plan to build our chicken production up to one thousand hens with seven hundred fifty layers and two hundred fifty meat birds. This should ensure that we have ample eggs for our own use and for the parishioners." On the very next day, "I want to obtain cattle in the spring."

Two and a half years after the Immaculata burned, a check for the loss arrived: "Mr. Belderok spent the entire day with

---

[211] 6/1/1981 diary

Mr. Frieden, my lawyer. We worked on the settlement for the insurance company for the Immaculata for 1.5 million dollars net. We already got $250,000 two years ago so the check was for $1,250,000." At Green Bay, Father and Mr. Beemster prepared a statement for the papers on the insurance payment.

Father left on June 15, 1981, for ordinations in Écône. His first stop was to visit the Piechaud family and review the statues that were being carved and the crowns. There were some antiques purchased and family visits during this trip: "Packing up set of china, sterling silver table setting for twelve, art, and some watercolors by Ferley. Leaving tomorrow for Hittle house in Frankfurt."

The ordination ceremonies were growing in attendance each year: "Thousands starting to arrive for the ordinations. The prince of Saxon and wife are present. The prince of Liechtenstein was also there. The Burgenmeister van Zoitskoner also came. It is thrilling that we now have five more priests for the Society. This afternoon, I drove to Switzerland with Fathers Grouch, Glover, and Wodsack. We are spending the night in our house in Switzerland just over the border from Austria."

And on ordination day itself: "Sun shone brightly over five thousand attendees at ordinations. Archbishop gave a marvelous sermon. It excited us all with its simple, truthful, and very logical defense of the Church and its teachings. I was, as always, struck with a deep pride and love for the Church as I saw these young men go to the altar and come back as priests of God. I cannot adequately express my emotions and inner spiritual feelings. Surely, Archbishop was inspired by the Holy Ghost today."[212]

On the following day, Father arranged for three sisters to come to the United States: "Met with Sister Marie Gabriel for two hours. We discussed plans for bringing the three sisters to America. They should arrive by the end of August. I met with several families who want to send their children to St. Mary's."

Upon Father's arrival in the States, on July 5, 1981: "Drove to St. Mary's for the Mass there. There are over seven hundred

---

[212] 6/29/1981 diary

packages and letters to be handled. Some include rosaries for Mexico." Father worked around the clock for three days handling the backlog of communications and had office people come by to see and they could not believe the quantity of mail and packages. Immediately, a women's retreat started for a week followed by a men's retreat. Father Bolduc was the only speaker for the men's retreat.

Father was forty-five years old in June and recorded a typical schedule that tires one just reading it:

> July 26, 1981: Sunday—Mass at St. Louis and flew to Green Bay for Mass. Discussed buying of the Jesuit land and he (Mr. Beemster) wants me to buy it right away as soon as I return.
>
> July 27, 1981: Flew to Detroit where Miss Elizabeth Cook and Betty G picked me up and drove to Miss Cook's home. Entire day going over plans for the property. Mass late this afternoon. Dug some plants for me to take back to St. Mary's.
>
> July 28, 1981: Betty G picked us up and drove me to the airport where I flew to St Louis. Drove to bank and made a twenty-nine thousand dollar payment on our mortgages. Mr. T. gave twenty-five thousand dollars and Mrs. K. gave four thousand dollars. Bought some books. Flew back to Kansas City.
>
> July 29, 1981: Meeting on plans for the Marian pilgrimage. Drove to Kansas City to pick up Mrs. E. and Father LeB. Drove back to St. Mary's.

This was followed by a weeklong retreat for priests starting on August 3, 1981, at St. Mary's conducted by Father LeBoulch. The Assumption Pilgrimage at St. Mary's was again held but was marred by a man who desecrated the chapel while the pilgrims were processing.

The school year opened on August thirty-first with a new addition: "First day of our third year. We opened the college today. This is a grand day for St. Mary's and will go down in history as a milestone in the fight to reestablish Catholic education. I was kept quite busy in the kitchen trying to arrange things for the correct dining procedure." There were eighty students enrolled in the Academy and thirteen in the college. It appeared from the diaries that Fathers Berry and Collins were now full time at St. Mary's.

There was a news release published in the St. Mary's Star newspaper about the school. A few excerpts were: "In September of 1981, a four-year liberal arts college program was commenced at Saint Mary's. The college is designed to give degrees in education, history, English, and Math; Father Bolduc stated that his goal is to rebuild the traditional Catholic educational system in America by emphasizing the five 'R's, reading, writing, arithmetic, respect, and religion. Asked what the goal of St. Mary's College was, Father Bolduc answered: 'To educate catholic youth along traditional Catholic lines making them aware of their rich Catholic heritage and preparing to take their place in the world as solid citizens that will permit them not only to make a living but to save their souls as well.'"[213]

Father flew to Durham for Mass and had an interesting event in the airport: "Coming from the airport, I saw a man beating another with a wooden club and we stopped, I got the club and a chain away from him."[214] Father had another interesting comment on September twenty-second: "Flew to Kansas City. A lot of work to catch up on. Paperwork is three quarters of this job. If I could get rid of that, I could start a half dozen more chapels." This was back in 1981, I wonder what the priests in 2020 would say to Father's comment?

A major event happened on the first day of October with the arrival of the sisters: "Fathers Collin, Berry and I went to Kansas airport to pick up the sisters. They were somewhat surprised at the size and beauty of the convent." Father commented that this was the first house of the sisters outside of Europe.

---

[213] See source 37
[214] 9/13/1981 diary

Father visited his hometown in October to celebrate Pop's eightieth birthday and his parents' sixtieth wedding anniversary. There was a fun entry on October twelfth: "Moved the slot machine out of the house today." The slot machine was an antique find of Father's that took up valuable space in a farmhouse.

The Angelus was still going strong in Dickinson, Texas, even without Father Bolduc's constant attention. He did have a special spot in his heart for this endeavor as seen on November 18, 1981: "Call from Mrs. Brown in Houston and on the spur of the moment, flew to Houston and arrived in time for a fifth anniversary of *The Angelus*. A lot of old timers were there. We had a ball. There was plenty of popcorn and we sang all night. The party was held at the Brown home and was done in grand style."

On December 11, 1981, Father commented about the growth of the Southwest District: "Although we have a large office staff, we still have trouble getting everything done and they are busy all day. Some of them work overtime and late into the night. We have become a vast multi-million-dollar corporation with some sixty chapels, a half dozen schools, a large boarding school, and a college, all in a few short years. I have two more large debts to pay and then the board will be fairly clean."

On the last day of 1981, Father again reflected on the happenings of 1981: "The year has been a good one. Many decisions, some of them distasteful, have had to be made. This has caused some hard feelings but has rid us of some who were not loyal to the cause and who were working against the Church. There will have to be more such decisions before the year is over but there can be no question that we have grown considerably. The college is doing well and will grow considerably next year. El Paso is the big object of our attention this year. I feel several of our boys from the academy will enter the seminary this year. I am counting on the visit of Archbishop Lefebvre to stabilize the Florida chapels. With Father P. working there, we should see much growth. He already has settled much of the factions caused by the J. conspiracy."

Father Bolduc went on to describe pressures on the priests to go against the SSPX with various conspiracies such as JBS [John Birch Society], communism, Masonry, and Zionists. "The greatness of the Archbishop and the SSPX will soon be known, and future generations of Catholics will reap the harvest of the seeds which are being sown today, often with great suffering and personal sacrifice."

There was an event in 1981 that I thought to include here as it shows that the entry for each day in the diary is only a page long and there were many happenings that did not make the diary. This event also shows the tremendous pressures Father Bolduc was up against that almost seem satanic. Father sued an individual in March for five offenses against himself. The following is copied from the online record of the court case background notes: "In March of 1981, B. phoned another member of The Society, Father Terence Finnegan, and accused Father Bolduc of (1) improperly transferring Society property to himself; (2) lying about his background and particularly his position in the United States Army; (3) being a traitor who had performed services for the Castro government in Cuba resulting in the death of a number of Cuban "patriots;" (4) being guilty of immoral conduct rendering Father Bolduc unfit to be a priest; and (5) being guilty of violations of criminal law and of "Canon law."

The trial notes go on: "Despite repeated efforts by Father Finnegan to discuss with B. the basis for these accusations, the defendant consistently failed to produce any evidence to substantiate his statements, even after a face-to-face meeting in Denver, Colorado, with Father Finnegan.

"Although Father Finnegan ultimately became convinced that B's charges lacked any foundation, initially the accusations against Father Bolduc caused Father Finnegan and other members of The Society to have serious doubts about Father Bolduc's integrity, honesty and fitness for his position. The accusations against Father Bolduc interfered with his ability to carry out the duties of his position as District Superior, to the point that he was relieved of that position in March 1984 and is currently awaiting reassignment." [I do not think this last sentence is valid as this suit did not seem to be part of the reason Father was relieved of his position.]

The case was resolved on June 15, 1984 in Father Bolduc's favor with two of his five claims against B., defamation and invasion of privacy being proven. The award was $47,001.[215]

---

[215] Source – email from Gary Pauly 11/1/17 – there is an attachment of the case notes

Chapter Twenty-three
Southwest District/St. Mary's (1982)

This year was a growth year for St. Mary's and El Paso but along with the growth came new problems. Fathers Collins and Berry needed a vacation and went to Florida for a week's rest.[216] Father Bolduc was teaching college classes on a regular schedule which took a good amount of preparation and presentation time. As more students arrived, the discipline problems increased: "Found the (three) girls in a laundry room in Belvue. Girls wanted to go to a big city to play electronic games. I was up all night."[217]

Father expanded the farming effort as seen on March 30, 1982: "Kevin bought four young Holstein calves for the college. We also bought a nice boar pig. Calves: five hundred dollars for five. Pig: one hundred dollars."

Father made at least a monthly visit to Wisconsin to say Mass at De Pere near Green Bay, Wisconsin. Mr. Beemster was not only a benefactor but a trusted sounding board for Father Bolduc. On one of his first trips to Necedah, Wisconsin: "Drove to Necedah with Mr. X. There are at least six factions here and a lot of diabolical influences. It is evident that the Necedah Shrine (not an SSPX chapel) is diabolical."[218]

Father had a friendship with the Benzinger family (of book publishing fame) that resided near Los Angeles, and he enjoyed visiting the Benzinger sisters and looking over their prints and paintings. Miss Marile Benzinger worked for Mrs. Post and knew her well.[219] In early July, Peter S. arrived in St. Mary's with the Benzinger collection. While at the estate, Father spent time proofreading the new book I accuse the Council by Archbishop Lefebvre.

---

[216] 2/8/1982 diary
[217] 3/13/1982 diary
[218] 2/15/1982 diary. Queen of the Holy Rosary Mediatrix of Peace Shrine is a Marian shrine located in Necedah, Wisconsin
[219] 3/17/1982 diary

There were many stories of Father Bolduc helping couples adopt babies. Some estimates, never verified, have the number of adopted babies at over one hundred. On April 17, 1982: "Flew to Kansas City. I cannot afford to be late for the appointment at the hospital this afternoon. I signed the baby out of the hospital with our lawyer present. Then Mrs. Belderok and I drove her to the Pryor house. What a happy day for John and Irene Pryor."

During the 1982 [school] year, Father worked on the Mass circuits, flew home to be with his mom for her surgery, and attended ordinations in Oyster Bay, New York.

In one of his conferences with the Archbishop, one of the topics was about attacks on certain authors: "Third conference by the Archbishop. He specifically said that he wants the attacks on Michael Davies and Walter Matt to cease."

Father met the Archbishop when he arrived at St. Mary's on May 4, 1982: "Pontifical High Mass and First Holy Communions. Confirmations fifty to sixty. May crowning. Reception for the Archbishop in the gymnasium. The Archbishop let us know that there will be no substitute for the Pope John XXIII breviary. He said we must cease the use of the Pius X breviary and utilize the John XXIII breviary and those refusing to do so were showing a defiance to the Society and the Archbishop himself. We had a blessing of the jeweled crown."

After the visit to St. Mary's, they flew to Vancouver for Confirmations, then to St. Paul, Minnesota, for the dedication of the church. Present were the Archbishop, Fathers Normandin, Vingliesu, Collins, Kelly, Cekada, Dolan, Jenkins, and Sanborn. After Confirmations in Green Bay, Father flew home to St. Mary's and had a talk with the two resident priests about the Archbishop's directives (see above) and they were very much opposed.

Father held the graduations at St. Mary's Academy on May twenty-nineth for sixteen seniors. There were two interesting entries in the diary on June twenty-eighth and twenty-nineth, 1982: "At 1:15 am I got a call to go to Kansas City from St. Mary's as Mr. H. was extremely ill. I drove there and gave him all the prayers and blessings of the Church. I returned in time for seven am Mass. Mrs. C. then drove me to Omaha, Nebraska, for a wake." He may have had two hours sleep during all this. There are many times when entries in the diary show that Father would have only three to four hours sleep.

This entry is followed by a note that Father had been a priest for eight years. It is amazing to realize what he accomplished in those eight years. Father had a tireless, never-ending quest for souls, started over sixty chapels, and directed the Southwest District and *The Angelus*.

On July 7, 1982, Father was home visiting Pop at the hospital. Father did what many of us should do as a prudential matter when the family members are divided between Tradition and the *Novus Ordo*: "Visited pop at the hospital. Took mom to see the lawyer, Mr. McLaughlin, and they drew up a paper so that they will have the Tridentine Mass when they pass on. I am named as being in full charge of their funeral arrangements."

The yearly pilgrimage was held in St. Mary's on the feast of the Assumption and was a great success: "Sunday—Solemn High Mass. Church was packed. Talks and our banquet. Best pilgrimage ever. Much credit must be given to Mrs. A. and Dave G. for their drive and directions as co-chairs."

The new school year had a difficult start as Mr. Belderok was sick for a long period and Father had to work "around the clock" to get school ready.

On September 3, 1982, Father left for Europe for twenty-four days. On September sixth, Father outlined why he was in Écône: "Had a long conference with the Archbishop. In all, sixty priests are here for retreat. The Archbishop's words about the upcoming general chapter were 'It is a little Council.'" Father Bolduc was assigned the council commission for the general chapter for the apostolic work in the districts. Father expressed his confidence in the Archbishop on September fifteenth: "The Archbishop knows people and knows how to direct them." On September seventeenth, a comment in the diary that was foreboding of a very problematic area for Father Bolduc and the Archbishop: "I had a very interesting talk with the Archbishop who gave me full support for what we are doing at St. Mary's, and especially my position in cutting the budget."

After the chapter, Father Bolduc visited his sculptor on the way home: "I stayed with the Peichard's who fed and cared for me like I was one of their own. They showed me the work on the medal and the progress on the statue of Joan of Arc. The third order medal is beautiful."[220]

The earlier-mentioned budget problems began to appear in the diary. On October 4, 1982, Father was speaking (on phone) with Father Williamson about the difficulties. This was followed by a visit on October eighteenth by Father Williamson to St. Mary's during which he reviewed the operation and finances of St. Mary's, and on October twenty-second: "I had a long conference with Father Williamson today. He gave me a short recapitulation of his visit and I gave him my opinions on what ought to be done."

On November twelfth, Fathers Berry and Collins left St. Mary's along with some of the teachers. It all came to a head in the middle of December with Fathers Williamson and Fellay at St. Mary's. On December sixteenth, Father wrote about a path forward: "Spoke with the Archbishop about our plans. He has now approved our plans to keep all of our schools and programs in operation. However, he wants a very strict budget."

This was followed by a meeting the next day: "Met with Archbishop Lefebvre, Fathers Fellay and Williamson, Mr. Belderok, and Mr. Redding. We discussed the financing and our plans to take care of the problems concerning the balancing of the budget." While all these talks were going on, there was a block building being constructed on campus for slaughtering animals and a bee house. It is still there today across from the church parking lot.[221] Some have used this building to point to Father Bolduc's spending excesses during a budget crisis.

To finish a difficult year, there was a problem with the priest assigned to New Orleans: "I was awoken at 4:30 am with a call from Mr. Belderok. There is an emergency in New Or-

[220] 9/20/1982 diary – the statue mentioned of Joan of Arc is now in Gilford at the Immaculate Conception Church
[221] 10/2020 – being used now as an administrative Maintenance bldg..

leans [and Father flew to New Orleans]. I met with Mr. Bellow. We went through the house [rectory] and found a hoard of incriminating evidence. It is hard to believe what went on here. I was unable to visit Fr. X (who is in jail) as there is no judge available. I celebrated Mass in Charlnett and then the Midnight Mass here. I don't feel well at all."[222]

---

[222] 12/24/1982 diary.

Chapter Twenty-four
Southwest District (1983)

There was a new priest at St. Mary's on January 19, 1983. Father met him on return from a trip to Kansas City. A week later there was a parish potluck welcoming Father De-LaTour. On the third of February, Father received some surprising news from Mr. Belderok: "The Archbishop had put Father DeLaTour in charge of St. Mary's, and I [Father Bolduc] am to go to Dickinson and establish the district headquarters there. I told Father DeLaTour that I would talk to him in the morning." Father DeLaTour asked Father Bolduc to address the people about the changes, but Father decided that he would rather leave quietly without fanfare. Father also cautioned Father DeLaTour that he could not handle the job at St. Mary's and that soon St. Mary's would be closed.[223] The Archbishop assured Father Bolduc that St. Vincent's would remain in the Southwest District and allowed Father additional time to pack and leave.[224] The suspected reason for Father's leaving St. Mary's was the budget and financial problems.

Father was hurt by this move as seen by this comment on February 10, 1983: "I have so much stuff here that it will take me a long time to put it all together. It is strange how many abandon you when the going gets tough." There was pressure on Father Bolduc to leave so the "healing" could start but Father told Father DeLaTour that he would take whatever time he needed. On February eleventh, a review meeting was held: "Had a meeting with Father DeLaTour and Mr. Belderok discussing all the various aspects of St. Mary's including legal, financial, projects, obligations, etc." On February twelfth, Father flew to Green Bay to make plans with Mr. Beemster and a lawyer. Father started to collect the nine years' worth of his

---

223 2/4/1983 diary
224 2/5/1983 diary

possessions at St. Mary's and Kansas City to ship them to New Hampshire.

After going to the district house in Dickinson, Father did not return to St. Mary's publicly for many years. His time at the district allowed him to set up a better accounting system, work on improving and writing articles for *The Angelus*, and continue his circuits for Mass at the various chapels. There were no signs that Father's dedication to the SSPX had faltered.

That was not so for other priests of the SSPX as seen on April 25, 1983: "I kept in touch with the situation in New York with the Archbishop. I had special prayers in hope that the priests there would support the Archbishop and the seminarians would remain faithful. I fear for Fathers Kelly, Dolan, Berry, and Cekada. They are so proud and arrogant that I do not think they can override the crisis. They will be led into blind disobedience because of it. I always said that when the chips are down, they would abandon the Archbishop." The events over the next few days were very difficult for Father and the parishioners. The crisis was nicknamed the "Oyster Bay 9" as nine priests left along with some seminarians.

On April 27, 1983, Father wrote: "I flew back from New Orleans. Many phone calls. All of this must be terribly painful to the Archbishop. How could those who have received the priesthood from him, treat him this way?" On the next day, the diary relates: "Talked with Father Williamson and the Archbishop. Fathers Kelly, Cekada, Berry, and Dolan were dismissed by Archbishop for disobedience. Fathers Sanborn, Zapp, Skierka have withdrawn from the Society. Jenkins and Collins—thinking things over."

On April thirtieth, the rest of the story unfolded, and it challenges the mind to think that ordained priests would act in such a manner: "We had the dedication of the Church and Mass this morning—Our Lady of Fatima and Mount Carmel (Old St. Mary's Church) in Goldsboro North Carolina. The chapel was packed. The mayor of Goldsboro presented the Archbishop with a certificate. Confirmations (seventy-two in all). The Archbishop met with some of the coordinators to inform them of the situation in the Northeast. Father Williamson informed us that the thieves in the Northeast had given him ultimatums. They now claim all property and all contributions as their own. They are calling all over the country, spreading vicious lies about the Archbishop. At last, the group of infiltrators have shown their true colors. The Archbishop vows to oppose them in their plans to take all property. They are cold, deliberate, calculating thieves and liars."

I can remember at this time going to Sunday Mass at St. Anne's in Redford. I was waiting for the first Mass to end to go to second Mass. The people leaving the chapel said that our priest had broken away from the Archbishop and wanted us to come with "The American Priests" as they now owned the chapel. As it turned out, they had put the deed in their names without informing the Archbishop. The St. Anne parishioners had a choice to make, and our family stayed with the Archbishop and had Mass at various rental locations.

During the tour of America for Confirmations, the Archbishop was working on editing Michael Davies' *Apologia Pro Marcel Lefebvre Volume II* and handed Father Bolduc seventeen chapters which the Archbishop had finished editing.

To inform all the chapels about the happenings in the Northeast was a large task. Father was also working on an issue of *The Angelus* which discussed the Northeast schism: "Worked on *The Angelus* and this is going to be one of the best issues ever."[225] A few days later: "The lies and misleading statements of the Northeast must be exposed. Priests of the nine are in California and Phoenix trying to drive up support for their cause."

On July 20, 1983, Fathers Schmidberger and Fellay were in Houston reviewing the Southwest District books. There were multiple issues, but the biggest issue was on July twenty-first: "Father Fellay continued to work on the books. He has some difficulty with me not signing the board minutes. Finally, the board minutes were changed to my satisfaction, and I signed.

---

[225] 5/30/1983 diary

The issue had to do with Mr. Beemster's claims." Mr. Beemster was claiming in a lawsuit that he had ownership of St. Mary's.[226]

On August 11, 1983, Father Bolduc was given permission from the township to build a church on the Bolduc homestead. There was a meeting of the board of directors of TCNH – Budd, Ernest, Maurice, and Father. At a meeting on September twenty-fourth, Mr. Beemster gave Father a check for one hundred thousand dollars for New Hampshire Traditional Catholics.

Upon returning to Houston, Father handled correspondence and took care of his circuit. There was an issue at the St. Louis chapel: "Flew to St. Louis. No one at chapel. Mrs. M.'s daughter drove up and had a note for Father Bolduc. It said I was not to examine any financial records. She also said her mother was on the way to St. Mary's with the records. I called Father Williamson and he was evasive but confirmed the message." There was a meeting a month later which added confusion to this situation: "Father Fellay brought a letter from Father Schmidberger which stated that he knew nothing of the St. Louis episode."

On September 12, 1983, the first SSPX Southwest District meeting of chapel coordinators occurred: "Spent most of the day meeting with Father Fellay. The ladies and I got all the things together for the meeting of the chapel coordinators." The three-day event was very well received.

While in Houston on October fourteenth, Father had an opportunity to enjoy one of his favorite events: "We all went to the opening night of the Houston Opera—the *Barber of Seville* was playing. The performance was good. Father Carl, Father Pienierd, Bro. Anthony, Sister Grace, Chris Graham, Miss Dipoletto, and Mrs. Bradford [were present]."

Father was still aligned with the SSPX. On November 30, 1983, we see this diary entry: "Mass at Old St. Mary's (North Carolina). Father Stark and I met about straightening out the finances at Raleigh and returning items that were part of the

---

[226] I have not verified this information. There is a lawsuit but finding out the claims would require some work in Kansas court records.

Msg. Gilbert's estate. Everything needs to be put in the Society's name and two signatures are needed."

Almost two decades had elapsed since the start of Vatican II and Father comments on December 11, 1983, about the Pope's actions: "Sunday—two Masses (Houston). Today the Pope went to attend and participate in heretical services at a Lutheran church. Surely God will not let this act of treason go unpunished. Catholics are shocked and Catholic priests break their neck trying to outdo themselves with one blasphemy after another."

St. Michael's: First Holy Communion with Father
Bolduc

Chapter Twenty-five
Independent Priest (1984)

In 1984, Father Bolduc left the SSPX. To read about all that happened is difficult, but we must forge through it so that all is presented. Father Bolduc started the year as Southwest District Superior for the SSPX by preparing all end of year statistical reports for all the chapels.[227] Issues arose early in January at St. Louis where the board of directors, including Father Bolduc, were asked to resign by Father Fellay. Father Bolduc accepted that—if the ills were resolved. On February 20, 1984, the St. Louis board voted against allowing Fathers Schmidberger, Fellay, and Laisney on the St. Louis Board.

Father did not go to St. Mary's, but parishioners were calling him about developments there. It appeared Mr. Beemster's lawyers were proceeding through with the suit against the Society. This suit involved who owned St. Mary's—the SSPX or Mr. Beemster.

On February 3, 1984, Father Schmidberger, the Superior General of the Society, asked Father to visit with him when he came to Switzerland. On Father Bolduc's arrival, one of the issues appeared. "Father L. picked me up. Went to the house in Reichenbach, said Mass and waited for the Archbishop and others to arrive from Zaitzkofen. The Archbishop does not like to admit the mortgage situation which exists at St. Mary's. However, there is no question that he okayed it. Later I had a meeting with Fathers Schmidberger and Fellay. [Here Father Bolduc referred to a separate journal which he kept on these meetings.] The Archbishop admitted that the document which they tried to force me to sign was false and intended to defraud Mr. Beemster."[228] Father Schmidberger had letters that concerned Mr. Beemster's suit that he wanted Father Bolduc

---

[227] 1/4/1984 diary
[228] 2/14/1984 diary. This is a strong accusation against the Archbishop, it is Father Bolduc's opinion.

to sign but Father Bolduc did not feel he could sign the letters. As a result, Father Schmidberger has said, according to the February 17, 1984, diary entry, that he would have to remove Father Bolduc from the position of Southwest District Superior. Since I have not seen the letter or heard Father Schmidberger's interpretation of events, I cannot comment on this.[229]

On February 21, 1984, Fathers Bolduc and Fellay returned to Houston where Father Fellay continued to review paperwork there. On March first: "Father Fellay told me that the decision has been made to replace me as district superior effective March 1. He also told me who my successor was, and I named him before he did—Father Richard Williamson." Father Bolduc suspected the reason of his removal had to do with the letter he was asked to sign regarding the Beemster suit. Father Bolduc received a letter from Father Schmidberger on March second with the order to report to Switzerland, which Father Bolduc found "impossible to achieve" with no explanation why he couldn't report as requested. He suspected they wanted him out of the country for the Mr. Beemster trial. On March fifth: "They insist that if I am not in Switzerland before March fourteenth, there will be consequences." Father spent the next several days packing and on March 15, 1984, he arrived in New Hampshire from Houston.

According to an email on October 21, 2020, Father Foucauld le Roux (Secretary General of SSPX, Menzingen) stated that there was a letter on February 25, 1984 from Father Schmidberger to Father Bolduc, relieving him of his role as Southwest District Superior in the USA on March 1, 1984. Further, Father Schmidberger wrote that Father Williamson was to take Father Bolduc's place.

In the April 1984 issue of *The Angelus*, a copy of the letter Father Schmidberger sent to Friends and Benefactors was included on page twenty-three. I think that the letter was well written, sincere, and complimentary to all the work that Father Bolduc had done for the Society. It stated that the Society

---

[229] Father Laisney commented as follows: "I was told in January 1984 that I would be US district superior from July 1st. Hence, it was normal that at an annual meeting there would be change of director accordingly."

statutes provide for a year of spiritual renewal after ten years of work. Father Schmidberger related in the letter that he asked Father Bolduc to go to Écône for a physical and spiritual rest.

When I asked the Archbishop at Écône in 1987, "Why did Father Bolduc leave the Society?" the Archbishop answered: "He would not obey."[230] The Archbishop was not specific. This comment could have been related to the budget/money problem at St. Mary's, not signing the letter re. Mr. Beemster, not going to Écône as directed, or any combination of these reasons.

On March 10, 1984, in a Letter to Friends and benefactors[231] of the Southwest District in the USA, Father Schmidberger explained the situation; he wrote that a priest is often in continuous external activities, very often under stress, and that he must find a balance with times of rest, prayers, and meditation. That was the official reason for that year of spiritual renewal. In a personal letter, Father Bolduc tried to say the reason was unfair. He felt that he had been expelled unjustly; but Father Schmidberger replied that it was a false reason and insisted on a year of rest. Then faced with Father Bolduc's disobedience, Father Schmidberger expelled him.

Father started buying animals for the Gilford farm and working on the hay cuttings and the garden. On March 24, 1984, Father flew to Green Bay for a meeting: "Mr. Beemster and I had a meeting with the lawyer. We agreed on the presentation to be made to the other side. I am impressed with Mr. Beemster's honesty and integrity. His goal is to bring the true Mass and Sacraments to the people and does not allow anyone to deter him from his course."

On March 29, 1984, Father got a call from Dickinson: "Miss Graham informed me of a board meeting at *The Angelus* to remove me from the board. I called Father Carl, and he was apologetic but could give me no reasons for his actions." Father did not know the reason for his removal from *The Angelus* board, but he was no longer an active member of the Society.

---

[230] Family trip to the Netherlands and side trip to Ecône in 1986
[231] See April 1984 edition, p. 23, of *The Angelus* for copy of letter to Friends and Benefactors

Father had not accepted the removal from the Society and was somewhat bitter.

In later years, Father told his brother Ernest that he had made a mistake by leaving the Society and should have swallowed his pride. That was good of Father; to admit mistakes and accept one's part in a dispute is a wholesome outcome. When Father Rostand visited New Hampshire—around 2014—the discussion turned to Father's leaving the SSPX. Ernest related that he and Father Bolduc had discussed that before he died. Father had said that he had to leave the SSPX, and he wished he had not done it. Father Rostand was so pleased to hear that.

It was a sad time for Father in many respects. His father (Pop) was dying. On April 16, 1984, there was an interesting quote from Pop: "Pop doesn't think he will get back from the hospital." On April 27, 1984, Pop died. The Bolduc family members had not agreed for many years on what was happening in the Catholic Church, most stayed with the *Novus Ordo*, but Armand, Ernest, and their parents attended the Tridentine Mass. Father's parents understood there would be issues regarding the funeral and the Mass: "Differences of opinion, but fortunately Mom and Pop had put their desires [regarding their funeral arrangements] on paper."

Father spent the rest of this year taking care of the farm in Gilford, going to chapels in New Orleans, Green Bay, and the Irish Hills. On May 9, 1984, the chapel in New Orleans decided regarding their relationship with the Society: "Flew to New Orleans. Mr. Bellow and Father Elias picked me up and showed me the document that the Southwest District wants them to sign. We decided to keep the parish in the hands of the parishioners." There was a court case regarding the ownership of the New Orleans chapel and the judge ruled in favor of the Society. The parish in Necedah is added to Father's circuit on August sixteenth along with Madison, Wisconsin. Father had some property in New Port Richey, Florida, located near his two brothers' and mom's house. On November 28, 1984, he had all his properties turned over to the Traditional Catholics of New

Hampshire (TCNH) corporation of which Father Bolduc was the President of the board.

Father Bolduc with Miss Elizabeth Cook in Irish Hills Michigan July 1983

Father at Saints Peter and Paul in Irish Hills. Steve Summers altar boy; Patrick Summer's First Holy Communion

Chapter Twenty-six
Missions (1985-2011)

During the next twenty-seven years before Father died, he worked at the same feverish rate as before as a parish priest covering multiple parishes. He had souls to save, and he was serving up to eight chapels across the United States.

Some chapels were visited weekly, monthly, or as scheduled. Ones that were noted in the diary were St. Michaels in DePere, Wisconsin; Immaculate Conception in Gilford; Our Lady of Victory in Necedah, Wisconsin; Saint Benedict Center in New Hampshire; Alberquerque, New Mexico; Madison, Wisconsin; Saints Peter and Paul parish in Irish Hills, Michigan; Toledo, Ohio; and Jericho and Lexow, Wisconsin.

The logistics of getting to these missions was very taxing, especially as Father got older. First, Father flew each Friday or Saturday from Gilford to Green Bay. To make connections from Concord, New Hampshire, he would leave Gilford at 2:30 a.m. to be at Concord at 4 a.m. In a typical month, he made four flights, usually on Friday, from Gilford to Green Bay and a return trip on Monday.

The diaries of Father complain of frequent delays and cancellations. On one flight, delays and the weather caused him to be twelve hours late. A flight from Gilford to Green Bay on February 1, 2000, lasted from 5 a.m. to 9:30 p.m. On a flight to Green Bay in November 1996, he wrote thirty-three letters while on the plane and in airports. In traveling to the different Mass centers, Father flew in and out of airports in large cities and he often commented on the sad situation surrounding these airports. In December, 1986: "The airports are still terribly crowded. I wish I could leave these crowded cities and never see them again. A lot of the people are comfortable, even pleased with living, walking, and existing in these garbage heaps. The little cottage in the wilderness looks better all the time."

Father included his typical December, 2008, schedule for a Sunday in Green Bay: "December twenty-eighth Sunday schedule—typical—four am, rise; five am, set things up in church; five-thirty am, start confessions; six-thirty am, Mass; seven-thirty am, Confessions; eight-thirty am, second Mass—always High and Benediction of the Blessed Sacrament. Ten o'clock, leave for sick calls: 1) Wyndemere Nursing home—Confession and Holy Communion; 2) to the L's—three people, Confessions and Communion; 3) to St. Vincent's hospital for two parents and neonatal daughter; 4) same facility—Trina and new baby; 5) Mrs. S. at the health care center next to Motel 6; 6) then to Menasha to Mr. Porto for Holy Communion; 7) to the Aurora Center in Oshkosh; 8) then to visit Mr. A. for Holy communion; 9) to Eureka—Mrs. Q. for Confession and Holy Communion; 10) then back to the rectory around five pm. The above schedule is maintained each Sunday and parts often each weekday. Sometimes some patients are sent home as they heal, and others are added to the list. I have maintained this schedule for many years." When a trip to Necedah for two Masses was started, the Sunday schedule was much busier.

In July of 1998, he commented on a typical Sunday's waking hours: "In a typical Sunday, I was up at two am and got to bed at ten pm." In January 1997, he made twelve sick calls in one day, which was typical. When it came to Last Rites, Father never delayed until it was more convenient as seen in November: "Was in bed on the first at eleven pm and Mr. M. came to get me for last rites, went right to the hospital." A long night's sleep is unusual for Father as seen in September 1998: "On the thirteenth, had the best night's sleep in a long time—six straight hours."

There were two main churches that Father traveled to for daily and weekly Mass. One is in DePere, Wisconsin, and the other on his home property in Gilford. At both these locations, he built new churches.

The process of building the Immaculate Conception church in Gilford started in 1985 and finished in 1989 with a December dedication. The church was designed as an old fashioned, New England-style white-steepled church where two hundred twenty-five churchgoers could attend the Tridentine Mass. The paperwork and approvals were not an easy process, due to the local diocese. Ernest Bolduc sent me six news articles from local and out of state papers describing some of the issues with which Father Bolduc had to contend with the local bishop of Manchester, New Hampshire. The press coverage was not favoring Father Bolduc as the title of a Concord, New Hampshire[232] paper in 1987 shows: "Conservative Priest Establishing Church for Dropout Catholics."

There was much resistance to a Traditional church being built as seen by this note on December 16, 1986: "I went to the meeting of the zoning board tonight. Mr. Philip T. McLaughlin was there to represent us. In the final vote, we won by a four to one vote, with one abstention. We were all overjoyed that justice had prevailed. I trust God will remove all difficulties, and allow all rancor on the part of these people to be put aside and let us go on to the worship of God, which is what we desire. We had been aware for a long time that there were several individuals and elements that were trying to prevent us from building our church. We know for a fact that Fr. X of the Lakeport Church of Our Lady of the Lakes had approached certain individuals in the town of Gilford and caused the change of the zoning which restricts my ability to build Churches there. This had been done after I made it known that I was building a church there. Even prior to the enactment of the zoning change, there had been discussions by various priests and laymen in which it had been stated that Father Bolduc would never build his church on his farm because Father X. had arranged with members of his parish who were on the zoning board and on the planning board who had agreed to see to it that the zoning of Father Bolduc's property would be changed. We had also heard that should Father Bolduc succeed in getting around the zoning change, that those in the position to do so would 'tie Father Bolduc up for years' and thus prevent him from building. Mrs. X was the main instigator in this mess. There is no question that she and Father X plotted to deprive me of my constitutional rights and actually violated my civil rights by discriminating against me because of 'race, color, or creed.'"

Father Bolduc was quoted in a local paper[233]: "Bolduc said he has the legal and moral right and the duty to save souls, with or without the blessing of the bishop. 'The bishop's opinion doesn't necessarily affect me. I am not obedient to the bishop. One's obedience is to the Roman Catholic Church and God.'"

In April 1987 the building plan for the new church was approved by the town planning board and they started work in July, digging and pouring the basement. By October, the Bolduc brothers—Budd, Ernest, Armand, and Father—along with Brothers Anthony and Gerry had put the first-floor deck on the church and readied it for winter. There was some good news: with all this hard work, Father related in his July diary entry: "I went from two hundred forty five pounds to two hundred pounds—hard work is the answer [to weight loss]."

Father had difficulties with the local diocese in 1989. In May, after a meeting with the local bishop in Manchester: "Went to meet with the local Manchester Bishop, Bishop G.—turns out to be a kangaroo court. I shall write a report in my other book which will be more complete. He had to admit that my celebret was in order. He had to admit that there was no "Mass in private" clause in my celebret."[234]

In September of the same year, the local Manchester Bishop continued his harassment of Father in a much more severe and open way: "There was an article in the Citizen [newspaper] that had errors, but they published my rebuttal. The Concord Monitor [newspaper] was up and interviewed everyone. Many people are upset over Bishop X's arrogance. He has informed local businessmen that if they allow anyone from the church to trade with them, they will be excommunicated and denied the Sacraments. He told Mr. X, the local undertaker, that if he performs a funeral from this Church or buries anyone from

---

[233] *Evening Citizen*, Laconia, N.H., Tuesday May 5, 1987 (source 6)
[234] A Celebret is a document given to a priest which proves that he is in good standing and has permission to say Mass, usually outside your own diocese.

this church, he will be excommunicated and denied the Sacraments." In addition, the Union Leader newspaper of Manchester, New Hampshire, published a statement by the diocese chancellor, in the November 1, 1988, edition, that: "Sacraments such as marriages, Mass and Confessions performed by Bolduc will be invalid."

In early December 1989, the Immaculate Conception church was dedicated with many distant friends in attendance: "Father R., Domenick Lazzaro [Army buddy], Mr. Nichols, Mrs. Burns and Hanrahan, the Looneys [Albuquerque], and Mrs. Beemster and Mr. Peot arrive. Deguire's already here. Theresa [older sister] has been sewing for the last month on vestments and altar coverings. Sister Cecilia is a big help. Open house with five hundred plus people coming. Stayed up until three am preparing."

At the dedication on December third, Father was very happy with the turnout: "Dedication—two hundred twenty people. Father sung the Mass—What a glorious day. Mom was the first for Holy Communion. There is much concern among the local liberal Catholics that we were able to muster such a large crowd—especially during bad weather. While they are talking of closing one or more of the two local churches because of a lack of customers and priests, we are building and packing them in. That ought to tell somebody something."

The other main church of which Father was pastor, was in De Pere, Wisconsin, and is called St. Michael's. St. Michael's was founded in 1970 by Mr. Henry Beemster. Besides the Archbishop and Father Bolduc, Mr. Beemster was very instrumental in getting Tradition rescued in the United States with his limitless generosity for Father Bolduc's projects. St. Michael's would become Father's home church that he eventually serviced daily and from it would take trips monthly to the other churches. As an example, in December 1992, Father spent twenty-two days in Wisconsin.

Mr. Beemster suffered a stroke and was hospitalized in November, 1985. His wife explained that he must be patient as his recovery might be slow, saying: "Remember Heinie, Rome wasn't built in a day." Mr. Beemster answered very quickly—"No, I wasn't the boss of that job."

In December, Mr. Beemster passed away. Father learned on the seventeenth that he was very sick and because Father was already at Necedah, he went right away to the hospital: "While praying at the bedside of Mr. Beemster, I placed my special indulgenced crucifix on his chest. He was in a coma and had been since Monday. After offering all the prayers for a departing soul, and giving the apostolic blessing, I took the crucifix and applied it to Mr. Beemster's lips. Mr. Beemster's whole mouth was open, slowly [he] closed his mouth and very deliberately kissed the crucifix. There were multiple witnesses to this event. Father was very moved as the crucifix holds a special indulgence given by Pope Pius X for any of the dying who kiss the crucifix. Mrs. Beemster was comforted by this as was her daughter, Mary Ann, and Mrs. Beemster's sister, Josephine."

In November 1997 discussions began about the new church in De Pere: "Had a meeting with Mrs. Beemster, Pete (Piot), Mr. Lacenski regarding the new church." Construction on the new church in DePere started in June, 1998: "Working on new chapel and building fund started. Cleared new building site. Mrs. Beemster, Pete, Sister Rita, and Steve Lacinski turned over the first shovel of dirt at the new building site. Church excavation started." The work in the Church went quickly as many families were there helping. In December, the cornerstone was placed for the new St. Michael's Church.

Finishing St. Michael's new church was the big project for 1999. There was an entry in the January diary: "The steeple was installed. Father blessed the cross and put a relic in the right arm of the cross. The progress on the GB church is way behind due to everyone wanting their own ideas to be implemented."

I talked to Ernest Bolduc on April 10, 2020, about the project. He related that they took the plans from the church in Gilford and made it longer and wider. Gary Pauly and Steve Lacenski were the two men primarily responsible for building that church. On meeting Steve at the fiftieth celebration of St.

Michael's, Steve corrected the previous sentence stating that St. Joseph was in charge of the project, and he was a helper.

Father insisted that they not use particle board in any way or shape in the church building. Instead, they used 1 inch boards at an angle. Money issues were noted in a March diary entry: "Most of the men working at the church are working on scraping and sanding and finishing the pews. We are financially in difficulty—need about one hundred thousand dollars. Will make strong appeal to the people and try to think of way to cut corners."

In September, there were twenty-two men working on finishing St. Michaels for the dedication on September 29, 1999: "Dedication—two hundred fifty people present. We had a Solemn High Mass after blessing the Church in and out. Paul Busseteri was MC [Master of Ceremonies]; I was the Celebrant; Father S. was the deacon and Father R. was the subdeacon. There were twenty-one altar boys. We did the entire service for the dedication of the church and finished with a Te Deum. The Church was spectacular. I gave the sermon although I had a sore throat and a cold. Some people that were not parishioners came to see the church and those items that we had salvaged from their church. They were happy that the items were being used. On the next day, the thirtieth, the three priests offered Masses at the same time on all three altars."

The new bells were installed on October 20, 2000: "Ernest and I flew to Green Bay for the dedication of the Carillon Bells. First ringing of the new bells. There were three hundred present at the reception. Mrs. Beemster's eighty-seventh birthday. Mr. and Mrs. Belderok visited." Father loved singing especially old songs: "Mrs. Beemster, Jack and Mary Ann Burke sang old songs—one of the most enjoyable evenings in a long time."

Father would visit Mrs. Beemster every chance he had as he enjoyed her company. In 1993, she had been in a nursing home and now needed to be near her daughter in St. Louis. In August, it was time for her to travel: "Went to the Reves Nursing home immediately after Mass and made it in time to give Mrs. Beemster Holy Communion. I gave her a hug and I kissed her, and she kissed me. I said I loved her, and she said she loved me too. Then those sent to get her walked in the room—they had been waiting at the door—and I left. I most likely will never see Mrs. Beemster alive again. She will most likely never have the Blessed Sacrament again—certainly not from the hands of a faithful Traditional priest." A week later Father says: "I miss not seeing Mrs. Beemster each day."

The De Pere properties were in Mr. Beemster's name but on June 19, 2000, there was note of those properties passing to TCNH: "Had a meeting at Mary Ann [daughter of the Beemsters'] and Jack's home in St. Louis as regards the Catholic Doctrine Center. The funds for the CDC are invested in St. Louis at a bank with Mary Ann in charge. She mentioned that there is a large amount of money in the account [trust]. She went over Mr. Beemster's will. The will states that at Mr. Beemster's death, all funds from this trust and all property are to go directly to me (TCNH). This includes all the property at St. Michaels, the church, the rectory and the parish house and all furnishings. Present at the meeting was the entire board, Mary Ann Beemster-Burke, Jack Burke, Mrs. Alma A. Beemster, and me [Father Hector L. Bolduc]. The board wanted to know what would happen to TCNH should anything happen to me. According to Mr. Beemster's will, Mrs. Beemster is fully in charge until her death but must administer the trust for CDC and cannot use any funds for her own use." In February of 2000, a lawyer took care of the paperwork for the transfer of the Beemster trust to TCNH."

In June, 2009, Father celebrated his seventy-third birthday and his ordination anniversary: "In Green Bay—had a thirty-fifth ordination banquet with two hundred fifty in attendance. Song fest—what a grand day. I am really blessed to have such a loyal bunch of parishioners."

There were monthly trips to visit Miss Elizabeth Cook and say Mass at Saints Peter and Paul chapel in the Irish Hills, Michigan. The Bolduc brothers and sisters worked on a beautiful coffin for Miss Elizabeth and Father delivered it to her in July. When our family would go to Mass in the Irish Hills, we would see the coffin in a bedroom across from Miss Elizabeth's bedroom filled with empty quart jars. Miss Elizabeth wanted her blood collected at death in case she was declared a saint.

There was a note regarding the May 1989 Irish Hills trip which is sad in a way: "Father, as usual, cleans the house and chapel, then cooks dinner for he and Miss Elizabeth, which he has to do for each trip."

Mass attendance was down considerably at this time due to Father's criticism of Archbishop Lefebvre's consecrations. There were animals owned by the caretaker in the house at this time and they caused a mess. Miss Elizabeth, age eighty-six, was bedridden at this point. Father received a call on January 24, 1998, that his beloved Miss Elizabeth Cook in the Irish Hills had died. He described the funeral on the twenty-sixth: "Laid out coffin in the chapel and had funeral Mass. Blessed grave site and snakes came out of the ground and across the snow—power of the priest's blessing." I was one of those at the funeral lowering Miss Elizabeth's coffin with ropes and the snakes slithered out of the ground and between my legs. Father was standing right there and said to us: "Even the snakes don't want to be down there with her." Father loved her very much, but she could be cantankerous at times.

Father did travel periodically to Kansas City and St. Mary's to visit friends from the 1985-2011 time period: "Spent a week and said Mass at Miss Hanrahan's and other's houses. One day, they had a surprise party for me with over eighty people attending. I did make many sick calls in Kansas City."[235]

In another trip, "we (Mrs. Burns, Mrs. Murphy, and I) took the Blessed Sacrament for a ride all around the city of Kansas City. We made a very large circle encompassing the entire city to place it under the protection of the Blessed Sacrament."

There are small chapels and homesteads that Father visited sometimes monthly. He visited the one in Jericho in March, 2006: "We then visited the old Catholic Church in Jericho where Mrs. Pauly's sister lives. It is a beautiful structure with lovely Munich stain glass windows. It has been closed and slated for

---

[235] February, 1985 diary

demolition. All beautiful Churches are being destroyed and when replaced, they are replaced with ugly building that look like warehouses or airplane hangars or gymnasiums. All part of the plan to inculcate what is left of the Catholic Church into the Protestant ridden 'global church.'"

Father was saying Mass at a new chapel in Sonora, Wisconsin. Finally, he was in the wilderness: "On July 24, 2008, traveled five hours to the Blessed Sacrament chapel to meet the Zaraza family at their home in the wilderness. They live poorly and frugally but live within their means—fervent Catholics. Stayed in the original house by the road—no electricity or plumbing—they gave me a shovel and toilet paper in case I needed it."

Father had been assisting at the Saint Benedict Center in New Hampshire with Mass, profession of the sisters, and funerals. In November, a leader at the SBC died: On the fifth, 2009: "Received word this afternoon that Father Francis of the Saint Benedict Center in Richmond. New Hampshire. had died. He was one of the greatest Philosophers of our time and of all time. He also fought the good fight against the enemies of the Church way back when it was unpopular to do so and right beside the great Father Feeney (Leonard). He protected the dogma of "Extra Eclessia, Nulla Salus" (Outside of the Church, there is no salvation). The Traditional Catholic Movement and the world will be poorer because of his death."

Father talked over the years about the famous "cabin in the wilderness." Sight unseen, he bought some very remote land in July 1996: "Mr. Pauly and Russel and I went to Cook, Minnesota (Roosevelt). Sang the whole trip. Bought property in Beltran State Forest. Took four days for the trip and traveled one thousand six hundred and fifty miles."

In 2011, Father was finally going to build his "retreat in the wilderness": "We need a haven where we (traditional Catholics) can go for a retreat, for hunting, and as an emergency against the financial and moral decline of this country. We must be ready when the pagan hoards descend upon us. The anti-Christian idiot we have in the White House knows exactly what he is doing and glad of it." Father, Mr. Pauly, and Trent Augustine went to the "retreat" house in November to see the property. It was remote but unfortunately, there was not one tree on the property.

Chapter Twenty-seven
Father Bolduc and his fellow priests (1985-2011)

Father Bolduc covered the missions with other priest's help; some were there for a few weeks while a few were helping for many years. From the diaries, many other priests assisted Father Bolduc but then a few months or weeks later, you would see a note that Father Bolduc returned from a circuit and the priest was gone with no explanation. I would guess that Father Bolduc set the bar high for himself and by example, for other priests that were helping.

There were mention of other priests that helped such as ones from India. This was a sore spot with some priests in the SSPX due to their claim of inadequate training of the Indian priests. Father Bolduc had many chapels that needed the Mass and so few priests to help with the heavy schedule.

In December 1994, a significant event for Tradition and Immaculate Conception Church occurred. A seventy-year-old widowed man moved to Gilford: "Mr. Richard McDonough sold his house and is moving into the rectory in the bedroom across from Father Denis." When Richard first set foot in Immaculate Conception church, he said, "Thank God, I'm home at last." Father Richard McDonough was the parish priest after his ordination at the age of 70 on July 29, 2000. In his later years, Father McDonough was able to say Mass, with help due to his infirmities, until his death on December 1, 2021.

Throughout 1989 and 1990, Father Bolduc went through his typical cycle: Tampa in the cold months; DePere and Necedah parishes on the weekends; and the Irish Hills and Albuquerque during the week, one day a month. Father D'Cruz helped out with Masses in Gilford. Father D'Cruz left Gilford in 1990 with no explanation recorded in the diary. After Father D'Cruz's departure, Fathers Paul and Denis joined Father Bolduc in Gilford. He commented that they now have three priests under one roof. It is an exciting time for Father, but it will not last, unfortunately.

Another priest who helped out for a considerable time in Neceedah, Wisconsin, was Father David Sansone. Father Sansone had health problems and left Necedah in 2012 after twelve years.

On August 21, 1993, there was a mention of the first priest from the DePere parish: "First Mass for Father Tim McDonnell, the first priest from St. Michaels. I guided him through his seminary years. First, he went to the SSPX. When they entered into schism and consecrated Bishops, excommunicating themselves, he left and went to the Society of Saint Peter (FSSP) in Germany. After a year there, he learned of the Institute of Christ the King in Italy and joined their ranks. I do not believe, as others do, that he will come to our assistance to help the chapels here who have few priests already overburdened, helping and serving them. I believe he will continue his education and will be a source of greater help to us in the far distant future. He will emerge as a bishop or official who will be in the position to greatly assist the orthodox church." There were Sundays in the future where Father Bolduc mentioned that Father McDonnell helped out but also In July, 1998, there were some developments with Father Tim [McDonnell]: "Father Tim cannot say Mass at St. Michael's due to pressure from the diocese which he has to listen to since he is a member of Institute of Christ the King."

In June, 1999, Father observed the twenty-fifth anniversary of his ordination to the priesthood. He had celebrations in Green Bay and Gilford. In Gilford: "Had the anniversary Mass on the thirtieth with Father Albert Gonzales as Deacon, Father Bolduc was the celebrant, Father Ricado Gonzales was subdeacon, Joe Dom was MC [Master of Ceremonies] and Father Jerecki was priest of honor. Mr. Richard McDonough was head server. Brother Francis and other brothers of St. Benedict center were here."

Father loved his faith and the Mass. In April, 2000, he told the author this himself: "I offered two Holy Masses as this is

First Friday. It is always so comforting to be able to offer the Holy Sacrifice of the Mass. I cannot imagine not being able to do so for one day." It infuriated him when others diminished the faith. In June, on the feast of the Ascension: "This great feast has been banned in this diocese as well as many others to appease those who deny Christ's Ascension. The bishops have truly lost the faith and are a sorry lot. That coward W. said in one paper that it was too hard for people to attend Mass as the feast isn't recognized in the secular culture. He is obviously an apostate."

The diocese church in New Hampshire often challenged the validity of the orders of the Traditional priests. In December, 2000, Father's diaries discussed how that turned out: "Got a report from Mr. N. of the meeting he had with the new Chancellor of the New Hampshire diocese. Father A. stated "that both Father Bolduc and Father Richard McDonough had valid orders and were valid priests and that all of that group (Society of the Virgin Mary) were valid priests. However, they consider us disobedient to the local Bishop."

On June 16, 2002: "Today the Pope canonized Padre Pio and made him a saint. He is the only person that I ever knew who has been proclaimed a saint. He was the man who directed my vocation to the Traditional Catholic movement. I was his spiritual child."

Father Bolduc always gave thought-provoking sermons. A treasure of numerous sermons by Father were collected by Gary Pauly on cassettes. I never noticed Father using a set of notes while he preached, and this was confirmed in a July, 2000, diary entry: "Wrote my sermon and memorized it as usual."

Father Hesse (canon lawyer) returned to Green Bay to talk to the parishioners: "He expounded why Catholics do not need to receive permission from anyone, including the local ordinary, to celebrate the true Mass. He also spoke on the problem of lay trustees and why they are condemned by the Church and Canon Law. This was the nineteenth anniversary of Father Hesse's ordination."

There was an interesting note in January, 2008, concerning the characteristics of a priest: "Picture of a Pastor/Priest: to stay long in any parish, the Pastor must possess the hide of a rhinoceros; the memory of an elephant; the persistence of a beaver; the friendliness of a mongrel pup; the stomach of an ostrich; the ubiquity of a crow; the stubbornness of an army mule; the patience of Job; the business ability of a corporation CEO; the heart of a lion; and the sanctity of an angel." The explanation of these observations is that an ostrich has three stomachs, crows seem to be everywhere at once, the Heart of the Lion just means strong heart.

Father LaFitte joined Father Bolduc in September 2010 and conducted a retreat for a week at a local hotel. It appeared Father LaFitte was to help Father Bolduc with the parish for an extended period, but Father LaFitte left the following January.

Closer to Father's death in 2012, word got out that he was dying. More than a few priests would visit Father in DePere or Gilford inquiring whether they could assume his parishes. After reading the diaries and other sources, charity demands that I not comment other than to say, he did not think any of those priests were right for the job.

Chapter Twenty-eight
Rome/SSPX (1985-2011)

In June 1988, Archbishop Lefebvre consecrated four bishops against Rome's wishes. Father Bolduc had heard rumors that this was going to happen but received a phone call on June sixteenth: "Mrs. G. called to let me know that she had verified directly with Father Williamson at the seminary and with Father Laisney at the St. Louis office that the Archbishop Marcel Lefebvre had decided to renounce Rome and consecrate bishops on his own on the thirtieth of June. What a tragic turn of events."[236]

On June 30, "Heard in the news that Archbishop Lefebvre had indeed consecrated bishops, something he had promised never to do. He thus became a traitor to the traditionalist movement and automatically excommunicates himself from the Church. This means that we who are left, who still uphold tradition and yet remain loyal to the Church and the Pope and do not give in to despair as he has, must work harder for the faithful souls left."

On July 25: "The breakup of the SSPX which I had foreseen has commenced. At least 16 priests and 20 seminarians have defected in the European theatre.[237] I am sure more will follow. I thank God that so many young men have been able to do the right thing under difficult times and the obvious pressures which they must surely be under. God Bless them, they chose to remain with the Church."

Father Laisney commented in a December, 2020, email that no priests left the United States District after the 1988 Consecrations. Fr D. was in the US District, and he left in 1989—be-

---

[236] Father Laisney commented in May 2022: "'to renounce Rome' was certainly not what WE said - perhaps what Mrs G. 'said.'"

[237] Father Laisney commented in May 2022: "The total number of priests who left the SSPX in 1988 was 16, plus 29 semarians. Now that is less than 10% of priests, much less than the pronostics (forecast)."

cause of the situation in St Mary's but also somehow because of the Consecrations. But it was 1989, not 1988.[238]

In the middle of September, Father Bolduc flew to Germany on the way to Rome. He met Sister Rose (from New York) and Father R (from Poland) in Rome. His intent for the trip was to develop alliances with others in the Traditional movement: "Met with two priests who had just met with the Ecclesia Dei Commission and had encouraging news."[239] Father met with other priests to discuss "the present problems of the Latin Tridentine Mass and how we can best effect a solution." Father prepared a document that outlined his biography, his priestly responsibilities, and several recommendations on how to improve the use of the Latin Rite of the Mass. It was apparent in these recommendations that he was not supporting the SSPX.[240]

He had multiple meetings with Cardinal Mayer of the Ecclesia Dei Commission: "Sister Rose and I went to the Vatican, and I celebrated Mass on the altar of St. Pius X at seven am. We then went to the office of Msgr. P of the Ecclesia Dei commission, and I had a long talk with him. Afterwards, I met with Cardinal Mayer, a humble, gentle soul. He was most interested in my situation and asked many questions. He was astounded about Pop's death and the refusal of the bishop of Manchester to allow him to be buried from the local Church. This afternoon, we went to the Polish sisters and ordered apostolic blessings. I worked late on the letter Cardinal Mayer asked of me."[241] Father signed for Cardinal Mayer an Ecclesia Dei document. Archbishop Lefebvre reviewed this document and could not sign it.[242] Here is a translation of the Ecclesia Dei[243] document Father Bolduc signed:

---

[238] Father Laisney V7 comments May 2022
[239] 9/21/1988 diary
[240] Father Bolduc letter to Cardinal Mayer 9/1/1988 "I came to Rome" (source 33)
[241] 9/22/1988 diary
[242] Statement by Father Patrick Summers—see original Bio page 120.
[243] Pontificia Commission Ecclesia Dei. English Translation done by Father Laisney

I, N.N., promise fidelity towards the Catholic Church and towards the Roman Pontiff, the Supreme Shepherd of the Church, Vicar of Christ, Successor of Peter in his Primacy and Head of the Episcopal College.

I accept the doctrine, which is taught in n.25 of the dogmatic Constitution "Lumen Gentium" of the second Vatican Council concerning the Magisterium of the Church and concerning the adhesion due to it.

Concerning some doctrines, which the second Vatican Council taught, or concerning the posterior renovations either in Liturgy or Canon Law, which seem to some people to be able to be reconciled with difficulty with precedent declarations of the Magisterium, I assume the obligation to follow a positive line of study and communication with the Apostolic See, avoiding all polemical note.

I also declare to accept the validity of the Sacrifice of the Mass and of the Sacraments celebrated with the intention to do what the Church does and according to the rites which are found in the typical edition of the Roman Missal and of the Rituals published by the Sovereign Pontiffs Paul VI and John Paul II.

Lastly, I promise that I will adhere to the common discipline of the Church and to her laws, above all to those contained in the Code of Canon Law published by the Sovereign Pontiff John Paul II, being safe those which have been conceded by the Apostolic See in the constitutions [...]

Done at Rome, on the 22nd of September 1988 – The above declaration was signed by Fr. Hector Bolduc.

As for the above document, Father Laisney[244] comments that it is loaded with dangerous things: the first paragraph, apart from the last four words, all the SSPX priests have virtually done in the antimodernist oath, with an interesting nuance: in the antimodernist oath, it is to the FAITH of the Church and

---

[244] Father Laisney in email, source 138. Father was the District Superior of the U.S. District from 1984 to 1990.

the definitions of the Councils and Popes (Trent, Vatican I...) that we pledge our faith and attachment: such attachment is not an abstract attachment to an abstract faith, separable from the Church (see sedevacantism); it implies the attachment to Church itself, founded on this Faith; it is a binding with "Peter Professing the Faith." Now in this declaration of the Ecclesia Dei commission, one promises fidelity to the PERSONS with no reference to the Faith itself—and that is dangerous.

The last words of the first paragraph are new, and presuppose a permanent "college of bishops," with all the ambiguous new doctrine of Collegiality on the matter, and this is not good.

The second paragraph introduces the ambiguous notion of "authentic" magisterium (in *Lumen Gentium* 25), somehow between the solemn magisterium (defining the doctrine) and the ordinary magisterium—that again, is a new and certainly not defined doctrine, under which they want to push the novelties. And that is most dangerous.

The third paragraph accepts that there "appears to be" some passages in the novelties that are "difficult to reconcile" with previous magisterium; but on those matters, one may not denounce clearly the novelties, one rather pledges to avoid any "polemic."[245] Practically after more than thirty years now, it appears that the "Ecclesia Dei" societies have done near nothing to denounce those novelties.

The fourth paragraph accepts the validity of the new rites, but fails to state that there are often many reasons to doubt—in practice—such validity due to many abuses, either the lack of proper matter (e.g. confirmation without olive oil for the Chrism, which the new rubric allow), or lack of proper intention because many modern priests are taught the wrong thing (e.g. that the Mass is not a proper propitiatory sacrifice...) which open the door to distorted intention.

The fifth paragraph is all on the new code of Canon Law, as if there were nothing problematic with it (e.g., can. 844!).

---

[245] Wikipedia definition—A *polemic* is contentious rhetoric that *is* intended to support a specific position by forthright claims and undermining of the opposing position.

At the same time, Father Bolduc received from Cardinal Mayer, who oversaw the Ecclesia Dei commission, the faculty to say (sometimes called a celebrate) the 1962 Mass:[246]

> Paul Augustine Cardinal Mayer, OSB
>
> By these present [letters] it is attested that Reverend [Father] Hector Bolduc, ordained on the 29th of June 1974, has the faculty to celebrate the Sacrifice of the Mass using the Roman Missal published in the year 1962, according to the norms of the Apostolic Letters "Motu Proprio" given on the 2nd day of July 1988.
>
> That faculty will be effective until a Commission established for this purpose will be able to publish general disposition after consulting the local Ordinaries.
>
> Done at Rome on the 22nd of September 1988.
>
> Augustine Cardinal Mayer, OSB
>
> President of the above-mentioned Commission
>
> (signature): Camille Perl, secretary

Shortly before leaving to go back to the U.S., Father went to Germany to discuss how to move the Traditional movement forward: "I arrived in W. and spoke with Fr. X. and Father X. We really have our work cut out for us. The bishops will be the stumbling block, especially as regards the 'collegiality' of bishops as the liberal and modernists greatly outnumber the conservatives. I had dinner at the St. Peter's Society new fraternity house here."[247]

Two days later there was another entry in the diary about the movement to Tradition: "This evening, we had a long talk about the present situation of St. Peter Seminary. We all agreed that there must be a universal decree establishing the Traditional Latin Mass and that a bishop must be appointed to administer their spiritual needs. We spoke of the advantages and disadvantages of being accepted by diocesan bishops."

---

[246]   Ecclesia Dei agreement 9/22/1988 (source 73), Cardinal Mayer document for Fr. Bolduc (source 74). Translation by Father Laisney.
[247]   10/4/1988 diary

Father returned to the States on October tenth and continued his work in Gilford and the circuits. Attendance at some of Father's chapels was reduced due to Father's negative talks on the Archbishop's consecrations.[248]

Father was still working on the plan to expand Tradition in the world throughout the year. In March, 1989: "I wrote several important letters to Rome." At the back of the diary, Father had addresses for many high-level prelates in Rome: "Joseph Cardinal Ratzinger (Congregation for the Doctrine of the Faith), Eduardo Cardinal Martinez Somalo (Divine Worship), His eminence Antonio Cardinal Innocenti (prefect of the Sacred Congregation of the Clergy), His Holiness Pope John Paul II, Augustin Cardinal Mayer, Msgr. Camillo Perl, Secretary, His eminence Edouard Cardinal Gagnon (President Pontifical Council for the Family)." Following these addresses, he noted: "And let's not—please!—be devastated either by Bishop L.'s reaction to all this, or by the Roman Mafia working for the Church's overthrow. Let us rely on Mary and the Rosary above everything! Mary, Help of Christians pray for us."

To see clearly where Father Bolduc's attitude is towards the SSPX, I have excerpted parts of a letter from August 25, 1990, to a Mr. Hugh Akins of Commack, New York[249]: "I have no association whatever with the SSPX and desire none. No, I am not a sedevacantist and have no use for them. My parish here in New Hampshire has about eighty regular attendees. There are two other priests who work with me and a third who covers in case of emergencies. There are two bishops who support us and our work. Both are Traditional and have no connection with Archbishop Lefebvre, or other groups who have 'consecrated' their own bishops, Cardinals, Popes, etc. I offer only the Latin Tridentine Mass according to the missal of St. Pope Pius V. I have not accepted the changes to the Canon and other parts of the Mass of Pope John XXIII as so many of the SSPX priests have. I have not added the name of St. Joseph to the Canon as requested by Archbishop Lefebvre. So that you are

---

248   12/1988 diary.
249   Letter to Hugh Akins 8-25-1990 (Source 145)

not mistaken, I greatly respect Archbishop Lefebvre and I am indebted to him for my priesthood."

The year 1998 was momentous as Father Bolduc showed visible signs of reconciling with the SSPX. From March through August, Father held Confirmation classes for those in Wisconsin who wanted to be confirmed. This seemed to be a result of Father's talks with canon lawyer Father Hesse in 1997. Gary Pauly had been asking Father for some way for those needing Confirmation to receive the sacrament and Father Hesse[250] confirmed that what the Archbishop did in consecrating bishops was canonically correct. In May, Father Bolduc had Father Hesse talk to the parishioners three different times regarding the correctness of the Consecrations.

On September 27, 1998, a bus left for Chicago for the Confirmations of Father Bolduc's parishioners. It had been since 1983 that Father Bolduc had left the SSPX with little communications with the Society. I think Father's terrible experiences with the hierarchy of the Novus Ordo church and his discussions with Father Hesse led him back to a favorable attitude toward the consecrations and the SSPX. Father Bolduc wrote a letter to Father Peter Scott (District Superior of the United States, SSPX) dated April 6, 1998, where he noted his appreciation of the SSPX: "It remains a fact that the SSPX is the only Traditional Catholic priestly organization which has not compromised on the Mass and the Faith."[251]

There was an encouraging note in the July, 1999, diary regarding Archbishop Lefebvre: "Wrote an article to Mr. De R. answering C.'s stupid attack on Archbishop Lefebvre." Father Hesse gave multiple conferences in October to the parishioners. One diary entry concerned the Society of Saint Peter (FSSP): "Poor Father B., he trusted the liberal New Ordo and

---

[250] Gregory Hesse, S.T.D., J.C.D. of Vienna, Austria, was ordained in 1981 in St. Peter's Basilica. He held doctorates in both Thomistic theology and Canon Law. From 1986-88 he served as Secretary to Cardinal Stickler at the Vatican. From 1991, he worked in Austria, Germany, and the United States giving lectures and producing theological articles that appeared in Catholic Family News, The Fatima Crusader, and other journals. He died of complications due to diabetes on January 25, 2006.

[251] Father Bolduc letter to Father Peter Scott—4/6/1998 (source 165)

now they are stabbing him in the back. You cannot trust the compromising liberals either in politics or religion."

Father kept his finger on the pulse of what was happening with the SSPX. In February 2006 he wrote: "Got a call from Father X. of New Orleans. He is concerned about a split in the SSPX as are many other priests. Both Fathers Schmidberger and Fellay are over here trying to take care of damage control. Many feel they are moving too fast in the direction of the Vatican and are afraid of another Campos, Brazil, fiasco. Some priests want a place to go to should they need it."

In October 2006, Father related an enjoyable story that happened to him at St. Michaels but also when he was a seminarian: "When I was very early into my first years of the Religious Order of the MIC (Maria Immaculate Conception—the Marian Fathers), there occurred an amusing incident which I have never forgotten. On an important feast in Stockbridge Massachusetts, Mass on Eden Hill in the beautiful little chapel, it happened that I was chosen to hold the Holy Water bucket while Father L. P. sprinkled the congregation with Holy Water. To do this more effectively, he climbed up the winding stairs to the top of the pulpit. There he dipped the head of the sprinkler into the bucket and proceeded to drench the people. On his second swing, the large head of the sprinkler full of water detached itself from the handle. It sailed through the air and struck a woman in one of the front pews on the head. It rendered her unconscious for a short time. I noticed the whole action and burst out laughing. I got the evil eye look from Father P. but I really could not help it. Why is it that things that happen in church ever at the worst solemn moment always seem more hilarious than elsewhere? On Sunday, October 1, 2006, the same happened to me except the sprinkler head flew off and slammed against the wall. I continued to sprinkle people with the water in the handle."

Father spent a couple days each year for the Rogation days blessing the farms. In May of 2009, Father blessed over twenty-five farms (fourteen in one day). In November, as he had done in the past years, he blessed the hunters and their guns:

"First day of hunting—blessed guns and hunters. Today, Wisconsin has the largest fighting force in the world—six hundred fifty thousand strong."

A seminarian in Winona must have been close to Father Bolduc, as in March 2009, Father went to a shop where they were working on Frank Riccomini's chalice. In April, Father LeRoux (rector at Winona seminary) and Frank arrived to pick up the chalice. I know of another SSPX seminarian that Father Bolduc helped finance through his years at the seminary.

Developments in Rome regarding the Latin Mass were reported in July, 2007: From July sixth—"There is much in the air about the Pope allowing the old Mass 'more freely.' This is nonsense. All priests have the right from God to offer the old "true" Mass according to the missal of Pope St. Pius V. It is the new Mass (mess) that had to have permission. When this *Moto Proprio* is released, it will amount to nothing as there will be so many strings attached as to make it ineffective from the start. The Liberals are determined to destroy the Catholic faith and the Mass. They are now in the position to do so. The only ones invited to attend the Pope's recent meeting in Rome were the two biggest liberals in the U.S.—O'Malley from Boston and Burke from St. Louis—who have made it clear that they hate the Traditional Mass and the Church."

There was some good news in January, 2009, regarding the SSPX: "Received word today that the Pope had removed the excommunication of the four bishops of the SSPX. Of course, we all knew that they were never valid in the first place."

Bishop Williamson made some statements in 2009 that caused him and the SSPX some difficulty: "The battle between the SSPX, Bishop Williamson and the pope continues. One doesn't know what rumors are true. One thing, and only one thing is certain, the devil is in the works and is doing his best to destroy what little is left of the Church. Our faithless (N.O.) Bishops allowed the enemy in the gates, these wolves in sheep clothing betrayed Christ and Holy Mother Church and now souls are being hammered out on the Devil's anvils in the diocesan offices." Bishop Williamson had to leave Argentina and moved to England.[252]

---

[252] 2/2009, the government of Argentina asked Williamson to leave the country (Google).

Gilford - Immaculate Conception Church

Gilford Bolduc House with sign

Chapter Twenty-nine
Gilford, New Hampshire (1985-2011)

During 1985, Father continued working on the Gilford homestead when the weather was warmer. He wintered in Florida. Family members including Father, Armand, Ernest, and Budd worked on shoring up and repairing the many buildings on the farm. It was heartwarming to read about the family coming together for various projects around the Gilford property such as in July: "We killed and processed one hundred sixty-seven chickens averaging six pounds dressed."

Farming and gardening in Gilford were a family affair. When hay was being loaded into the barn, there were fifteen family members helping. Brother Anthony[253] arrived to help Father in Gilford with the gardening and other farm chores: "Processed two hundred thirty chickens, harvested two thousand pounds of potatoes from twenty pounds of seed potatoes, processed pigs with eleven family members—rendered the fat into seventy-five pounds of pork sausage—had the hams smoked elsewhere." There was a cute side story about the potato harvest in October: "On hearing that we had an exceptionally good crop of potatoes this year, Mom said: 'I knew we would have a good crop, I cut the potatoes.' She said the secret is to leave at least two eyes on each potato piece. If one doesn't grow, the other one will. She cut them in the garage doorway where she has cut them for more than sixty years."

Father Bolduc loved his mother as a loving son. He couldn't do enough for her but that didn't stop Father and Ernest from making practical jokes at her expense. Father always enjoyed a good joke either on himself or on others. His mother was no exception to having fun with as related in these stories by Ernest: "Back in the 1980s, mother sent Father to the Big Banana (a vegetable and fruit place) to pick up things and some lemons. Mother made the best lemonade ever. When he

---

253 Mark Schaeffer

Father Bolduc in Vegetable Garden 2003 Gilford N.H

Father at Gilford farm processing chickens(Bob, Theresa, Helen, Hector, Bob, Linda, Gerry)

returned with the goods, he had put wooden lemons in place of the real ones. Mother, being old and with less strength in her wrists, had to roll the lemons with her stocking feet until they were soft and then she would clean the lemons. Of course, the wooded lemons did not soften. She called Father to return these lemons to Big Banana as they were hard as rocks, and at that time, Father started to laugh, and mother then realized that the lemons were wood. At that point, she shouted 'it's you and Ernest who planned this.' She then laughed and laughed. She was always a good sport and enjoyed tricks played on her."

Ernest related another story about his mom: "Another time, our mom and dad lived in Florida in the winter, and Father would fly most weeks to be with them. One week, Father again wanted to play a trick on mom. He had me (Ernest) send him some brown wooden eggs that my company made, just like the lemons in the story above. It seems that the folks' refrigerator, if not opened enough, would freeze the food. So, this morning Father had put the wooden eggs in place of the real ones. Mother got up to cook breakfast and could not crack the eggs and felt they were frozen. She continued to try to crack them when Father opened the door slightly and started to laugh. Right then she knew what it was all about and started to laugh and laugh as she uttered it 'You Hector and Ernest again.' She was a good sport."[254]

In Gilford, Father helped his brothers manage the farm and brought extra animals on to the farm such as four burros[255] which he had delivered from out west. Besides the burros, the cattle, chickens, pigs, and turkeys provided meat for the family and for sale. I found records of four hundred sixty chicks bought and processed during this year. The gardens were "Father Bolduc" large (e.g., one hundred twenty-five raspberry bushes) and the fruit from the fruit trees filled the canning jars bound for the fruit cellar. There was a note in May where he made eleven cases of cherry wine from the fruit trees.

---

[254] Transmittal letter Ernest Bolduc 1/18/2018 (source 88)
[255] 5/7/1986 diary

The family homestead in Gilford is still a productive farm and garden as seen in August of 1996. They enjoyed the fruits of the garden as they canned five hundred jars of jellies, jams, tomatoes, and other vegetables. As always, it was a family affair, a nice trait of the Bolduc family. In the same month, Father received the approval for the cemetery by the church: "The cemetery has been approved, now I can be buried where I was born."

The farm and gardening kept Father occupied in a labor of love. While maintaining the barn, he had a fall in July, 1987: "I started scraping the eaves of the barn on the twenty-seventh. The ladder slipped from under me, and I fell thirty feet to the cement platform in front of the barn. Brother took me to the hospital. I hurt my right ankle and leg, my back and right hip, and buttocks. My hammer was in my right jean pocket, and I landed on it. Lucky, I had no broken bones. I have a lot of pain and soreness. The doctor couldn't believe that I had not broken anything. I have bed rest with my foot elevated for three days." In September, he got back to work on the barn: "remounted the tall ladder and painted the eaves." In later years, Father had many joint and back issues that may have been a result of this three-story fall onto cement.

The work in Gilford continued, starting in April, 1990, with the sugar bush operation: "I was home for the boiling of the sap for the first time in more than twenty-five years. I got a good cold drink of sap. Boy was it good. Armand and Ernest boiled in the evening. Armand looks just like Pop. The similarity is so great that when I first walked in and saw him in his bib overalls, I had to do a double take. Even his mannerisms working at the evaporator are the same."

Father would talk often about the syrup operation in Gilford. In April, 2004, he related a story in the diary: "When I spoke with Theresa on Good Friday, she reminded me of one of our Good Friday chores on the farm. At home we were not permitted to talk or have any entertainment from noon to three pm in honor of the death of Christ. However, we could work. One of the most common jobs reserved for Good Friday was washing sap buckets. This was before the days of plastic sap lines and gravity feed. We had hundreds of sap buckets and covers to wash in hot water and place on boards or planks upside down to dry. Because we were not allowed to talk, the work went faster and got done quicker. Of course, my father could talk and did talk. The hot water for washing the buckets had to be hauled in pails from the farmhouse, quite a distance (maybe one quarter mile), especially through the snow and or mud."

After seeing buffalo on his many trips, Father had to have some of his own and that finally happened on November 5, 1990: "The buffalo came, and I was there when they were unloaded—named them Bill (Cody) and Annie (Oakley)." He bought them on November second in Wisconsin and had them shipped to New Hampshire.

December 1990 was a very sad one for Father Bolduc. His mom passed away after a short bout of pneumonia. Father wanted to stay with his sick mother so Father D'Cruz flew to Wisconsin for the Masses there on November twenty-nineth. On December third, he wrote: "mom worse—looks irreversible. Budd, Sam, Maurice left Florida for New Hampshire. I brought the Pius X crucifix and mom leaned up and kissed it—all in the room were moved. I rush home (from the hospital) each day to say Mass for Mom's recovery. Getting one to two hours of sleep. On the seventh, mom died—I have lost my saintly mother whose love and prayers have supported me all these years." The funeral Mass was on December eleventh and conducted by Father: "The church was full and overflowed into the choir loft." On December twenty-eighth, Father wrote in his diary: "Have just finished the first Christmas season without Mom. My only consolation in her death is that she can help me and my course more from heaven than she could here. I shall have a monument made in her honor." Father's mother was laid to rest in the cemetery in April of 1991. This delay was due to the hard winters in New Hampshire.

Father killed two hundred twenty-one turkeys (averaging thirty-five pounds) in November, 1991, for the Thanksgiving

Father's buffalo in Gilford pasture

Father Bolduc's pride and joy "Buffalo Bill" 1999 Gilford

holidays. The traditional Thanksgiving feast at the Bolduc farm was enjoyed this November, 1991, with the families. They certainly had enough turkey with a thirty-five pounder and forty pounder: "Doris did a lot of work and Ernest made mom's pork stuffing from mom's handwritten recipe."

As I read through the diaries, I was always amazed at how some of the Bolduc family members were always there on the farm to help with various projects like gardening, canning, animal slaughtering, building repair, etc. I talked to Ernest about the involvement of Ernest, Budd, and Armand on the farm: "They took care of it when Father was on circuit. When Father was at home, they worked on a myriad of new projects and repair work on the farm. They were up almost every day to take care of their beloved homestead. They knew Father as a brother and a priest. They had a lot of respect for him and when he said 'no' it meant no, and when he said 'yes' it meant yes. There was never any question about Father's thoughts."

Bigger and better gardens continued to be grown in Gilford. Some of the crops that Father was harvesting are shown in his September, 2002, diary: "plums, tomatoes, pears, beans, peaches, apples, cucumbers, raspberries, strawberries, grapes, peas, parsley, beets, onions, cabbage, Swiss chard, cumquats."

The sad event of 2004 and 2005 was Theresa's sickness and death. Theresa was seven years older than Father and had a major influence on him. How Father handled her sickness reveals how Father treated those he loved. As the 2003 year neared its end at Thanksgiving: "Theresa has mild lympho-blastic syndrome which can lead into Leukemia. On the twenty-fourth: "Theresa here, how wonderful to see her for thanksgiving dinner. I put the turkey in the oven at four am and it was cooked by eight-thirty am. We had thirty for dinner, including the Lams with two professors from China."

Father received a call from Ernest in February of 2004: "Theresa has two weeks to two months to live. I had feared such a call." In May, Father and Theresa had a private talk: "She instructed me concerning all aspects of her funeral and wishes following her death. She wants to die here in this house where she was born and to be buried in the cemetery here." In June, Theresa celebrated her seventy-fifth birthday. Father visited her monthly in Vermont but for Thanksgiving, she traveled to Gilford: "Theresa arrived—what a blessed day—it has been a year since she has visited. Theresa and Father were the only ones at the early Mass. Had two thirty-five plus pound turkeys for thanksgiving dinner and a smaller than normal group— very good time had by all. Have a tight chest and a headache."

On one of Father's visits in March, 2005, Theresa told him about his youth: "She also spoke about my learning to read at an early age saying that I could read books through when I was two years old. She says she would sit me down on the step by the unfinished room and I would read as she taught me. I could read books and memorize them through before I was four years old."

On a monthly visit on November 21, 2005: "Visited Theresa with Persis and Sally T. When I stepped into Theresa's room, her arms and hands went up and beckoned to me. She hugged me and I her. She could not speak but answered my questions by either nodding or shaking her head. What a pitiful sight. She looks like a living corpse. There were tears in her eyes and in mine although I had to hold mine back. Her body was very hot. I gave her the full last rites and anointed her. Prayed for her and with her. I said our three Hail Mary's with her, and she mouthed the words. Her courage and determination have not left her. She is still very much in control. Her hearing is very acute. I know Theresa wanted me to stay longer and I couldn't. Will I ever see her alive again? I kissed her and she pressed her lips to my check. I gave her a blessing and walked to the bedroom door. I turned and her eyes were fixed on me. I waved and she moved her hands in response. Then we took our de-parture with heavy hearts. Bob, her husband, called the next day with the news that Theresa had died. On the twenty-fourth, the family had Thanksgiving dinner with thoughts of Theresa who was the center of Thanksgiving for so many years.

Thanksgiving 2006 was a large affair with over sixty-five people present. Father cut up fifty pounds of potatoes and twenty pounds of carrots. He also made seven gallons of soup for needy parishioners in Green Bay area.

There were three buffalo killed on September 26, 2003 and a butcher was hired to cut up the fifteen hundred pounds of meat. There was a clipping in the *Laconia Evening Citizen* on October twentieth, advertising the meat: "For sale—Buffalo Meat—High in taste, low in Fats and Cholesterol. Steaks, Stew meat, hamburger, roasts. Packaged, Frozen, five dollars per pound. Bolduc Farm—500 Morrill St. Gilford."

Farmers can become somewhat insensitive to death when it comes time to slaughter animals for food. However, that does not mean they do not love small animals that cause no trouble as shown in this story about a mouse in November 2005: "Yesterday, while pulling rocks out of the back pasture, under one of the very large rocks a small mouse scampered. How she escaped being crushed I will never know. I almost killed her but missed with my boot. Then I thought better of it and helped her out of the large crater left by the stone. She ran to a brush pile and disappeared inside. Near the empty hole left by the rock, I found some acorn shells and seeds. There is no question that her winter hibernation had been destroyed. I felt sorry for the poor little thing so today I picked up a sack of acorns from the front lawn under the old oak tree and took them down to the wood pile along with some apples. I left them where she had entered the wood pile in hopes she would find them and pack them away for the winter. Perhaps I had been influenced by having just finished reading the adventures of Danny Meadow Mouse by Thornton Burgess. I hope she makes it through the winter."

Ernest was now managing the farm using a local farmer to cultivate the fields.[256]

---

[256] 2023

Ordination chalice of St. Pius X, Silver gilt,
Baroque style , jeweled

Blind stich vestment."

Chapter Thirty
Collections/Treasures (1985-2011)

Father continued searching for rare treasures as he got older. I think he did this for the preservation of beauty and antiquity, to make some money for his missions, and as a refresher after spending so much intense time as a priest.

People ask how Father accumulated so many treasures. The Benzinger estate is an example of how he gathered treasures and monetary assets. For those that don't know the Benzingers of California, the first Benzinger printing house opened in New York City in 1853 selling religious books in Polish, German, and English. There were two Benzinger sisters in California that wanted to convey their collections and monies to Father Bolduc.

In March, 1985, Father spent a week in the Los Angeles area working with the Benzingers as they wanted to give their properties and collections to Father. In July, there was an emergency visit to Los Angeles to administer Last Rites to Miss Marieli Benzinger.

Father had been given ownership of the Benziger estate near Los Angeles and made a trip in December, 1988, to pack up certain valuables and ship them to New Hampshire.

In 1989, Father was still traveling to California to work on packing the Benzinger estate for shipping to New Hampshire. In January, he packed a twenty-four-foot truck and a car with items. In April, the last trip was made: "Ernest came with Father for one trip to Green Bay and then flew down to Los Angeles to work on the Benzinger estate—boxed up seventy boxes and packages and mailed them. Ernest was overwhelmed at the size of the house and the entire project. Ernest helped for a day and then returned home. Had Lucy, Celia, Andrea Thompson, and Michael helping clean, filling two dumpsters from the whole big house." In May, Father received the check for the sale of the Benzinger estate.

Francis Woodman Cleaves was a Sinologist, linguist, and historian who taught at Harvard University, and was the founder of Sino-Mongolian studies in America. A deeply committed teacher, he retired, reluctantly, in 1980. He later returned to teach Mongolian, without remuneration, for several years following the untimely death of his successor, Joseph Fletcher. Cleaves never married, but he maintained a large community of cattle, horses, and golden retrievers on his farm in New Hampshire. In contemporary argot, one would say that he "lived off the grid," foreswearing even a telephone and accessible only by mail or personal visit. Knowing Father Bolduc, it is natural that these two historians were friends and that Professor Cleaves trusted Father with his collection.

In September, 1990, Father met with Professor Francis Cleaves which led eventually to filling half of the church basement with a "one of a kind" collection: "Had two meetings in Gilmanton with Mr. Francis Cleaves who is involved in Asiatic Studies. He has a collection of books and manuscripts pertaining to the Chinese and Japanese."

In October, 1994, the Cleaves library was moved from Alton to Gilford, New Hampshire: "Went to Alton to fill four pickups with boxes from Professor Cleaves. Went back and got seventy boxes. On the twentieth, professor Cleaves was in Gilford to start unpacking the boxes."

It appears the Cleaves library is very rare as visitors from all over the world come to Gilford to study the collection.

A large library in the basement (approximately 24' by 80') of the Immaculate Conception Church held the Asian collection that needed to be catalogued. In July, 2001, progress was made: "On the eighth, Victor and Ruby Lam were here and brought with them Professor Yang Nan from Pekin University in China who moved in here and who will be cataloging the Chinese books in the Professor Cleaves Asian Library. The Lams will set up the computer in the library."

I had noticed while in Gilford, many black filing boxes in one of the storage sheds and their contents were revealed in an August, 2002, diary entry: "Moving all of the Cleaves library of the Chinese dictionary—hundreds of file cabinets boxes." Each letter of the approximate fifty thousand Chinese letters has its own card inside these cabinet boxes.

Need I remind anyone that Father never went anywhere without looking for antiques? The overflowing buildings in Gilford are a testimony to this statement. The year 1991 started with an unusual entry in January: "Went to dump to collect old bottles." This dump trip does seem an odd hobby for a priest. However, on April 10, 2020, I talked to Ernest Bolduc, and he was moving those five thousand seven hundred plus antique milk bottles because the carriage house floor was starting to buckle under their weight. He also had about the same number of collectable bottles, worth much more than the other five thousand seven hundred plus bottles.

In November, 1999, Father was excited with a find: "Mrs. S. got me a bread bucket like I had never seen before. It is blue Spatterware on the outside. Very clean on the inside. Looks like it may be stainless steel. Has a country scene painted on it." I could not possibly estimate the number of bread buckets or washing machines that are in Gilford at this moment.

Father was very excited about a missal he found in February 2011: "I purchased an altar missal of 1579—what a magnificent addition to my collection—a real treasure." He had it reconditioned by professional book restorers. The missal was issued just after the Council of Trent.

Father sold, through an auctioneer, in June 2007, two famous historical documents for $190,000.

Father had great difficulty in August, 2011, picturing the proposed new Internet world without books: "People are predicting that in twenty years, there will not be any books in stores. All will be on the internet and computer. I cannot imagine that. How will someone get a first edition or an autographed copy? Hope I won't live to see that day."

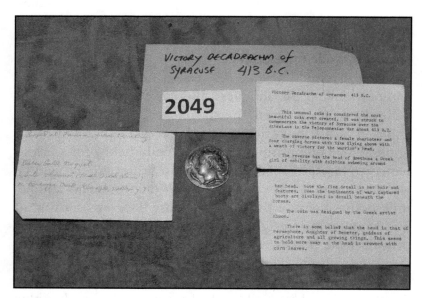

Greek coins 413 B.C. one of best designed commerating
Spartan victory in Pelapponesian War #2049

ivory and walnut base monstrance. Gift from archbishop
lefebvre to Father Bolduc.

Young Father Bolduc

Father Bolduc in garden - concord grapes - notice shirt tag - "Superior Septic"

Chapter Thirty-one
Father as a person (1985-2011)

Father valued the truth as he saw it and when anyone violated that truth, he was not bashful about letting him know his thoughts. There was a note in the December, 1998, diary which included a press clipping written by Father Bolduc in a Green Bay newspaper: "The author of the October fifteen People's Forum letter, 'Let's learn from history' obviously could use some of her own advice. Ben Franklin certainly did not come close to leading a 'perfect' life as the writer would have us believe. I am certain that one of his mistresses would have concurred. As for the 'proud attempts' of the Indians, it is common knowledge that the Indian tribes in this country and in Central and South America practiced slavery as well as cannibalism, some to a greater extent than others. Saying that Communism offers no threat to our government or to others is sheer stupidity. Does the writer really believe that the one hundred million plus victims who died under Communism were willing volunteers? The greatest blunder and untruth is the writer's attempt to link the name of Christopher Columbus with that of Hitler and Stalin. While seeming to attack ignorance and bigotry, the writer's letter reeks with both. M. R. [author of article] is right on one point: Ignorance and prejudice are a cause of much of the world's problems. Her letter is proof of that. There is an old saying, 'it is better to let people think you are stupid than to open your mouth and prove it.' Before writing any more letters, R. should purge herself of her own prejudices and ignorance." Let no one say that Father Bolduc minced his words.

Father Bolduc was dreaming again in February 2000: "Started working on my plans for my cabin in the wilderness." He did hope that he could go to this cabin and be able to read and pray but in November, he restated his reality: "I keep thinking of the woods and if I shall ever be able to go there and build my little camp. So many projects at home in New

Hampshire and the ever-increasing work of all the chapels make it doubtful. I cannot abandon those who rely on me for the Sacraments." All of us appreciate his dedication and hard work helping take care of our souls right up to his dying day.

Whenever Father wanted to document a thought but do it secretly, he would abbreviate using coded capital letters that described the thought. There are many of these private messages in the diary, I have only decoded a few of them. On December 2, 2000, he demonstrated a sample of his coding scheme: "YYURYYUBICURYY4EE—Two wise you are, two wise you be. I see you are two wise for me."

Father performed his share of weddings over the years, but there were two this year that he commented on. In June 2001: "I went to the reception, and I wish I had not. Going to bless the food is one thing, having to put up with the noise, suggestive jokes and insinuations is something else. There is also the matter of improper dress. One young girl had so little on that there were 'cat' calls and rude remarks by the so-called announcer." Fortunately, the wedding in August was much better: "The wedding was the finest wedding I have been involved in (Charlotte U. and Dennis L.). The bridal party was dressed appropriately, and the choir were splendid."

Additionally, not all funerals were to Father's liking such as the one for Armand's mother-in-law in February of 2002: "Several people standing up and giving speeches about the deceased. It shall not happen again!!!"

In 2004, Father commented on a new movie that was out in February: "Heard about the new Mel Gibson film—the *Passion of Christ*. How the Jews and other liberals tried to kill it but by the grace of God it is a great success and most likely the greatest movie ever made. The anti-Catholics are frothing at the mouth and all the liberal 'Catholic' bishops are issuing words of caution. What a triumph for Mel Gibson and for God. Attended the *Passion of Christ*—Nothing more need be said except it was the greatest movie ever made and will most likely remain so for ever. 'O what our sins have done to Christ.'"

Father led a march for life in January 2006 against abortion in front of the hospital with two hundred twenty-four people in attendance. Dr. Paul Byrne from Michigan gave talks to Green Bay and Irish Hills on brain death and organ transplants. And one for the record book in April: "Baptized William Francis Bowman—the one hundred forty-first grandchild of Mrs. Tom Kinjiski."

Father treasured talking to some of the older parishioners. He wrote in January, 2002, about Wisconsin: "Went on sick calls. Mrs. Gill seems as always. She loves her old farmhouse and her nice wood furnace. She talked to me a lot about the old days. Once when she gave birth to one of her children in the early morning hours, she had to get out of bed and help the men butcher hogs a few hours after giving birth because she had to cook and make the blood sausage. This tells a lot about this strong, proud farm housewife." He would also talk to Miss Elizabeth up in Michigan for hours; they were kindred spirits.

As Father advanced in years, he reminisced and dreamed in 2002 more and more about his "cabin in the wilderness." In May: "Packed material in boxes for the "woods" and Gilford. On May nineth, "the pounding of the rain on the roof caused me to picture myself in a small cabin in the wilderness with a wood stove fire burning and me in a comfortable chair listening to the rain on a metal roof—one day." In October: "The air and the sky were clear and crisp. Wonder how it is in my wilderness property. I long so much to be there. Nothing but wildlife, the water, trees, forest, etc. Just one week would suffice." Father paid for another wilderness property in November on Little Black Lake in Ontario, Canada. There were many entries in the diary about the wilderness but in December of 2003, Father realized that the wilderness dream was becoming further and further away. The many boxes for the wilderness filled three semitrailers and some items are now stored in the guest house in Gilford.

In the year 2003, the streets, airports, and homes were full of the new gadget called a cell phone and Father did not like them at all, and commented in August: "I really wish I could do without that dastardly phone. The cell phones are a real curse. God must have permitted them to be invented to punish mankind. One cannot be at peace anywhere or enjoy quiet, read or write or rest. At the airport, people walk around with one of these contraptions stuck in their ear. They discuss even the most personal problems openly for everyone to share. Something should be done about controlling their use in public places."

Father had an ending comment in his diary in December, 2007, regarding the coordinator for the Necedah chapel and his history of keeping diaries: "Virgil Bulcher came from Necedah with the collection money. He is a good, hardworking, trust-worthy person. This is the twenty-one thousand, nine hundred and fifteenth entry I have made since I started keeping a journal diary sixty years ago." Is it not interesting that he accounted for fifteen leap years? With about one hundred words per page, that is two-point-two million words. The Catholic Bible has around eight hundred thousand words.[257]

Sister Rita was dying in July, 2008, so Father gave her last rites: "It hurts to see this great soul in such condition. I have to keep a strong front for the sake of the family. I left after a while so I could weep in private. On the twelfth, Sister Rita Laurence Selisein died—will miss her terribly."

Father loved to be around the children as seen in March 2008: "Little James (Drew) was there along with Simon. I cautioned Simon not to go to the den where they found the bear hibernating this past December. Little Simon (three years old) had gone in the den and touched the bear. I told him that as it was getting warmer, the bear might wake up and that bears are always hungry after a long sleep. He said 'It's okay, Father, I've got my brown scapular.' Oh, the innocence."

In July 2008, Father made a trip to New Orleans for Mass and a little fishing: "Little Nicholas, one of the twins, came fishing with us. I mentioned that my knees and hips and legs were hurting because of all the strenuous exercise I have done

---

[257] https://www.readinglength.com/book/isbn-0199362777/

in the past. Nicholas observed—'Father, your mouth must sure hurt a lot—you've been talking so much.'"

In February, 2009, Father again complained that he was spending too much time on the phone with about six phone calls per hour: "Some people would say 'what would we do without the telephone.' I say 'what would we do? We would get a lot more work done, and our souls would be much at peace.'" And, "When people spend a lot of time on the phone, watch out. They are not doing God's work and hindering others from doing theirs."

Father still pined throughout this diary about his wilderness cabin. In November, 2009, during a violent storm in De Pere: "It is during these severe storms that I think of being in a one room cabin in the far-off wilderness with a wood burning stove, plenty of dry firewood, a comfortable chair and lots of good books. Let the wind blow and pelt the snow against the windowpanes. Let the wind howl and blow the snow without stopping. Let the extreme cold snap and crack the ice and the let the wolves howl. That would be paradise on earth."

Father commented in July, 2010, on God's beautiful nature: "Once again at the celebration of the evening Mass, the sun in the heavens shown directly on the tabernacle containing the Son of God. As we ended Holy Mass, the light was directly in the center of the tabernacle. How wonderful to behold. Now we know that the church is built True East and True West. This could only happen during the Summer Solstice when the sun is in the extreme of its southward motion. I find it very comforting, and I point it out each year to the parishioners." A few days later in the diary, Father comments again on the sunset: "A magnificent sunset this evening. A blood red sky against the trees and hills to the West. It started just before nine pm and continued until 9:10 pm. As the sun got lower on the horizon, the sky became streaked with purple, pink, and violet streaks. Absolutely incredible. What wonders come from the hand of God."

Each diary year had two or three comments on the dream of living in the wilderness, but I think Father had one of his final comments in February of 2010: "New verse for that poem I wrote in Book Three (Ed note—ledger/journal). 'Although I thought of my wilderness cabin often, In the end, it was realized in my coffin.'"

In June, 2011, Father celebrated his seventy-fifth birthday. He was not able to rest well because of the arthritis and other ailments. Taking care of a large parish like St. Michael's required a priest who was willing to forgo sleep when necessary: "Call (in June) from D. L. at 1:30 am—mother just died—I rushed to the hospital—body still warm—gave her emergency form of extreme unction. No sleep now for forty-five hours." Father's typical day lasted from 3:00 a.m. to 11:00 p.m.—a twenty-hour day. During those hours he daily said his office and two Masses during the week, three rosaries, visited the sick, answered thirty letters and twenty-five phone calls, and had private counseling sessions.[258]

[258] Diary entry 6/2011. The rosary comment was on 2/2011.

Gilford small chapel

Gilford Barns with silo

Chapter Thirty-two
Politics (1985-2011)

Father was not shy about his thoughts on the political situation throughout this period. Father started the year with a political tirade on January 20, 1993, about his feelings on Bill Clinton's inauguration: "Black Wednesday—today marks a dark hour for our country. An evil man has been sworn in as president. A) A draft dodger heads our military; B) a traitor who demonstrated against the U.S while our men were fighting in Vietnam, and therefore is responsible for the death of thousands of American Service men, is now commander and chief; C) a traitor who traveled to the Soviet Union at a time that they were arming, and financing North Vietnamese now sits in the White House; D) a man who has promised to kill as many unborn children as possible and whose wife has been even more forceful in this matter is sitting in the highest position in the nation; E) a man who openly had numerous adulterous relations with women while he was married and in public office is president although he is unrepentant for his blasphemous and unusual conduct; F) a man who has no moral principles but rather encourages perversion and amoral homosexuality and lesbian ways of life, which sins call to heaven for vengeance, is president; G) a woman who has made the most disparaging remarks about the American family and motherhood and housewives now is the 'first lady.' She not only knew of her husband's immoral and adulterous actions but approved of them and encouraged them as long as she could achieve her goal of climbing up the ladder. What is unforgivable is the large number of liberal Catholics who cast their votes for this monster while the Bishops remained silent or even encouraged his election. God will certainly be waiting for these liberal, modernists, hypocrites and will certainly extract a dire payment on our Nation because of it. Mary, help of Christians, intercede for us. Christ ever just, have mercy on us."

The year 2001 started on a high note with Clinton's leaving the White House: "Bush takes over on January twentieth. Sure glad to get rid of those corrupt and immoral Clintons. However, their corruption remains in those of like ilk who remain in places of importance. Our poor country. But does it deserve better because of the scandal of abortion?"

In September 2001, the United States was under attack: "On September eleventh, the attack on the World Trade Center buildings and the attacks on the Pentagon and Camp David. The squabble between the State of Israel and Palestine is responsible for this outrage. Both are terrorist organizations and should be banned from existence. Will Justice ever come about for the terrorists? I do not doubt President Bush's resolve, but I do doubt the resolve of our so-called allies and the cowardly liberals who infest Washington, D.C., like a plague of locusts."

On September 11, 2004, Father's vented about the attack on the U.S.: "Today we mark the anniversary of one of the most cowardly acts in history. It even eclipses Pearl Harbor as it was directed wholly against civilians. All terrorists are Muslims. All Muslims are cowards. They are all pagans, and their god is the devil."

The 2008 election results in November did not please Father: "Obama won the Presidency. I took the flag down and inverted it to show a country in distress. Also flew it at half-mast to show a nation in mourning. A sad day when an abortionist and enemy of our nation is elected to preside over a country he hates. Offered Mass—one in reparation for the election of Obama."

Father started 2009 with a very somber note in the diary on January twentieth. The diary page is outlined in black magic marker as this is inauguration day. "A great day of mourning here in the U.S. as a faithless, anti-life, anti-American, closet Muslim became President of this country. He is already being called President Death because of his hatred of the unborn which he has determined must die in greater numbers. He is a curse from Hell sent by God because the people of our great land deserve no better. God has sent this Satanic monster from the depths of hell to punish us for our sins of infidelity to him."

Chapter Thirty-three
Father Bolduc's Health (1985-2011)

Father had a rough start with his health this year as seen in a diary entry on March 21, 1991: "I had my first good day of work this year since I've been sick so much." It was no secret that Father was working long hours and was fifty-five years old. On September 27, he arrived in Gilford from Albuquerque at 8:30 p.m. and left for Green Bay the next morning at 3:00 am.

Father's health was continually a challenge and <u>he never seemed to take time to get better</u>. In February 1997: "Throat sore and swollen—no sleep. Went to the hospital—104 degrees temp."

On the first trip in December 2002 to Green Bay, Father was sick: "Had a sore throat plus chest pains. No sleep all night. Pains in the right lung. On the second trip, found out it was pneumonia. Gave me twenty tablets at five dollars a tablet!!! (Notice the exclamation points.) Picked up masks so that I didn't infect anybody."

In 2004, Father's health this year was becoming worse with comments throughout the diary: "Tired with periods of forgetfulness; don't feel good—back pains, stomach all upset; Still dizzy and weak; don't feel well—sweated all night and feel cross." There are signs of impending bigger health issues.

Father's health continued to be an issue in the first five months of 2005 with diary statements like: "I had to leave the altar during Mass"; "Can't get my breath. Chest feels like a heavy weight on it"; "Haven't had a night's sleep in weeks—can't catch my breath." Finally, in June, after a doctor's visit: "Had a call from Dr. McCarthy that I have an enlarged heart and fluid on both lungs. He says that it appears evident that I suffered a heart attack some time ago although I have no knowledge of it. Thank God it isn't worse." After hearing this news from the doctor, there were signs in the diary that he was taking this seriously: "Got my daily twenty minutes exercise on the stationary bike." In August, Father had a heart catheterization which found two blockages which the doctor decided to treat with diet and medication.

Rheumatoid arthritis afflicted Father in 2006 and he had trouble moving. Once, in April, he could hardly move until mid-afternoon and once he had to call the Pauly's over because he fell to the floor trying to get out of bed. He slept in a chair most nights because lying in bed was too painful. It did not help his arthritis—or anything else—in August when a buffalo escaped and charged Father and knocked him unconscious.

His health continued to deteriorate in 2007, especially his eyes. In October: "Eye exam—hardening of the arteries—back of eye—causing blood vessels to burst and leaving blood on the retina—therefore trouble seeing." His difficulty with his eyes caused several letters to be returned due to illegible addresses. In September, Father ended up in the hospital with bronchial pneumonia. There were continuing arthritis issues according to the fall he took in July: On the thirteenth: "My arm is bruised and has a puncture (right arm) from falling out of bed last night. Hit my head and arm on the table next to the bed. Landed on my knees. They were already sore and now are worse."

Most days in 2008, Father was not feeling well in the joints. It was so common that he mentioned an exception to this daily pain on February twenty-second: "Yesterday was pain free TBTG [Thanks be to God] and OLGS [Our Lady of Good Success]."

Father mentioned in December in 2008 that he had another fainting spell. He traveled from Gilford to Green Bay and had a terrible trip: "Had a 6 am flight to Green Bay, left at noon and got to Detroit. At Detroit, plane was delayed and at 10:00 pm, three others and I rented a car and drove to Green Bay arriving at 4:30 am. After that arrival, had Mass at eight and a funeral at eleven. Went to sleep at 9:00 pm after having been awake for forty-three hours."

In October 2009, the swine flu was spreading across the nation and Father was suspicious of the government's actions:

"The pig or swine flu is going around now—the government is trying to pressure everyone to get a shot." Father is resistant to go to a doctor because of this epidemic: "Have the cold still—if I went to the doctor, they would call it swine flu and try to give me a shot. This is all an artificial health emergency, a panic to get control of more people. [N.B. As I write this tribute to Father Bolduc in early 2020, we are in a lockdown due to the Covid 19 pandemic, and I am suspicious of the motives of our Michigan governor. We must wear masks, should not have public Masses or Sacraments, and have an upcoming election in November which really makes me question the Democratic governor's aims. Father would have been furious if he would have been alive in 2020 when they succeeded in taking control of the peoples' health decisions.]

2010 was a difficult year, especially regarding Father Bolduc's health. Father Sansone was quite sick at times after a few long stays at the Mayo Clinic. In February, Father began passing blood in his stool and received a diagnosis from his doctor in Green Bay: "Doctor McCarthy called and said they found a tumor in bowel tract that is malignant and aggressive cancer cells. He wants me to have chemotherapy which I absolutely refuse to have. Surgical removal is the only solution as far as I am concerned. See large (ed. note journal/ledger) book #18 Blue cover for more comments. Father Macek arrives (to help fill in). On the fifth, had a CAT scan."

On the eighth, Dr. Smith, the surgeon at St. Mary's hospital gave me a thorough exam. He advised me to have chemo and radiation treatment, but I told him it was out of the question. He referred me to other doctors to explain why this treatment approach is right. I have no intention of having them pour that poison into my body. Called Ernest and updated him. Surgery set for March third. Mr. Phil White called, and he has not been feeling well. His legs are quite cold all the time. He had Chemotherapy a year ago and now has lots of problems that can be traced to that. I will never submit to that treatment."

During this time, Father continued his work in Wisconsin and made trips to Michigan, Gilford, and Ohio. On February twenty-first: "I felt weak and had constant pain from my problem and had to wash my clothes even on Sunday."

The surgery was scheduled for March 3, 2010. Father's diary details each day of his surgery and the following recovery. What surprised me during this period is that Father made all the arrangements and traveled all on his own without any parishioners in Green Bay knowing about the sickness and surgery.

> March 2, 2010: 'Up at three am and offered Holy Mass. Took a taxi to Motel 6 close to St. Mary's hospital. I started taking my cleansing dose at 8am. What a disagreeable tasting medication. Reading *The Angelus* and the *New American*. Started reading the *History of the Western Civilization*. The time passes slowly. Can't wait for tomorrow to get this all over with. I shall set up my portable altar for Mass early tomorrow."
>
> March 3, 2010: [Ed. Note – The writing in the diary was almost illegible. Father had been drugged and had his operation when he wrote the following entry]: "Up at 12:15 am and offered Holy Mass. At 4:00 am, checked out of the motel and walked over to the hospital. They took me in at 5:00 am and prepped me. When I woke in recovery, I cannot recall anything about the operation. All seems well. I can't feel any pain. I am tired and can't sleep. Lots of nurses in and out."
>
> March 4, 2010: 'Cannot have food or water. This is the third day. A lot of complications today, they were going to take me for a walk, but my blood pressure got very low. My eyes are blurry. Several times I felt like vomiting. Couldn't read. I would like a big, tall glass of cool water. Ernest called like he did yesterday. They are making maple syrup today. I wish I had something to do. Had my Mass in my bed late at night."

March 5, 2010: 'Got a shower and change of clothing and bedding. Still not a drop of water. Father Macek wanted to know if he should stay longer—I say yes. I talked to someone about how to take care of my pouch—ostomy. I offered Mass at 11:15 pm."

March 8, 2010: "Rested well—not really slept. All I have left plugged into me is my IV. Dr. Jaslowski tried his best to get me into Chemo. I said NO but will "think" about it. I walked back and forth three times today. Twice alone. Had another small heart episode. More EKG's. More blood tests. At 8:14 pm, I had my first taste of food in 7 days. A small cup of cranberry juice. Got my Mass in this evening with no trouble—TBTG."

March 9, 2010: "Ernest called at 8:20 CST this am to inform me that my brother Charles A Bolduc (Sam) had died an hour ago. Complications of heart and cancer. May his soul rest in peace. Had my first taste of food since March first. A small mug of chicken soup and a popsicle. No sooner had I finished them when I violently vomited both up. Luckily, I had taken care of Holy Mass for Sam earlier. The good Lord knows what He is doing."

March 12, 2010: "Just after the doctor's visit at 7:00 am, I passed my first solid matter into my pouch. A banner day. Doctor Smith released me this evening. I took a cab home. Father Macek was surprised to see me walk in. I felt very weak and worn out. TBTG I was able to say my Mass each day—my record of daily Mass is still intact."

March 13, 2010: "Got up early and offered Holy Mass at 4:30 am. Before I got far, I was very sick. Headache, sweating all over, tired, weak. Had trouble getting through the Mass. Afterwards, I collapsed in the front pew and fell asleep. I woke up when Father Macek came over for the 8:00 am Mass. I am sick. Slept most of the day. My pouch came detached from my skin. I cleaned myself up and drove myself to the emergency room. Father Macek found me at the hospital and drove me home."

March 15, 2010: "I had Pauly's and Lacenski's over to explain what had happened. At least now that someone knows, they will not think I was just being lazy. Nurses have been extraordinary."

March 17, 2010: "Had stations of the cross but I became disoriented and had to be helped back to the rectory. I am slowly getting the hang of things."

March 31, 2010: "Mass at 4:00 am. Read the entire Passion and did not get tired. I keep getting stronger. Went on all local sick calls. Got food for the house and got caught up on lots of correspondence. Worked hard all day. Got a lot done. Received many phone calls and made a lot of calls."

On April fifth, Father Macek left, and things returned to a more normal course. Father was researching localized cancer treatment with XRAYs. He commented that the cancer business is a hit or miss enterprise and was looking more favorably on radiation treatment as a follow up.

In May, he had more follow-up tests: "On the fifth, I got the result of the Cat scan. They found no presence of cancer in any of my organs or in the area where the cancer had been removed. Also, none showed up in any of the lymph nodes. However, there might be some microscopic cells lingering somewhere. It appears that cancer research and treatment is the most inaccurate and unreliable thing going."

On June twenty-eighth, Father had his final radiation treatment: "Backside burns due to radiation. It was intense. They can find no trace of cancer in my blood or body—Thanks Be To God (TBTG). My hind end is extremely sore."

2012

This year, 2012, I will return to the yearly format as it is Father's last year alive, and the diaries were very descriptive of Father's life. You will notice, he didn't slow down and attempt to reduce his priestly work. Father celebrated his seventy-sixth birthday and continued doing his duty. This was what he hoped and prayed for. To give the reader an idea of his activities during this year, I have included a summary of his January diaries: "One trip to Green Bay for twenty-six days. Baked two pies for shut-ins. Packers football team won their fifteenth straight—TBTG. It eclipses world news. Everywhere you go, it is the main topic of conversation. One cannot help but wonder what good could be done in the world if all those who go to the football games—went to church! This is the sixty-fifth year of keeping a diary—since 1947. Nursing homes are filled with flu symptoms cases. I have to be careful and wear a full mask and wash my hands. On the seventh, Whites, and I out to dinner after the HNS meeting—going to bed right away as my heart is really pounding fast and did so all night. Tired—bad knees, hips, and small of the back. Wapaun prison visit to Kirby and Christopher—Confessions and Holy Communion. On the eleventh, had Wednesday night devotions, as usual, but I forgot, and parishioners had to come knocking at the rectory door. I have a lot of work to do but just don't have the 'stick to it' ability. Made six gallons of chicken soup. Ernest called—bypass (highway) land may be coming back to us—from the 1950's—TBTG—there is some justice in the world. Wedding. On the sixteenth, I feel tired all the time. The slightest bit of exertion leaves me exhausted. Bones in knee and hips and small of back are hurting something terrible. Funeral. Sleep three to three and one half hours normally without naps. Long talk with Father Sansone—I think progress is being made. Mass at Jericho. Slipped at airport in Green Bay on ice and went head over heels—had trouble getting back up. On the twenty-seventh, very, very tired and out of breath. Baked four pies. Inventorying the Jungwirth home materials which are now moved to church basement. One trip to Irish Hills and Toledo—Mr. Childs picked me up in Detroit. Gilford—eye clinic with shot in the eye, dinner at the Farm." It was amazing all he could accomplish with the number and severity of health problems he endured.

In February, the bad news arrived with some pushing for information on Father's part: "Blood work and CT-XRAY. No Cancer. BP 120 over 45. After the visit, I heard Doctor J. talking to someone about me and said, 'Oh no.' Later that afternoon, I got a call from Dr. J. He informed me that [after] a further exam of my XRAYS that there was a question about a small white dot that had been seen six months ago—most likely scar tissue. He also said that there was a cloud or film around my liver. He suggested that I have a biopsy of that location. On the third, I insisted I see the CT scan and he pointed out spots on my liver. Could be cancer. We agreed to wait two months and do another scan—not a biopsy."

In March, work continued on the Minnesota retreat house with Gary Pauly and Joe Ullmer heading up the project. Father accompanied them on the trip, most likely to be in his wilderness and think about the future. Father called a friend to commiserate on his health problem: "Had a long talk with Father Finnegan—He has always been a true friend and wonderful priest."

The April Easter liturgy was very tiring but rewarding: "Holy Thursday—all night adoration. Good Friday—Way of the Cross. For Easter, had the 8:30 am Mass which was a High Mass with incense and was magnificent with twelve altar boys in red cassocks and white surplices. The church was beautifully decorated with flowers. It was really a tribute to our love of Christ and His proven claim to be the Son of God by His Resurrection."

Father took on another project this year which was not a surprise as he refused to quit even as the clock was running down. This year is the two hundredth anniversary of the founding of the town of Gilford. In May, Father gave final approval for his design of the bicentennial medal, and they were delivered in June—twenty four carat gold—ten silver and five hundred brass medals. The medals were made for the August eleventh Gilford bicentennial celebration. Struck in a gold tone, the medallion bears the town seal on one side while the bicentennial is remembered on the other, along with a reminder that

Gilford is the lone town in New Hampshire to take its name from the site of a battle in the Revolutionary War.[259]

Father had a CAT scan and wrote on May ninth: "Had an appointment with Dr. J. He confirmed that the cancer has metastasized and is now well established in my lungs and liver. He recommended chemotherapy and I of course refused. He also wanted to take a biopsy and I refused it. He says it is only a matter of months and will get very painful. I told him I will let the cancer go its own way and take whatever comes. Will keep this to myself and will say nothing about it. I will put my things in order. Must finish the project up north (Minnesota retreat house). Must get the project at Brooklyn Irish Hills finished."

The Irish Hills project was to build a church on the property, either in the existing structure or a new building. As for the money needed for the project, Father said: "I know which two documents I will have to sell." The project never started, and the Irish Hills property has been sold.[260]

On May sixteenth: "Then I had a meeting in the basement of the Church with eight men of the St. Michael's parish. I discussed with them what to do when I leave here. Formed a parish committee. They are all solid men of the parish and have been here for a long time."

I have taken all these diary entries about Father's impending death with calmness but became somewhat emotional with his comment on the twenty-ninth: "Held little James Hector Drew and we talked about his favorite animals—I will miss him." On the thirtieth, the Ullmers helped pack one hundred boxes of books for shipment to New Hampshire.

By June, Father was seeing the effects of the cancer: "My back (lungs and liver) is acting up as well as my throat." Father Joe Pfeiffer arrived, and we talked until late into the night." Father Bolduc learned a lot about the SSPX happenings. In July, there was an SSPX chapter meeting during which Bishop Williamson was expelled. Father Joe Pfeiffer gave a long ac-

---

[259] Source 61 (picture of medal) and source 79—*Laconia Daily Sun*, 8/22/2012, p. 11.

[260] Property sold in January 2021. Miss Cook's gravesite will remain on the property.

count of the chapter meeting. I suspect most of the account was speculation as the chapter meetings are very confidential.

A Father D. arrived to take care of Necedah as Father Sansone had left. Father D. also left by the end of the month. Father Bolduc had many visitors in addition to Father Joe Pfeiffer. It was possible that word had spread about his sickness. On July seventeenth, Father Bolduc went to the funeral home to take care of his funeral arrangements.

Sometime during this period, Father Bolduc called Father Rostand, the District Superior of SSPX. Father Rostand said of the call: "Father Bolduc knew that his end was approaching, even though it came much sooner than expected. He contacted the US District to discuss the future of his chapels. As mentioned, he was called too soon to finalize anything. We were supposed to meet. It was then natural for us to send Fr Duverger as soon as possible after we learned the death of Father."[261]

On August eighth, Father visited the oncologist who was surprised that he was still alive. They made another appointment for November. On the ninth, Father again talked to the SSPX U.S. District Superior. They had a nice talk. Father Bolduc noted in his diary to see big ledger for details. This conversation will come into play after Father's death. On the tenth: "New pills upset stomach—have stopped them. I pray for enough time to find a suitable replacement for me here at St. Michael's and Our Lady of Victory in Necedah. I called Father McDonough. He is offering his sufferings for me, and I am offering mine for him. Who will outlast?" For the rest of August, Father was having trouble keeping food down: "Sunday—only food is bowl of soup—did more harm than good." On the twentieth: "Father Finnegan arrived. He gave me last rites and heard my general confession which I have been preparing for since I heard he was coming. What a great friend I have in Father Terrance Finnegan." On the thirty-first: "Vomiting in bed every half hour. Got fifteen minutes sleep. Had to empty the pouch six times during night. Feel miserable and tired."

---

[261] See email from Father Rostand 3/27/2018.

The month of September deserves a day-by-day account since these are his last entries:

September 1, 2012: "Today I heard a pair of owls answering one another. It was very early in the morning and the first owls I had heard for a long time—several months at least. I don't feel good but managed to say Mass and [make] some sick calls. Tried to do some paperwork but ended up resting as much as I could. There is a little chipmunk that lives near the church. He is quite friendly. I put some corn kernels out for him."

September 2, 2012: "Sunday—very nice day. I had confessions and offered the low Mass and then confessions and the High Mass, my regular Sunday schedule. Right after the Benediction of the Blessed Sacrament, Virgil and I grabbed our bags and left for local sick calls. Then to Necedah for the 3:00 pm confessions and 4:00 pm Mass. Then right back to Green Bay as I leave early tomorrow morning. The Paul Ryan convention speech at the Republican convention will, I believe, be the deciding factor for the winning of the election this fall. God must not abandon us to another four years of Obama socialist rule or there will be no more freedom left in this country."

September 3, 2012: "Flew to Detroit where Jack Boyle picked me up and drove me to the Toledo Moriarty house chapel. We had holy Mass. The largest crowd we have ever had there. Then we all went to Applebee's for lunch as usual. Afterwards, we made a sick call to a hospital. Mr. Garno and Jonah drove me to the Irish Hills in Brooklyn, Michigan. Went on sick calls there and then offered Holy Mass. I am very tired and uncomfortable. Catching up with me. I am going to bed as early as I can as I am in need of a lot of rest." [Ed. Note: I was at the Mass in the

Irish Hills, and he had to stop during the sermon to catch his breath. He also leaned against the wall during the sermon due to his general weakness. His sermon was like all of his sermons, fiery, educational, and inspiring.]

September 4, 2012: "I was up early and offered Holy Mass. Mr. Childs picked me up at 6:00 am and drove me to the Detroit airport. I flew to Manchester right on time. Ernest picked me up and drove me to the Tilton, New Hampshire, home where we visited Budd. I gave him Holy Communion. He seemed a little sleepy but talked to us. Back on the farm, I went through some mail. Went down and picked up a load of gas and diesel fuel. This evening, we went to Ernest's and Ellie's house with Armand and had a delicious meal, as always. Later I picked up today's mail and went through it. Going to bed very early as I am tired and don't feel well. Rained lightly most of the day is still raining at 7:00 pm."

September 5, 2012: "Woke at midnight to the sound of rain on the roof. Opened the window slightly so I could hear it better. Believe it or not, I did get back to sleep which was very difficult for me and most unusual. I woke again to a hard rain. Then got up for my Mass at 4:00 am., did some reading. Went to the Church to serve and assist Father McDonough and his Mass. Soon after Mass, Ernest showed up and drove Father McDonough and I to Manchester where we met Mrs. Aline Lotter about our wills and trusts. I signed lots of papers. While driving home, we stopped in Belmont and got a cup of ice cream from Jorden's ice cream shop. At home, I drove to the gas station for a second load of gas. Now the tractor is filled, and all the gas cans are full. Gas is now in the three dollars and seventy cents range." [Ed. note – a good farm boy, even at the end, the gas cans had to be full.] "I had a bowl of corn chowder for supper. Dan Schroeder stopped by for a visit this evening."

September 6, 2012: "Had some rain during the night. In the eighties and sunny all day. Celebrated Mass at 4:00 am. Nice and quiet. Did some writing. Ernest and Ellie came up. Armand also was here for most of the day. Ernest and Ellie went on the Mount Washington [boat] today to assist those who have trouble breathing. Armand cut grass this afternoon and evening. I went to the bank, and bought food supplies. This afternoon, Armand and I went to Gilmanton where we visited a farm where they raise buffalo. I purchased a two-and-a-half-year-old bull for four thousand dollars. He will be delivered soon. This evening, I cooked a spaghetti and meatball supper. I ate a good plateful. The most I have eaten in months. I worked on mom's rose bush. Went to the arbor and ate several bunches of concord grapes."

September 7, 2012: "Up most of the night since I got two phone calls about flight cancellations. Got to Green Bay real late. Had Mass before leaving New Hampshire just in case I would end up being abandoned at some airport. I offered Mass on arrival. Then had a wedding Mass at 5:00 pm and First Friday Mass at 7:00 pm. My fourth Mass of the day. I had fourteen messages when I arrived. I answered them and went to bed."

September 8, 2012: "Closed the all-night adoration at the morning Mass. Offered the Mass here and then went on sick calls. Then I went to the Pauly's and Mr. and Mrs. Pauly drove me to Jericho where I offered Mass for the group there. I went through some of my mail that had accumulated during my absence. Worked on letter writing this evening and prepared for tomorrow's Mass. Got a call from Steve Curtis who was involved in a fender bender."

The following two entries were related to me by Virgil Bulcher since Father didn't make any more entries.

> September 9, 2012: Sunday—Said his two Masses at DePere and then after teaching the High School students, went three hours west with Virgil. Said Mass at Necedah and told Virgil he was tired and needed to clean up and go to bed.
>
> September 10, 2012: Father Bolduc did not show up for Mass. The altar boys got Virgil and told him that Father Bolduc had not shown up and that something must be wrong as the chapel doors were not open and that Father Bolduc was never late. Virgil went to the rectory and found Father Bolduc unresponsive and cold lying in bed with one arm under his pillow and his head on top of the pillow, and the other hand stretched out and open. Cause of death: Cardiorespiratory failure, and metastatic Colorectal Cancer.

Father Bolduc in casket 9/13/2012

Father Bolducs funeral Mass at St. Michaels 9/14/2012
Fathers Finnegan, Cyprian, Elias

Appendix A

Ernest Bolduc comments on Father Bolduc's sickness and death

When Father Rostand visited New Hampshire—around 2014—the discussion turned to Father leaving the SSPX. Ernest related that he and Father Bolduc had discussed that before he died. Father had said that he had to leave the SSPX, and he wished he had not done it. Father Rostand was so pleased to hear that.

Father went to a doctor in New Hampshire to see what was wrong with him. Dr. McCarthy said it was hemorrhoids. Father told him that those were removed. The doctor relooked at the information and [did] more tests and said Father was right, it was colon cancer. Father was dying of colon cancer. He went to Wisconsin and had an operation—which removed the cancer. He did not want anyone to know. He arranged for a priest to take his place in Wisconsin. Father was confident that things were going well after the operation and Father had that little bag that he had to empty regularly. Then things started to get worse, and the cancer spread throughout his body.

He never told Ernest anything. Ernest commented at dinners that Father was not eating much. Father said he did not want to fill up that "little bag." Father had told Ernest the year before his death that he hoped to semi-retire soon as he could arrange for someone to take over his duties. He said that he should have at least ten more years to take care of the things that were hanging. Ernest said: "Now I am taking care of those things."

Ernest never accepted the fact that something was going to happen to Father Bolduc since he was younger than Ernest. On his last trip home, they were coming home from the airport and Father said if Jordan's ice cream was open, he would like to have a cone. Father got the largest ice cream cone possible. As he was eating it, Father said that the ice cream felt good in his throat. Ernest asked him what was wrong with his throat and Father said that it just felt good. That was a clue, but Ernest missed it. When they got to the rectory, Father wanted some of the corn chowder from the soda shop that Father thought was the best corn chowder. Ernest got him two buckets. Father smelled the corn chowder and said it smelled so good. That was the second clue. He ate every bit of it. This also went over Ernest's head. Other than that, Father did his normal work such as writing letters to those with whom he corresponded.[262]

---

[262] See Sony 2/25 recording, 56 minutes in—Ernest Bolduc.

Appendix B
Gary Pauly – Father Bolduc's death and funeral (2012)

We, St Michael's Board, were told by Fr. Bolduc on August 22, 2012, to call Fr. Finnegan(Our Lady of Quito, Phoenix, Arizona), Fr. Rostand (SSPX District Superior) and Fr. Cyprian (Prior at Our Lady of Guadalupe Monastery) when he died.

On the morning of the September tenth, when I received the call that Fr. Bolduc had died, I was three hours from home working on my son's house. A board member had made the call to me, and I told him I would make the necessary calls.

I called Fr. Finnegan and arranged for him to come and say the funeral Mass. Then I called Fr Rostand and managed to get to him right away and explained that I had Fr. Finnegan coming to say the Funeral Mass and I wasn't sure what I expected of Fr Rostand. I did not think that Fr. Rostand expected my call. I told him I needed a priest for next Sunday and while he was thinking about that, I would have to make a call to Fr Cyprian. Well, Divine Providence took care of that call for me, for Fr Rostand said: "Fr Cyprian is right here" and he put him on the phone. I explained that Father had died, and we were to call Fr Finnegan, Fr Rostand and Fr Cyprian.

The chances of contacting these three priests all in an hour were impossible, but that day was special. Fr Cyprian was caught off guard too, I think, and we talked a bit and he said he would call back. He was in Kansas City, Missouri, on his way back from Wisconsin having just buried his own father. He called back and said he, Fr. Elias, and Fr. Duverger would be at St. Michael's Church the following morning by 8:00 am for Mass.[263] We had three Masses a day the rest of the week.

Father Cyprian and Father Duverger placed Father in the casket with his purple vestments and prepared him for the funeral.

---

[263] See Gary Pauly's email of 2/27/2018.

On the day of the funeral, Fr. Finnegan said the Mass assisted by two Benedictine monk priests—Fr. Elias and Fr. Thomas Aquinas. Fr. Cyprian and Fr. Duverger sang in the choir, and there were two other monks who came from Our Lady of Guadalupe Monastery—Br. Roman and another brother also sang. The sermon given by Father Finnegan was strong and beautiful. I copied down one point that I think was very reflective of the Archbishop's thoughts on Father Bolduc: "The Archbishop said that Father Finnegan was going to the U.S. (after ordination) to work under Father Bolduc—he gets the job done."

Father's body was shipped to Gilford. The casket was on the same plane with Gary and others. There was a High Mass with incense in Gilford with Gary as the Master of ceremonies. The church was as full as it ever was with a beautiful Mass.

Gary related that one person in attendance said: "If I was to become a Catholic, it was because of that Mass." There was a military burial at the church's cemetery. A large box of letters of condolences from all over the world was also present in Gilford.

Appendix C
Pioneers' Testimonials

The following are interviews with acquaintances of Father Bolduc during the years from 1973–1984. Father called many of these people pioneers because they were part of the Traditional movement when it started in the United States. I interviewed most of these people by phone with a recorder capturing the information and then I would summarize the conversation since there were more than twenty-four hours of information on the recorder for all the interviews. It was an enjoyable experience hearing their testimonials since I only knew Father Bolduc's life in pieces. I must comment that the testimonials were memories sometimes from over 40 years ago. The purpose of these interviews with the below people was twofold: To explain their path to tradition and to discuss their personal impressions of Father Bolduc as a priest and a person.

Father Finnegan

Father Finnegan was raised a traditional Catholic in Rapid City, North Dakota and was called to be a priest during his High School years. A younger priest encouraged Father to leave High School and go into the minor seminary but fortunately, an older priest (Monsignor Richard Schlur) advised Father to get life experiences first before entering the seminary to able to handle the attacks on the faith occurring during the late 1960's.

Father went to St. Thomas College in Minneapolis, Minnesota, and majored in Music. During college, Monsignor Schlur was a teacher who would talk about the great difficulties in the Church and the grade schools at that time. Father Finnegan respected the Monsignor and learned from him that the Church was in trouble. He graduated from college on September 27, 1970, with a piano instrumental major. He took a job as a music and religion teacher at a Catholic school run by

Benedictine nuns, teaching grades sixth through eighth. The seventh-grade kids told Father Finnegan that Jesus was their brother and God was God. To them, Jesus was not God. Father was shocked. When he was young, he was taught the truths of the Trinity by first grade and the natures and persons of God by second grade. Here were these seventh grade kids talking heresy, though there was no malice in their hearts.

Father had decided that at the end of this school year, he was not going to continue teaching but was going to go to the seminary. He went back to his friend, Monsignor Schlur and told him of his plans and the Monsignor advised Father that it was suicide to do that. He said that Father had to go back to college and learn Latin and Philosophy because if Father Finnegan went back to the seminary, they were going to be teaching heresy. Father went back to college for a sixth year to learn Philosophy and Latin. They examined all the false systems that were contrary to Aristotle and St. Thomas Aquinas. Father Finnegan realized the wise counsel he had received from Monsignor Schlur since "I cannot go to a seminary, keep my mouth shut, and at night study and get ordained. It requires a brilliant mind, and I was not that. I need to go to a seminary where they teach tradition." Father had heard of Écône, and he was invited by the seminary to attend.

Seminary days

Father Finnegan, at the age of twenty-six, went to the Écône seminary in the fall of 1973 and that is where he met Father Bolduc, who was then thirty-seven. Father Bolduc had done studies at Catholic University of America for ten years under the sponsorship of the Marianist Fathers. At the Catholic University, Father Bolduc met Father Clarence Kelly. They were both conservative seminarians who ran a paper that criticized the modernist heresies. Father Kelly realized he needed a Traditional seminary and left for Écône. Father Bolduc realized that the liberal seminaries were not going to work and went to Écône in 1973.

Father Finnegan related how Father Bolduc went through natural and supernatural sacrifices at the seminary. Father was rejected by his peers. On the natural level, he entered the seminary at thirty-six when Father Finnegan was twenty-six and other seminarians were nineteen and twenty. He did not have any fellow seminarians that had been through the life that he had. Father Bolduc had seen the world, was a curator of art and antiques, had made much money, and had been in the Army. You cannot hide that background—he was speaking of grandiose things. Father Finnegan was friends with Father Bolduc because they were both "older" generation seminarians.

Before he was ordained, Father Bolduc had to go off to Fribourg to study history—this was the Archbishop testing him. After a while there was a crisis in a Paris suburb, where they had just started a new parish. The Archbishop asked the seminarian Hector Bolduc in the spring of 1974 to go and help the pastor[264] up there. The pastor was young and having trouble. Father Bolduc went there and did everything he could to help. Father's Canadian French was not close to the French language in France. The pastor did not accept Father Bolduc with open arms because Father Bolduc was so experienced and single minded. It was a rough time for Father Bolduc as he could not understand what the Archbishop's plan was for him. There had been no plan for his ordination announced and Father returned to help out in Paris. It was now Easter vacation and Father returned to the seminary. The Archbishop told Father he would be ordained this summer of 1974—he was jubilant. At his ordination on June 29, 1974, his mother, father, and one sister were in attendance.

Father Bolduc's first assignment was to the seminary in Armada, Michigan. There was a certain personality difference between Father Ward (the rector) and Father Bolduc. Father Ward was more of a monk type and Father Bolduc wanted action. Father Bolduc believed that there were people that did not have the Traditional Mass and he wanted to help as many people as he could with the Mass. He was unique in that way.

---

[264] Father John Cottard

Father Finnegan thinks Father Bolduc's part in the SSPX in the U.S. was supernatural. Father Post was the first priest ordained for the U.S. in 1972 at Powers Lake, N.D. Fathers Kelly and Ward were ordained together in Écône in June, 1973. The Archbishop assigned Father Bolduc to Texas due to the personality conflicts in Armada and he was accepted very well there. The Texas parish grew amazingly fast in an incredibly beautiful church with two brothers as coordinators. Father Bolduc was on a Mass circuit and when he got back home, the locks were changed on the church and rectory, and they stole the sacramental records. The brothers were jealous of Father Bolduc—it was most unjust and Father was most distraught. This was around 1975 or 1976. Father Bolduc showed up at Écône and was throwing his arms around talking to the Archbishop. The Archbishop was being a good father and trying to help Father Bolduc. Now a certified letter came from the families in Texas asking to get Father Bolduc back. They said they just had not the courage to take on the two brothers. The Archbishop agreed to send Father Bolduc back but with the warning that if they did not treat his priests right, Father Bolduc would not be there. The parishioners obtained a beautiful church from the diocese without the diocese knowing they were Traditionalist. Mr. John Brown convinced the diocese that he wanted to buy the church and land, demolish the church, and then put up a used car lot. The name of the church was Queen of the Angels church in Dickinson, Texas. The diocese was furious and stripped out the altar, communion rail, and the side altars. Father Bolduc brought down an altar and communion rail and statues from a hospital in Kansas City. The grand opening was extraordinary. The Archbishop was there along with Fathers Kelly, Sanborn, and Dolan.

You would think that Father Bolduc would rest now but he went on to found chapels in Kansas, New Orleans, Raleigh, Tulsa, Topeka, Florida, South Carolina, North Carolina, Little Rock, Arkansas, Oklahoma City and Monett and Springfield, Missouri. We were called suitcase priests. Wherever Father

Bolduc could start a fire, he would start a fire with zeal and love for God and true Catholicism.

Spiritual

It has been over 40 years since Father Finnegan's ordination. The original statutes of the SSPX were drawn up by the Archbishop with his experience as the Superior of the Holy Ghost Fathers and consultation with Cardinals. Father Bolduc was living the spirit of the statutes but not the letter of the law. As an example, the statutes call for prayer in common but with what Father Bolduc was doing (which was his inspiration from God), he could not say prayers in common with other priests as he was always moving and there were no other priests around. He was laying the groundwork for what is happening now (i.e., Priests able to say prayers in common).

Father Bolduc would say the divine office in the early morning hours. He would get up exceedingly early and say the whole breviary. He wanted the day hours to be available to work with people.

Father Finnegan's first assignment with the Society was in Dickinson, Texas, in 1978. At that time in 1978, there were four[265] SSPX priests in the Southwest Region of the U.S. Father Bolduc was most always gone on one of his circuits. Father Finnegan was thinking that when he got ordained in 1978, he would be working with Father Bolduc arm to arm and shoulder to shoulder. Unfortunately, that was not to be, with so many Catholics wanting the Traditional Mass and so few workers.

When Father Gerard Hogan was transferred from Our Lady of Sorrows in Phoenix, Father Finnegan was assigned to Phoenix in 1979. The chapel in Phoenix was purchased by the SSPX and needed regular Masses to support this newly purchased church. But every weekend, after Father Finnegan would say two to three Masses at Our Lady of Sorrows, he would travel to California to say Mass in Walnut Creek, drive to Sacramento and have an afternoon Mass, and drive to Lake Tahoe for an evening Mass there. On Monday morning, after

---

[265] Fathers Bolduc, Post, Pulvermacher, and Finnegan

morning Mass in Lake Tahoe, he drove back to Sacramento and flew back to Phoenix. He was exhausted.

Expulsion of Father Bolduc

Father Bolduc was given an ultimatum in 1984 that if he was not in Écône, he was to consider himself out of the SSPX. Father Bolduc did just not want to go. We will have to find out in heaven, but Father Finnegan knows enough about the man to know it just was not God's will that he go to Écône. They were going to take a man that was a real operator and put him on ice. Father Finnegan thinks the intention of Écône was to help him, to give him rest and strengthen him and then give him an even bigger assignment. When Father Bolduc left the SSPX, the SSPX had a foothold in the U.S. It would have taken others fifty to one hundred years to accomplish the same results without him.

Father Finnegan left the Society 1992. When Father Bolduc left the Society, the Society Superior told Father Finnegan that he could have no contact with him. Father Finnegan was irritated with Father Bolduc because he left. Father Finnegan was so busy, so he left it alone. In April, 1992, Father got a phone call from Father Bolduc. Father Finnegan was not officially out of the Society but had decided that he was going to leave. He was under obedience not to talk to Father Bolduc, but Father Finnegan had left the SSPX in his mind so was glad to talk to him. Father Bolduc just wanted Father Finnegan to know that if he needed any help, just let him know. Father Finnegan was surprised by the call: "how did he know? No one knew."

Father Bolduc talked to Father Finnegan two weeks before he died in 2012. Father Finnegan had learned Father Bolduc was dying and called him to see if he could come and see him. Father Bolduc said to come (at this point, Father Finnegan is audibly incredibly sad). Father Finnegan visited him, and they went over everything else, the misunderstandings and everything. They exchanged confessions and Father Finnegan gave Father Bolduc the last rites. Father Finnegan commented that Father Bolduc was such a holy priest, hearing his confession was like listening to a confession of a little child. That was the purity of his soul.

Father Finnegan related that Father Bolduc is with God now. As a man, he had to build up quite a bit of strength in his life. He was physically a very strong person, and he could do a lot of work. One of his disappointments at the end of his life was that he was dying. It came as a surprise. It was hard right up to his last day, he got up and went to work. "My impression of Father Bolduc was that he was like the angels, he was always on the move. He did his priestly duty to the last day."

Father Finnegan is now[266] in Phoenix as an independent priest at Our Lady of Quito, which services some one hundred seventy parishioners. He has an Oblate there that has helped him since 1992 when Father left the SSPX.

Father Post

Fathers Post and Bolduc were both assigned to the U.S. district of the SSPX within a year of each other, but they were covering different areas of the country. I include Father Post's remembrances because he fought for Tradition at the beginning, and I wanted present day Traditional Catholics to understand the great obstacles these early Catholics had to overcome to secure Tradition.

In 1953-60, Gregory Post was in San Francisco and thought he was going to be a secular priest but decided to postpone that vocation to go to college to be a Language Arts Instructor. In 1964, he wrote to several religious Orders and ended up studying with the Discalced Carmelites for four years, the last two in Washington D.C. (1966-1968) at the Catholic University. In 1968, he was not happy with what was going on in the seminary such as color TV in the library, no curfews, unlimited beer and funds. As an example of the abuses, on one Sunday in August, 1967, the Newman clubs got together for an outdoor procession and then a Mass. At this Mass, they carried

[266] 9/2020

on a pole a picture of snoopy the dog rather than the crucifix. Instead of Christ up there, they had a picture of a dog.

This was a very confusing time in the Catholic church and Gregory left the seminary and joined his family who were moving to Post Falls, Idaho. Once in Post Falls, they met Father Edward DeBusschere who was a Canadian chaplain. In 1969, Gregory's mother talked to Father about saying the Traditional Mass on Sundays and Holy Days in Coeur D'Alene, Idaho, in a building on the property of Mr. and Mrs. Ken Peters. Gregory (now 29 years old) served as sacristan for the small chapel.

Through a Roman professor, Robert Anderson, Gregory was able to communicate with Archbishop Lefebvre and a meeting was arranged for Pittsburgh, Pennsylvania in 1971. Gregory had a nice talk with the Archbishop and they decided to meet in Powers Lake, North Dakota, at the Our Lady of the Prairies church run by Father [Fredrick] Nelson in August, 1971. At the ceremony in Idaho, the Archbishop blessed seventy-five people in wheelchairs, without pausing, with a monstrance— the Archbishop was very spiritual. After this meeting, Gregory received the acceptance letter from Écône and with donations from the Idaho parishioners, Gregory flew to Écône on October 5, 1971. There were three Americans there—Father Kelly, Father Ward, and Gregory. The Archbishop talked to Gregory and reviewed that he had received the minor orders in the Carmelite Order. The Archbishop laughed because Gregory had already had ten-and-a-half years of seminary training. He was then sent to Fribourg where he attended the University of Fribourg which was still conservative. Gregory received from the Archbishop the subdiaconate and diaconate after one year at Fribourg. At the end of the school year in 1972, the Archbishop said that he was going to Powers Lake and at Powers Lake he would ordain Gregory.

On Monday, August 28, 1972, Gregory became Father Post on the feast of St. Augustine in the chapel of Our Lady of the Fields. Father Post then said his first Mass in Idaho and then back to Switzerland to finish his last year of Theology at the University of Fribourg where the traditional seminarians were the only ones with cassocks among the two hundred seminarians there.

Upon return to the U.S., Father Post, after suggesting to the Archbishop that there were many faithful in California, was permitted to set up a chapel in San Jose, California. In 1976, the coordinator in San Jose was trying to rule the priests and Father Post split with the coordinator and put a down payment on a house in Campbell, California. The parishioners worked on the building transforming it into a rectory and Mass center which eventually served one hundred fifty parishioners. The Traditional Mass in the San Jose area is now at Los Gatos, California, the retreat center. At this time (2020), California has eight SSPX chapels.

Father Post went to Father Bolduc's ordination at Écône, and his first solemn high Mass in Laconia, New Hampshire, in August 1974. Father Bolduc would come over and visit Father Post in California and both priests talked about their spiritual challenges leading their parishes and their mutual coin collecting hobbies. Father Bolduc was very forceful person and he secured property in St. Mary's, Dickinson, Kansas City, and other locations. There was no fooling around with this modern nonsense. He was an excellent Traditional priest.

Father Bolduc was Superior of the Southwest District and Father Kelly in charge of the Northeast district. They each had a magazine that they published and were not charitable towards each other. The Archbishop, at the first general chapter meeting in 1976, split the U.S. into the above districts from one district because of the disagreements.

In 1983, the Northeast district pulled away from the Archbishop (the Oyster Bay 9) and took possession of the chapels in the Northeast District. This takeover of these chapels was not just, but it happened.

Dave Gayner

Dave first met Father Bolduc while they were working on St. Joseph's church in Armada, Michigan. He was later transferred to a new job in Topeka, Kansas, and was working for Southwestern Bell when an employee informed him that there was a Jesuit property for sale in St. Mary's, Kansas. He had heard me talking about finding a place to have Mass said.

For a while, Dave's family had been attending Mass in Kansas City at a rented hall with Fr. Bolduc as the pastor. Later Father began to say Mass in his basement in Topeka, KS. Dave decided to take a trip out to St. Mary's and view the property and was amazed with the beauty he saw. The stained-glass windows on the Immaculata, the statue of the Virgin Mary in the circle, and the beautiful green grounds. He knew at once that he had to phone Father Bolduc and tell him about the gem he found. Father was enthusiastic and wanted to see the property immediately. They both made the trip together to St. Mary's to see the property. Father was excited to see this property and immediately had a vision and pure faith that this property would belong to the SSPX. He envisioned a school and a huge parish that would flourish for time to come. The two of them stood out in front of the property and made a joke that maybe they would use only ten percent of all the buildings.

Father Bolduc phoned his Superior, Fr. Kelly, about the property. Father Kelly and Fr. J. both flew out to view the property. Father Kelly told Fr. Bolduc that this property would never work, it was too expensive, and he was not to pursue it any further. Father decided to make an executive decision to continue to pursue the property, because he KNEW God would provide.

Father Bolduc then contacted the Land Investment Company based out of Denver, Colorado. The president, vice president, and their attorney flew out and met Father and Dave at a very humble restaurant located in Rossville, Kansas. During the meeting, the investment folks were telling Father they needed nothing less than nine million dollars. Fr. Bolduc proceeded to tell them, that he had no money, only eighteen dollars in the checking account and that they needed them to donate the property. Their jaws dropped, and the president of the company was indignant and very agitated—along with the other two, he immediately got up and stormed out of the restaurant. Dave apologized to Father because he was embarrassed that they reacted this way towards a priest. Father then told him, not to worry, they WILL donate it. Father's faith never waved. Dave, on the other hand thought Father had only a pipedream.

About four days later, Father phoned Dave and said, "They're donating the property." He was shocked and ashamed that he didn't have the same faith as Father Bolduc. Father then gathered the courage to call his superiors and inform them that the property was donated.

When the property was acquired, parishioners from Kansas City made several trips to help clean up the property. The Immaculata was cleaned by Dave's and Shibler's daughters one week before Mass was to be said in it. Unfortunately, the church burned down before this could happen. There were three buildings that were cleaned and painted so that several folks could move in and stay there. If it wasn't for the faith of Father, St. Mary's College wouldn't exist. If it wasn't for the fruits of the parishioners, who worked so hard to get the property going, it wouldn't have been done.

The next issue was paying for the deposits for the gas, water, electric and sewer. Again, there was only eighteen dollars in the checking account. The city wanted one thousand dollar deposits for each utility. Dave informed them that there just wasn't the means to pay it. Through the grace of God, those fees were waived.

We had a huge issue that needed to be reconciled. There was no heat for the buildings. Boilers needed to be put in. There was a Traditional Catholic by the name of Mr. Henry Beemster who donated all the money for this to be done.

Later, Dave found out from Carlita Brown, who had typed for *The Angelus* and several books, that Father Bolduc acquired the Queen of Angels Church in Dickinson, Texas. The church had a huge hole in the dome. Father looked at the church and said, "We can fix it." Father was able to buy the church because of the donation from Mr. Henry Beemster. After which time, we were told that St. Vincent's Church in Kansas City was up for sale. Father Bolduc worked through prayer and had this protestant bishop purchase the property for fifty thousand dollars[267] as a straw buyer. The local diocese found out that Father Bolduc had purchased this property and they were very angry.

Today St. Mary's College is using 100% of the rooms and all of the buildings and has nearly one thousand students in the grade school, high school and college.[268]

Lee Ullmer—Wisconsin

Lee and his family had always been traditionally-minded Catholics. He, his dad, and his brothers owned and operated a cheese factory in the small town of Isaar, Wisconsin. The parish church was less than a block away from their homes. In the late 1960's a new bishop was assigned to the Green Bay diocese and Lee and his family started noticing changes in the Mass. Even though some of the older priests were sent to the little country churches, and offered a more conservative Mass, they felt it was too risky to continue attending the parish church.

The Ulmers had the privilege of knowing other Catholic families who were also very concerned about the new changes. One of the men, Mr. Henry Beemster, had purchased land along the Fox River, just outside of De Pere, Wisconsin. There was a small two-car garage on the property that he converted into a chapel. It was named St. Michael's.

Around 1974, Lee and his wife Karen and their young children began regularly attending Mass at St. Michael's. Fr. Altenbach, an independent priest, was serving both St. Michael's and another small chapel in Oshkosh, Wisconsin. They first met Fr. Bolduc in 1975 or 1976 when he came to St. Michael's and attended a Holy Name Meeting.

Lee and Karen moved their family to Oregon in 1978 but came back to Wisconsin in 1984. It was about that time that

---

[267] Father Laisney remembers this price as being $65,000.
[268] See Source 117; see email from 3/27/2018.

Fr. Bolduc left the SSPX. He was then able to service St. Michael's, as well as several other Traditional chapels across the country. Lee respected Fr. Bolduc and loved him for what and who he was. There was nothing that stopped him if there was a soul that needed help. You could call him any time of day or night and he would come. He was able to converse well on any number of subjects (farming, business, armed service) to anyone, thereby endearing himself to a great many souls.

Father would do anything to save souls—he was selfless. Whenever someone had a problem, he was right there to listen and advise. He also communicated by handwritten letters, with a great number of people across the county.

One time Lee asked Father if he could visit the husband of one of Karen's old classmates, who at that time was in the hospital. He had become very bitter against the Church. The next day Father told Lee the visit had gone quite well. The gentleman was very interesting and polite. He and Father had been able to speak on a number of various topics. Another time he asked Father to visit a crusty old Marine who was very disenchanted with the Faith. Father, of course, willingly obliged. The man explained to Father what he had done wrong in his life and that he was sorry for doing it. At the end of the conversation, he asked Father if he should go to confession. Father told him he already had. The man did recover from that illness, and just could not say enough about Fr. Bolduc. Father became well known at the hospitals in Green Bay, due to all the visits he made.

In 2008 and 2009, Father Bolduc assisted Lee and Karen in becoming Franciscan Third Order members. After completing the paperwork that was required by the Capuchins in France, Father inducted them into the Order. He was very happy to help with this.

Fr. Bolduc was raised on a farm in New Hampshire, and he had a custom to visit the farms of St. Michael's parishioners on Rogation days to bless the crops and animals. Father always encouraged the parishioners to be as self-sufficient as they could; by raising a few animals and planting vegetable gardens. As the old saying goes: "You can take the boy away from the farm, but you can't take the farm out of the boy."

It appears, when talking to other Traditional Catholics anywhere in the U.S., they would tell you that they knew, or at least had heard of, Fr. Bolduc. Bishop Tissier de Mallerais came to St. Michael's to confer the Sacrament of Confirmation twice since Father Bolduc had passed away. He was overjoyed to see Father's church.

Marty Stenson—Oshkosh Wisconsin—1972

Marty is fifty-four years old and presently on the board of St. Michael's in Wisconsin. He was a young boy, second grade, when his father came home from church and said: "We're done, we're not going back into that church (*Novus Ordo*)." The Stenson's at that time were a family of twelve and lived a block away from the local church. It was a shock and sad event and very vivid in Marty's memory. Marty had just received his first Holy Communion and was appreciative that his father recognized the errors of the local church. His father found a local traditional priest in Father Altenbach who came to Oshkosh to say the Mass. Other families came to the Mass that was in the basement of a farmhouse. Father Altenbach was based in Green Bay at St. Michael's and drove down the hour to Oshkosh. Eventually the Mass in Oshkosh disbanded in 1974 due to a rift in the farming families and the people from Oshkosh had to travel an hour to De Pere.

Mr. Henry Beemster, a very prominent businessman in Green Bay, saw the errors in the *Novus Ordo* churches and decided that he and others would start their own chapel in the Green Bay area in 1969. There was a handful of priests servicing the chapel in Green Bay. The first time Marty remembers Father Bolduc was in 1978. He was a younger priest, and he would strike up conversations with Marty who was a teenager. Marty respected all the priests, but Father Bolduc talked to Marty and Marty realized that priests were really "men." Marty was confirmed in 1978 by Archbishop Lefebvre. Father Bolduc was the Archbishop's "right hand man."

From 1978 to 1982, Father took care of St. Michael's routinely. Marty loves baseball and his favorite team was the Brewers and in 1982, they were contending for the division championship. The Mass was usually in the morning but this day it was moved to the afternoon. That conflicted with the "big game." Marty was eighteen and the server with a big decision. He could call in sick and see the game in the afternoon. He remembers that day well. He decided to serve Mass. After Mass, the conversation moved to the big game and Marty explained the situation and his decision. Marty got the impression that Father was incredibly happy that Marty had made the right decision. Father Bolduc was not a big sports fan, but he made Marty feel that he was interested in what Marty had to say. Marty's connection with Fr. Bolduc was solidified even more.

The Beemster's had asked Father Bolduc to be their permanent priest at St. Michael's. Marty and his wife were married by Father Bolduc. Father Bolduc commented that Marty's wedding was the most beautiful one he had performed. Father Bolduc has baptized all of Marty's children.

Father was a hardworking priest. When Marty was the Holy Name Society President in 2010, Father was wearing down. He asked Marty to take him on sick calls. They started at 7:30 in the morning and got back at 7:30 at night. They went all over the State of Wisconsin. He had a list of people that needed the Sacraments and Holy Communion. Father never said he was too busy to do something. Marty was fortunate to spend time with him the last few years. When he called the St. Michael's board together at the end, we knew what was coming. It was a sad time. The good news is that he is working for us where he's at.

Father Bolduc was not only their spiritual adviser and confessor, but he was also easy to talk to. Whether he was really interested in what you were talking about, he made you feel he was. Father was also humble and would admit mistakes. His last sermon at St. Michael's was emotional. He passed within the day.[269]

Fran Ullmer—1973—Wisconsin

Fran went to a Catholic school and graduated in 1964. He remembers being in the service in Vietnam and the chaplain said that "we're going to be doing something different, we're going to be facing you during the Mass." Fran and friends wanted to know why—what was wrong with the older way. They would brush them aside. It was a privilege to go to the Latin Mass.

Fran was married in local church but a friend of his was going to St. Michael's. Fran has served the Latin Mass since the age of seven and once their family went to St. Michael's, they knew they were home. Father Altenbach was the priest at the time and Mr. Beemster was one of the servers at St. Michael's.

They were cheese makers when they were growing up, so sometimes they could not get to St. Michael's for morning Mass, so Father Altenbach would also have Mass in Oshkosh and they would drive down there for Mass. Father Francis Hannifin would also come up to say Mass.

Fran had fifteen children, the first one was lost because of Agent Orange. Father Bolduc married all the children. Some were big weddings, and some were small. Fran and his wife have eighty-one grandchildren. When Fran and Kristine got married, they said "Lord would you bless us as with as many children as you trust us with but Lord, would you also help us raise them?" Fran thanks God for his kids and the way they are and the way they act. When they meet, they give a hand-shake and a hug. I say, "Dear Lord, if there is anything I have left to wish for, it's that we all make it to eternal happiness." I do not worry that I have a lot of money, I had a good wife that stayed home to take care of the family. We owned Ullmer's dairy equipment company. My son now runs that company.

---

[269] See Sony audio recording—3/5.

We have some in-laws that aren't going to church, we still love them, and they respect us and we love them and pray for them.

When Fran was a commander of the American Legion, they had a Memorial Day celebration, and it was Fran's turn to invite the priest. Fran thought it would be nice if Father Bolduc gave the invocation. Fran was a member of the American Legion post in Wisconsin, which was called the Polish American Legion post. Fran invited Father to join the local post and Father said that he was a member of the post in New Hampshire, which is Post 1 in the U.S. Father Bolduc also reminded Fran that he was not Polish. Fran said no problem and Father joined the Wisconsin Polish American Legion. Father gave a talk at the celebration and enjoyed talking to all the veterans. Father could talk to anyone. When Father died, Fran, Gary Pauly, and Lee Ullmer and their wives escorted Fathers body out to New Hampshire for the funeral and gave him a twenty-one gun salute and gave the flag to Ernest (Father's older brother).

Whenever there was a sick person, Fran would approach Father about visiting them in the hospital. Father would never ask which Catholic church they attended or were they Traditional. He just wanted to know their full name and which hospital and he was on his way. He never said, "I'll try to get there tomorrow." He said: "I never want to know that someone died before I could get there because I was tired." Many times, Father would come up to Pulaski and we would get into Fran's truck and go to see Jackie Bruskiewicz and others that were sick and needed confession and first Holy Communion. Jackie said she was confined to her home with Rheumatology of the whole body from March eighth to July thirteenth, and Father would come every day with few exceptions. Father told her that it may be a problem during Holy Week. Jackie said she understood. Father came on Good Friday morning and gave her Holy Communion. Father told one of Jackie's relatives that she probably had suffered enough that when she dies, she will probably go to heaven. Father wrote Jackie a note when he found out he did not have much time and said he would sure like to see her one more time before he died. Jackie made it in to see Father one last time. Whenever Jackie talks about Father, she breaks down and cries, she loved him so.

Once, around 2010, Father had some books that he needed to get up to his home in New Hampshire, and Gary Pauly and Fran drove them out there. Once there, Fran drove and Father showed him where he went to school, the general store, and where he shopped. Father was very proud of where he grew up. Father showed him the collection he had assembled and described in detail how he got each item. He never blew up the story to make himself sound important. Ernest asked him a number of times, "What did you pay for an item?" and Father evaded the question time and again.

When it was deer season, Father would have an early Mass and afterwards he would come out and bless the hunters and their guns for a safe hunting season. Father commented to the hunters that this army of hunters in Wisconsin was probably the biggest army ever assembled in one state on the opening day of deer season.

Fran was just honored to know Father. Fran served Father's last 6:30 am Mass in De Pere. Fran was cleaning up the prayer books and Father came down the aisle and was surprised to see Fran still here after second Mass. Father had a nice smile on his face.

Father had told the parish board previously that he only had a few months to live, and he had selected those people on the board and wanted them to hold down the fort and take care of business. When the meeting was finished, Fran told Father that with news like that, he might get a lot of hugs from Fran. Fran then hugged Father, kissed his hands that held our Lord, and said that he appreciated all Father did for his family. You know, a man hug.

Father handled his dying very patiently and quietly. Sometimes, during the last few months, when he was walking or in the car with Fran, he would grimace a little from the pain. He really did not want you to notice. Fran said, "What's it like

Father?" and Father said, "It's like someone sticks a knife in your stomach."[270]

Father Schmidberger

Since you asked me to give information about Fr. Bolduc to gather memories about him, I will do so to the best of my knowledge and very sincerely.

I met Father Bolduc in Écône in 1973/74 when I was a seminarian there, and we had quite a number of good conversations. He then acquired the chalice of St. Pius X, an absolute jewel with one hundred eighty-seven precious stones. Father had been ordained the twenty-ninth of June, 1974, by Archbishop Lefebvre. Then he was appointed to the United States to help in the apostolate there. Very soon he got in conflict with his confreres because they had an extreme attitude concerning the Pope and the new rites of the Sacraments. As a result, Archbishop Lefebvre divided the US in two districts: one northeast with Father Kelly as Superior and one southwest with Father Bolduc as Superior. Fr. Bolduc acquired Saint Mary's (Kansas), the former big Novitiate of the Jesuit Fathers. He also succeeded in buying the wonderful Church, St. Vincent, in Kansas City. He himself established the District Seat in St. Mary's. The eighth of November, 1978, the Church in St. Mary's, dedicated to the Immaculate Conception, burned down. The insurance reimbursed the damage of more than two million dollars. Father invested this money in the school since the finances of this institution were far away to be balanced. Father had a very important benefactor in Mr. Beemster from Green Bay—but Archbishop Lefebvre told Mr. Beemster, not only Father Bolduc will make the Society bankrupt if he continues like this, but also will make bankrupt Mr. Beemster. The Archbishop asked Fr. Bolduc to leave St. Mary's and appointed a French priest Rector of St. Mary's, Fr. de la Tour. Father Bolduc established the seat of the Southwest District in Dickinson,

---

[270] See Sony recording—3/4 42 minutes 2-20-2018

Texas, where we had bought the wonderful Church, Queen of the Angels. He engaged Indian Priests to help him in his apostolate, promising them a priory, a car and a fruitful apostolate. But these priests have been almost incapable to celebrate the Traditional Mass and they had sometimes had a very poor theological background.

Father also was not very helpful for Fr. de la Tour in St. Mary's, but gave him a hard time. When I became myself Superior General in 1983, St. Mary's was established as an autonomous House. In 1984 Fr. Bolduc left the Society of Saint Pius X; as far as I know, he established himself in Green Bay, where he took care of the chapel, and with some Indian Priests he took care of some other chapels. After some years of real separation, there was a certain approach to the SSPX; he sent the children of his chapels to the Confirmations performed by our young bishops. Some years ago, we learned about his passing away by tongue-cancer. So, we will keep him in our prayers.

As you see by this little report, there is light but also the one or other shadow in his life.[271]

Carlita Brown

Carlita Brown is now (2021) living in Brazoria, Texas, two and a half hours from the Traditional Mass. She attends and enjoys Father Francois Laisney's live stream Masses from New Zealand. She and her husband, John, were intricately involved in the start-up of traditional chapels in Texas—involved in every detail that goes into new chapels, including helping to paint the buildings. Carlita was Michael Davies' "go-to" person for getting *Apologia Pro Marcel Lefebvre* typeset and published. At this point in her life, she is retired and helping take care of her first great-grandchild.

Carlita related that Mr. Henry Beemster of Green Bay funded the purchase of St. Jude's Shrine.[272] There were many people who worked tirelessly to restore the church to make it fit for the celebration of the Holy Sacrifice. A visit by His Grace to

---

[271] Source – Email from Father Schmidberger.
[272] In the Houston area

St. Jude's Shrine to confer the Sacrament of Confirmation and Blessing of the Church was planned when the restoration was complete. The lay board had promised that when Archbishop Lefebvre visited, they would give the deed to the property to the SSPX. They did not keep that promise and shortly afterwards they "fired" Father Bolduc. Father Clarence Kelly, then District Superior for the Society ordered Father Bolduc to leave Texas, but Father refused. John and Carlita rented a banquet room at the local Travelodge and called a meeting of parishioners—an overwhelming number of whom attended. Father Bolduc was forbidden to attend by Father Kelly. At the end of the meeting, everyone was invited to the Brown home for "coffee"—where Father Bolduc just happened to be that evening. Father Carl Pulvermacher (who had arrived during the restoration of St. Jude's Shrine) and enough people left St. Jude's that it was necessary to have two Masses at the Travelodge on Sundays. Father Bolduc and Father Carl resumed the Mass schedule—one in Houston for Mass while the other traveled an extensive circuit of traditional chapels—alternating weeks "at home." Sometime later, perhaps a year, Queen of Angels property in Dickinson was purchased—again through the overwhelming generosity of Mr. and Mrs. Beemster.

Carlita told about the local bishop writing a letter to be read to the diocese's congregations, telling them not to go near St. Jude's Shrine. One afternoon after the letter was read at the local churches, Fr. Carl and she were painting on the exterior of the church when a young man—a high school boy—walked up and said, "What's going on here?" Father put down his paint brush and talked to him. That young man was Nick Novelly—present-day Treasurer at St. Mary's. He and his mother were at Mass the following Sunday—and the rest, they say, is history!

Carlita said that Father Bolduc was the most hard-working and driven person (inside the priesthood or out) that she ever knew. He accomplished his goals regardless of obstacles. She related a story about the birth of *The Angelus* magazine. When the last coat of paint had been spread and the last nail driven on the restoration of Queen of Angels, a group of workers—some of whom had worked from dawn till dusk for months—were relaxing on the front porch of the rectory. Someone asked, "What are we going to do now?" Father Bolduc spoke up and said, "We are going to start a magazine!" Father Carl said, "I learned to run a printing press in the seminary!" and Carlita said, "I'm a pretty good typist!" Within less than a month we had a shiny, new printing press and an IBM Composer! Both were very pricey pieces of equipment, but Father Bolduc saw to it that we had what we needed! Father Carl printed every issue of *The Angelus* (until the operation was moved to Kansas City), a missal for use in traditional chapels, all the countless pamphlets that were produced by Angelus Press, as well as all three volumes of *Apologia Pro Marcel Lefebvre* and Michael Davies› *Pope Paul's New Mass*. These publications were a labor of love for parishioners at Queen of Angels who hand-collated every issue of *The Angelus*, all the pamphlets and books for several years—until Father Bolduc bought us a very expensive collator!

Carlita relates that one of the most heartbreaking episodes of Father Bolduc's leaving the Society came when Father Fellay asked the Board of Angelus Press to remove him as Editor and member of the Board. At a meeting with Father Carl, Father Fellay, Richard Shanks (attorney for *The Angelus*), John and Carlita, the vote was taken to remove him from both positions. Tears fell and if a heart could be shattered, it was. Memories of that evening meeting still brings pain to her.

Carlita related that one of the most remarkable meetings she ever spent with Father Bolduc, was when Father Clarence Kelly (then District Superior of SSPX) was visiting in Dickinson. At the time, the office was in a small room off the main dining room of the rectory. That is where she spent her days. Tension in the rectory between the Fathers was so bad it could have been cut with a butcher knife. It was incredible. John and Carlita took the two priests out to dinner and the tension was terrible. While on the way to the restaurant, on a dark, two-lane highway, traffic had come to a dead stop. Both priests decided to investigate. Three people had been critically injured in a head-on collision. Father Bolduc administered Last Rites to one of them and Father Kelly administered Last Rites to a second victim. Both had died at the scene. The third victim was taken by ambulance to the local hospital, and they followed. When they arrived at the hospital, security tried to stop the priests from entering the operating room where the third victim lay. The priests, in unison, pushed open the big double doors, went in and gave Last Rites to the man shortly before he also died. The four of them continued with plans for dinner and, during dinner, both priests were amiable—small talk like you would expect at an ordinary dinner. They talked to each other, they were friendly—they were Brothers in Christ, having acted as they were supposed to. The next morning when she got to work, the tension and animosity for each other had returned. That evening has stayed vivid in her memories for nearly forty years!

Carlita thinks that one of the issues between the two priests was Father Bolduc's refusal to obey his superiors. If Father Bolduc had a different opinion and wanted to do something they didn't want him to do—he did it anyway! To his credit, Father Bolduc never "bad-mouthed" Father Kelly or gave any explanation for the animosity between the two.

Carlita believes that Father Carl was a saint. He was kind, hard-working, humble and generous. As a Capuchin monk, he held a pilot's license and flew himself in a Cessna all over the upper Midwest, ministering on Indian reservations. He was sent to Australia for the Order where he spent several years as a pastor to a large congregation. When Vatican II happened, and Father Carl failed to conform to the "reforms" he was consigned to kitchen drudgery in one of their houses. He found his way to the Society and was loved and respected by all who knew him. To draw a comparison between the two priests—Father Carl and Father Bolduc—it can be shown in their submission to their superiors. Father Carl had been at Queen of Angels for many, many years and done invaluable work for Angelus Press and for Queen of Angels. For some reason, unknown to any of us (including Father Carl) the Society transferred him to a small chapel in south Florida. He was heartbroken to leave all of us and the home he had come to love but he bowed his head and went without a disparaging word for those who sent him. He came home—back to Queen of Angels—to die! Another note about Father Carl—he was a great favorite of Archbishop Lefebvre. The affection each had for the other was evident when His Grace visited Queen of Angels on numerous occasions.

Carlita believes that Father Bolduc's refusal to obey his superiors was a tragedy for all involved—not least for him— but for the Society as well, and for all those who had loved and admired him for years—some of whom will still not attend a Society Mass. She believes that Father Fellay (in his numerous visits to Dickinson) and Father Schmidberger (Superior General at the time), who also visited Dickinson several times, acted in good faith and had good cause for dismissing him. Never did she hear any priest of the Society make any derogatory remark about Father Bolduc. They were saddened and frustrated by his refusal to return to Écône for a year. Based on what Father Bolduc had accomplished in the years before his dismissal, one can only imagine what he might have accomplished with a year's rest and retreat. Tragedy is the only word to describe it.

Claudia Shibler

Claudia was one of the first teachers at St. Mary's and retired after more than thirty-six years teaching the children of St. Mary's academy.

The Shibler family knew of Father Bolduc in 1975 when they went to a weekend conference in Troy, Michigan. At the conference there were nine Traditional priests, one of which was Father Bolduc. The priest that all the attendees were talking about was Father Bolduc. He was a great speaker, and everyone enjoyed his conferences, and any sermons he gave. People found it easy to understand his talks, as he did not talk above them and used simple terms, that all could understand.

Father Ben in Hillman, Michigan, told us where we could go to the Latin Mass. It was in Milwaukee, Wisconsin, where Fr. Altenbach was the pastor who also said Mass in De Pere, Wisconsin. Once a month, we would make the nine-hour drive one way across the Mackinaw Bridge to go to Mass. We would leave on a Saturday, stay overnight, attend Mass and drive home. A short time after we started going to Mass in De Pere, we had a second priest who started saying Mass, as Fr. Altenbach was quite old and needed to have someone take over this chapel. That is when we saw Father Bolduc again, as he was Father's replacement. It was so nice to really get to know the priest that we had already known from the Troy weekend. He always found time to come to the house and talk with us, in fact that is when we were told about the buying of the property at St. Mary's on June twenty-third. We were told that he planned to start a Catholic school, as soon as possible, and invited all of us to come to St. Mary's.

The first ones to see St. Mary's were Mr. and Mrs. John Shibler and their sons Edward and (youngest son) Steve, whom they left at St. Mary's when they returned home after their short visit. While they were at the campus the men did a lot of work clearing all the overgrown brush from around the buildings. They found it funny whenever someone would yell "found another door!"

They were told of a famous snake on the property, as the man who was in charge the eleven years that it was vacant, had evidently named the snake "King George," as he saw it quite often. One night walking up the stairs leading to Bellarmine, just as he came to the last three steps, he looked up and there was King George, staring him right in the face. It startled him at first, but he knew black snakes really can't hurt you, so he just waited for George to scoot away.

The only religious on the property were Brother Augustine and Brother John Fox. Brother Augustine was the manager and kept the records, and Brother Fox took care of liturgical business and managed the two gardens. Brother Fox was also in charge of training the three boys on the property how to be altar boys.

Father Bolduc was down to earth and made everyone feel comfortable. When he could spend more than just Sunday at the college, he would put on his work clothes and get us all moving, and you did not stop until Father stopped. It was always a good workout when Father came to "visit" and the children really enjoyed working with Father. He made it fun, and they got to see another side of Father. One time, he came up to my son and roughed up his thick curly hair. I guess it was his way of showing that he did a good job. At other times he would make sure there was some ice cream or some other treat for everyone.

Our family, as stated above, arrived at St. Mary's October 8, 1978. Father called us the "Pioneers." All who came at the beginning lived without many conveniences as only one building was fully functional and the other buildings only had electricity. Even now when we talk about our Pioneer days, our children will say that they were happy to be a part of the first beginning of St. Mary's. There was also happiness in being with others who, like us, were just coming back to the Latin Mass and now we were now able to go to Mass and other religious functions. We said prayers together in the morning and later Sister Mary Barbara, Ed Shibler, and I were the choir for High Mass.

The day the Immaculata burned, Fr. Bolduc came from Dickinson, Texas, as soon as he was able, and we were glad he came. The firemen were shooting those large fire hoses through the stained-glass windows. They had already blown out all the windows on the west side, but Father told them please stop breaking these million-dollar windows. Father Bolduc said later that for whatever reason Our Lord did not want us to use the church and that we would rebuild. The next morning, Father said Mass on the front porch, and we knelt on the steps (just outside the two big doors, which were open). We could still see smoldering embers through the doors.

I must tell now of something wonderful that happened the day of the fire. First thing you need to know is the priest in town had told his parish not to step foot on the Society's property, and so they did not. The day of the fire while I, and almost the whole town, were on our knees crying and praying, suddenly I saw ladies from town (who kept going all through the night) serving coffee and sandwiches to all the fire fighters. We could not have provided for these hardworking men, as we did not have the means or enough food to care for them. I am sure Father Bolduc thanked everyone who helped us on that terrible day.

Our first year here, living in the farmhouse on the school property, we had such a rough winter, which we have not seen since 1978. It snowed so much and then it would drift, and it could get up to five to seven-foot drifts. Our road was covered, and we had no heat. The children and I were still working on removing the snow at our end when we saw "something" coming up the hill. It was still at the bottom but seemed to move rather quickly. It was hard to tell what it was because the snow was flying so high, whoever was coming was completely snow covered. It was not until they were almost at the top that we could see that Father was standing on a snow blade and hanging on to an arm lift in front of the hood. I asked my husband, who was driving, why Father was standing on the blade. He said that Father insisted that he should be the one, as he weighed more than Bill and he was not sure if he'd be able to keep the truck on the road. The furnace was fixed (just a pilot light went out) and now we have some more stories for our grandchildren.

Steve Kaiser

Steve grew up in California and they stopped going to Mass due to the heretical sermons. They stayed home and said prayers. Steve's mother heard about a traditional priest in Powers Lake, North Dakota, (Father Fredrick Nelson) and sent Steve up there for a couple of summers to help out. In California, Steve's family had one of the first priests in the U.S. being ordained by the Archbishop, Father Post, who said Mass once a week. After High School, Steve's mom suggested he go to St. Mary's and see what was happening up there. Steve came to St. Mary's in 1979 and started working on the Pilgrimage (around the Assumption). Steve was eighteen and worked in the maintenance shop and thought the work was very meaningful and he also had daily Mass. It was a pleasure being at St. Mary's and the whole family joined up with Steve thanks to Steve's mother who prayed constantly.

Father was very kind and was dearly missed when he left St. Mary's which was devastating to Steve. He was a great priest and was concerned about everybody. He was a great example for us—he was tireless in his efforts for the parish and to get the school started. It was a real parish life here—there was probably a tenth of the people. For Steve, Father was a great example and he loved him.

He was just a dynamic figure for us young people and was the best we had at St. Mary's. I wish he had never left. Steve worked for fifteen years at St. Mary's and is now doing independent furnace work. Father Bolduc was very instrumental in acquiring Dickinson and Kansas City—there was a cloud of dust following him. When you work with someone like Father Bolduc, you have confidence that he cared, that things were going to get done and done right. His office was always open, and it was a very Catholic environment. He may fall asleep while you are talking to him because he was so tired.

Father had a plan for St. Mary's when he arrived—he hit the ground running. It might have been his military background; he had a plan. Financially he had to struggle as the parish was not rich. Nothing seemed to slow his thinking down.

In purchasing the Kansas City church, he had to be creative since the local diocese wanted nothing to do with him. Father talked to a local preacher who owned the school on the same grounds about buying the church and then selling it to Father. The diocese sold it to the preacher and the preacher sold it to the Society. Father gave the preacher an incentive for his help.

Steve invited Father Bolduc to Father Thomas Aquinas' (a Benedictine monk) ordination in 2010. Father Thomas is the son of Steve Kaiser and was baptized by Father Bolduc. Father Thomas and Father Cyprian attended Father Bolduc's funeral in De Pere, Wisconsin, in 2012.

Father was a determined person—generous. People could offend Father and he would take it for a time but there was a point of no return where you better duck because he is going to swing.

He was an avid collector and he would sell antiques to keep St. Mary's going. He was a tremendous figure.[273]

Mrs. Irene Pryor (RIP)

Mr. and Mrs. Pryor came to St. Mary's from Powers Lake the week after the Immaculata burned in 1979. They wanted their children to attend a Traditional Catholic school. They had been in Powers Lake, North Dakota, in 1976 and 1977. It was a great place but there was no work or school for their children. Their first child, Maximina, was adopted by Mrs. Pryor and her husband with Father Bolduc's help. Father had arranged for an unwed mother to come to Manhattan and have her baby so that the baby (Maximina) could be born in the same county as the Pryor's. Father paid for all the expenses (birth, legal, travel).

Mary Jane Graham came to the business offices with a basket for Father Bolduc. Mrs. Pryor was there with Maximina. After taking out the basket's contents, Father Bolduc said, "Wouldn't it be funny to put Maximina (who was two months old) in a basket with a note and place the basket on the convent steps?" The note said: "I am desperate mother, please bring my daughter up in the convent." Maximina still has the note. Father did this and then Mrs. Pryor and Father sat on the college steps and waited. The sisters saw the baby and were running around and after a few minutes, Father went down there and they ran up to him all flustered and said "Father, Father please come, please come, please come." Father went into the convent and after a few minutes of confusion, said: "Oh, this is Maximina Pryor, Irene must have wanted to play a joke on you." For a year after that, the sisters wouldn't make eye contact with Irene. To the best of her knowledge, Father did not start an orphanage and never told anything about the birth mother to the new parents. Father would always take the baby when Irene bought her on campus—she was referred to as Father's baby.[274]

Joe Salenbein—1980

Joe and his family came to Father Bolduc at Miss Elizabeth Cook's chapel in the Irish Hills, Michigan, in the early 1980's. Joe's church was one of the first churches to implement all the *Novus Ordo* changes.

Father said that one of the devil's goals was to get rid of Extreme Unction, of which Sacrament Father was much an advocate. Joe took Father to his Uncle George to give him the last rites with the famed Pius X crucifix. [Father was helping some nuns with some maintenance work and as a thank you, they gave Father the Pius X crucifix.] Pius X had blessed this crucifix and had inscribed on the back that whoever venerated this cross would not suffer the pains of hell. Father passed the crucifix around to be venerated with all the relatives and Uncle George wanted to keep it. After Father left, Uncle George told Joe "That man did something for me." It was within two weeks, on Sunday morning, a phone call was received by Joe that Uncle George had died. After Joe got the call, he could smell incense throughout his house. Joe took that as a sign that Uncle George had "made it" at least to purgatory. Joe got to venerate that cross at least three times.

After one Mass, Father told Joe that he made enough holy water to fill a small lake. He was big on holy water and blessings. The people drove up from Toledo and Father blessed their cars. He carried a red prayer book with blessing prayers in it and lost it and the next day, it miraculously showed up.

Joe related some of his favorite "Father's sayings":

[274] Sony 2/14—13 minutes

"Just keep praying, Let God do the rest".

"You may not live to see God answer your prayers, so don't be discouraged, God will take care of it."

If someone would give Father Bolduc some static, he would say "I'll just go to my boss and my boss is Jesus."

"Are you going to call Jesus a liar?" was reference to what God said in the Bible which was contrary to what the person was saying.

"They are destroying the Church a little at a time."

Father talked about his ordination day, while he was laying prostate on the ground, and he said that there will never be a day that I will not be with Jesus.

Father, when he was getting ready to be a priest was asked to investigate Martin Luther. He found a letter that Martin Luther wrote that since he had given up his priestly powers and could not give his dying mother the last rites, he arranged for a Catholic priest to come to give his mother the last rites.

Virgil Bulcher—Our Lady of Victory Chapel (OLV)—Necedah, Wisconsin—1981

Virgil's children, then so small, played their little violins for Father. It was a festive day as it was the anniversary of Father Bolduc's ordination to the priesthood. He was thrilled and delighted watching them play their little instruments. He loved music and sang in the choir. It was not long that Virgil began taking his turn in driving Father Bolduc from and back to De Pere. On one evening going back to De Pere to his rectory house, Father began singing old and popular famous songs. Virgil was amazed as to Father's memory. It was not long before they often missed the turnoff to De Pere while singing and talking.

Father had a marvelous memory. He would read a book from end to end, put it down, and remember all of what he read not having to go back and re-read it. He loved books, collected many books as well as libraries of books. He got the name of "Hector the Collector." He told me "You never have enough storage." He was always in the right place at the right time. It seemed things would just fall into his hands. Of course, he became known wherever he traveled for acquiring old very precious things. On another occasion, he recited a poem he had learned in school when he was very young. This was an exceptionally long poem[275]. Without missing any of the lines or stanzas or stop to think what is next, he kept going and going and going. He loved the opera, Carmen, and his big voice would sing out the various parts of the opera he loved to sing.

The first story Virgil remembered was when Father was driving an army tank. His partner was always the driver of this big army tank. His partner could drive real well, sober or intoxicated. He just had the "knack" shall we say. On one day, the partner did not show up and the commanding officer said "Bolduc, you drive." Father told him he could never drive that thing. Father got it going but said he never caught on how to drive it. Father said he could hear trees snapping and popping and he finally arrived first at the destination. The others were still coming when the officer caught up with him, he said: "Bolduc, you are right, you can't drive."

Father got to meet Padre Pio in a roundabout way. It happened that he wanted to see and meet Teresa Neuman, the stigmatist. Having arrived, he met a French speaking spokesperson of her. Apparently, they both spoke some German. The two went to lunch and the spokesperson asked Father if he knew about Padre Pio. Father said he had never heard of him (this is while he is still in the service). This person gave Father Bolduc a letter of introduction to Padre Pio. When Father arrived in Italy at the monastery, he would sing in the choir for benediction. It was not long before Father was serving Mass for Padre Pio. He asked Padre Pio if he had a vocation to the priesthood and Padre Pio said that he will let Father know before he leaves. Later, when he was about to leave, Father asked Padre Pio about his vocation. Padre Pio told him he would begin his studies at St. Mary's seminary, but it would not end there.

---

[275] Probably the poem "Evangeline"

Father Bolduc would change Padre Pio's bandages on his hands after Mass in helping to vest. Once Father asked him if he could touch his wounds in his hand. Padre Pio said yes. When he touched his wound, Padre Pio cringed, and Father Bolduc immediately began to apologize. Padre Pio just simply smiled and said, "That's alright, that's okay." Father Bolduc commented to Virgil that he had saved many things that he felt were precious in his life but oh, how he regretted never saving one of Padre Pio's bloody bandages.

Father Bolduc told Virgil how he saved the Archbishop's life on various occasions. The first was in Mexico. He and the Archbishop had just gotten out of the car in the midst of a crowd of people who had gathered to greet him. Father was the Archbishop's right-hand man at this time and had noticed a peculiar person coming towards them that caught his eye. He became very suspicious and cried out loud to the police authorities "Get that man." The policeman went up to the person and hit the man on the forehead with his head and knocked him into a daze and took him in for questioning. Later, Father found out that he was a hired assassin from South America.

Father Bolduc and Virgil's father were great friends. They were both farmers, loved the farm, especially the horses and the land. One day, Father stopped on Highway 21 on his way to Oshkosh and asked the farmer in this field of rich black fluffy soil if he could run his hand in the soil. He pushed his hand into the soil and pushed it all the way up to his elbow.

On the last Sunday before his death, he turned around after saying the Credo and said: "I am offering this Holy Sacrifice of the Mass for your eternal salvation." That Sunday my thoughts when I saw him move, somewhat staggering at times, how long is he going to last, how long will he be amongst us? After Mass that evening, Father said he was going to have a bite to eat and read a little, then go to bed and have a good rest.

The next morning the church was quite well attended. This time was different, though, as Father Bolduc was not in the confessional as was his custom. Virgil knew something was wrong and sensed the ultimate. He discovered the door to the rectory still locked and opened it and before opening it, said a loud "Father are you okay?" He repeated it and then opened the door and went in—nothing was stirring. He repeated his previous question before he opened the bedroom door and saw him lying there on his side with one hand resting up by his head. He asked Father if he could hear him? Looking closer, he could see he was not breathing. He went over to the church and asked his wife, Mary, who is a nurse, to see if she agreed. Yes, Father had died in his sleep. He went back to the chapel and told the people in church. "Now is the time to pray the rosary for Father Bolduc, he is dead." They immediately fell on their knees praying the rosary for him.

Father Francois Laisney

Father Laisney took over as District Superior of the U.S. after Father Bolduc left the Society.

Father Bolduc was ordained in 1974, before Father Laisney entered Écône in October 1976. Father Bolduc did come to certain ceremonies in Écône, such as ordinations when Father Laisney was a seminarian. Father Bolduc was among the priests and Father Laisney saw him without having really the opportunity to get to know him at that time.

Father Bolduc was district superior of the Southwest US District, until February 1984, when he left the Society of St Pius X. From what he understood, the problem was the management of St Mary's. He had arranged for the acquisition of St Mary's, with the help of Mr. Beemster, from Green Bay, who was his great benefactor. However, being generous, he (Father Bolduc) had offered jobs on the campus to quite a few faithful as there was MUCH work to be done to renovate that big complex! He offered too many jobs to attract people to St. Mary's so that St Mary's was running with a large deficit every month. After the fire of the Immaculata church, he got insurance money ($1.5M) and asked Archbishop Lefebvre for the permission to put it in a savings and use the interest for operating costs. Archbishop Lefebvre warned him to keep the principal but gave him permission to use the interest. However, with the large deficit, he was eating at the principal and fast. In an email from Father Laisney on November 2, 2020 (source 130), he points out that the principal was down to $300,000 sometime after only a year. This came to the point that Archbishop Lefebvre was obliged to remove St Mary's from his responsibility, and put Father de la Tour there, to avoid a complete bankruptcy. Father de la Tour was obliged to lay off quite a few faithful and reduce the remaining salaries to the bare minimum for those he absolutely needed to survive. He succeeded by giving them much spiritual food, and little by little increased the salaries to an honest level. The first year the General House (at Rickenbach at the time) had to foot the bill (which after the severe cuts was still around a $40k deficit) and the next year, Fr Schmidberger simply put St Mary's back under the district (when Father Laisney was district superior so that he had to foot the bill and eventually the budget of St Mary's was balanced). One can say that Fr Bolduc was quite generous—though sometimes imprudent in his generosity. He was also responsible for the acquisition of St Vincent, of Dickinson and other places. That was quite good.

Father Laisney arrived in the USA on May 11, 1984, and after Father Bolduc's departure. Father Bolduc withdrew to Green Bay and his New Hampshire family estate and did not fight against the Society of St Pius X at that time. Later, when the SSPX U.S. District was under Fr Scott, he reconciled with us and even had a SSPX bishop give confirmations at Green Bay.

I am sorry not to be able to help you more than that. May God rest his soul![276]

Ralph Fryzelka

Archbishop Lefebvre was aware that a sizeable group of Traditional Catholics existed in the Detroit area. So, he sent the first three Americans that he ordained to Detroit in the summer of 1973. They were Fr, Anthony Ward, Fr. Gregory

---

[276] Father Laisney email – 3-7-2018 (Source 116)

Post and Fr. Clarence Kelly. Fr. Ward stayed in the Detroit area where we rented a house in Royal Oak for the beginning of a seminary with four seminarians. Fr. Post headed West to familiar territory where he started missions in California. Fr. Kelly went East where he eventually purchased property at Oyster Bay Cove, New York.

During the summer of 1974, the Society bought the big red brick house in the country at Armada, Michigan and, after some remodeling, made it the home of the seminary. Fr. Bolduc was ordained in 1974, came to Armada, spent a little time there, but was soon off to set up missions in the South and West. I believe the Dickinson, Texas, location was one of the first properties that he acquired.

Ralph Fryzelka and his family were fortunate to be part of the Traditional group in the Detroit area when the first American priests came in 1973. They benefited from the Mass held every Sunday at a school in Royal Oak. One of the difficulties that Traditional Catholic families faced was where to send their children to school. Public schools were already exposing students to wrong ideas. Catholic schools were moving away from Traditional teachings. Some parents settled for protestant private schools as the best choice available.

Ralph moved his family to Midland, Michigan, after he found a private protestant non-denominational Christian school. It turned out to be a good choice as his Traditional Catholic children experienced no animosity from the teachers. They were even allowed to use their Douay-Rheims Bibles in the Bible class. However, Ralph felt that he wanted to do better for his children. When the news spread about St. Mary's, he visited in 1979 and 1980. As others had, he called Fr. Bolduc and Father told him to pack up and come which he finally did in 1982.

David Gaynor, a Detroit area Traditional Catholic, had moved to Kansas City where he lived and worked. He became aware of a campus in St Mary's, Kansas, formerly a Jesuit Seminary, that had been abandoned by the Jesuits and then sold, as happened to many properties owned by religious Orders following Vatican II. Dave contacted Fr. Bolduc who then came to visit the property. Fr. Bolduc was known for his negotiating skills. After some negotiation and, I think, a visit by Archbishop Lefebvre, the immediate campus was acquired in 1978. The property was in a poor and trashed condition however they could see the potential. As Traditional Catholics around the country heard about St Mary's, they called Fr, Bolduc. Whoever called, Fr. Bolduc told them, "Pack up and come." No questions asked. Initially I think that a third of the people came from Michigan and a third came from California as that was where most of the missions had been established. And, yes, an interesting assortment of people showed up. Most to work and contribute but a few to enjoy easy living. The ladies cooked and set up a meal at noon in the building that later became the convent. Everyone showed up to eat whether they had made it to work or not that morning.

There was a tremendous amount of work done to clean up and restore the campus to operating condition. Some of the men that moved to St. Mary's were hired by the maintenance department. The Shibler family came from Northern Michigan with several of their children, some married. They brought their truck, bulldozer, strong work habits and went to work. Gas lines were run to all the buildings and furnaces installed. A kitchen/dining room was built in one of the school buildings.

The beautiful church was one of the first buildings that was worked on. Unfortunately, it was destroyed by fire during the work. Fr. Bolduc, immediately after the fire, set up an altar on the front steps and had a Mass. It was his intention that the church would soon be rebuilt. A corner stone was constructed soon after to symbolize that intention. Maybe there was a silver lining to that cloud of the church burning. It could be that insurance proceeds from the misfortune provided much needed funds to help restore the campus.

A school was started for the families moving to St. Mary's with children as well as a boarding school for those who wanted to send their children from around the country. There were very few Traditional Catholic schools that had been started anyplace so it was an alternative that families increasingly took advantage of. Some of the people that moved to St Mary's provided the teachers that the school needed. Claudia, of the earlier mentioned Shibler family, was one of the first teachers and she continued to teach for many years.

Fr. Bolduc had more than a full-time job with keeping an eye on the activities on the St Mary's campus, and he continued to travel much of the time servicing missions that he had set up in earlier years.

Dennis and Gabrielle Murphy—1974

Dennis' father was an osteopath in Kansas City, Missouri, but because of the drugs prevalent in the public schools he was trying to find a more conservative parish and practice. In the summer of 1971, he decided to move his practice and family to Monett, Missouri, in the Springfield, Missouri, area.

Dennis' parents were not happy with the *Novus Ordo* teaching and were looking for a more conservative priest. Father Dunffy, of St. Louis, advised them to stop going to the *Novus Ordo* Mass if they wanted to conserve the faith of their children. The Murphy's started to look for a traditional priest and Dennis's mother discovered the work of Archbishop Marcel Lefebvre. In 1974 they had heard that there was a retired priest in Oklahoma saying the Traditional Mass. After a few attempts, a group from Monett area drove to Oklahoma City, a four-hour drive, for the Mass. To their surprise the priest saying the Mass was a Father Hector Bolduc, who was in his late 30's, recently ordained by Msgr. Marcel Lefebvre. They introduced themselves to Father Bolduc after Mass, and Father told them that he was willing to go to Springfield to offer the Mass for them once per month. Father Bolduc and Dr. Murphy agreed that it would be better to have the Mass out in the open, so people would know of its existence. They bought paper advertisements and conducted a TV interview for the Springfield area. At the time, most traditional priests were laying low trying to protect themselves from losing their pension. After Father Bolduc initiated the Mission of "Queen of all Saints" other priests came to offer their monthly Mass. Father Terence Finnegancame alternatively with Father Carl Pulvermacher to service their chapel. Father Bolduc was always searching for new places to say Mass and Dennis' Father would tell Father that what they needed was "an island," an island where they could all be traditional Catholics. A few years later, in 1978, Father Bolduc announced to Dr. Murphy that he had found their "island" in St. Mary's, Kansas. Father added: "We are going to get people from all over the country to move to St. Mary's."

Dennis came to visit St. Mary's, in June 1978, after the purchase of the property before the loss of the Immaculata Chapel. Father Bolduc did not live at St. Mary's all the time; he was gone much of the time to cover other chapels. The workmen lived at the beginning in the present-day convent which was the only building with water on the campus at the time. Before moving to St. Mary's in July 1979, Dennis was working in a factory by Monett and he heard distinctly on the radio: "Flash, the Immaculata chapel, in St. Mary's Kansas, just burned to the ground. It was the jewel of the Jesuits, because of its beautiful stain glass windows." When Dennis told his mother, she called Dickinson, and they confirmed the sad news that it had just burnt down. The Immaculata was almost done being renovated by several crews among which were Carl Stromberg and Albert Gonzales.

The first retreat offered by the SSPX in St. Mary's was in July 1979. The retreat masters were Fathers Williamson and Petit. The retreatants slept in Loyola Hall—in small rooms on mattresses that were lying on the floor. Many retreatants were from the northern States like Michigan, and they did not know anything about chiggers, so they were convinced they were attacked by bed bugs. Unfortunately, many retreatants got chigger bites after walking through the tall grass. After the retreat, Dennis was asked to stay and help to convert the old Jesuit refectory into the present chapel and to have Bellarmine Hall and other buildings ready for the first official school year in the fall of 1979. Dennis had an electronic degree from a Vocational school and is still working at St. Mary's (with electrical work) having worked there for the last forty years as a maintenance worker.

Dennis' wife, Gabrielle came from Québec in 1981, after having tried the SSPX convent at St. Michel en Brenne for one year. She wanted to help as a volunteer to get ready more buildings. Father Bolduc convinced both to enroll in the first year of St. Mary's College in the fall of 1981. Dr. Murphy, who had a stroke in 1977, could not practice for several years and Father Bolduc called him in 1980 and told him he was needed to teach at the Academy and to help him start the new College.

Father had built a concrete block building on the west side of the campus in the hope to use it for honey processing, eggs and chicken slaughtering, and butcher shop. It was his dream to be self-efficient, but the government refused to allow it. This building is now used for the facilities and maintenance department.

Father Bolduc was selfless, he never stopped doing things, starting new projects constantly. He often sang old popular songs. He and Brother Augustine would be singing all the time. He had a great sense of humor and was caring about everyone. He wanted to make sure the youth were behaving themselves and would occasionally drop into a gathering to check on them, especially at the popular bonfires.

Mrs. C. Redding—1974

My husband and I and our seven children met Father when he was saying the Holy Mass at different locations in and around Detroit around the 1970's. We had been attending Holy Family Church in Detroit with Fr. Bonfil (by way of Mr. Bartnik (RIP)). When Fr. Bonfil said that now they would be changing the Holy Mass in Latin to the *Novus Ordo*, he advised us all to leave and go with the group in Royal Oak. This is when we found Fr. Bolduc saying the Latin Masses around the Detroit area. Father Bolduc was transferred to St. Mary's, Kansas, and we lost track of him. My daughter was a boarder at

St. Mary's in the 1980's and said that on the July fourth holiday, Father would bring out the firehoses and he would have a wonderful time with the students. He was so down to earth and so spiritual at the same time. After a few years, my husband lost his job and called Father Bolduc for a position in St. Mary's, as two of our children went there for the boarding school. Father Bolduc hired my husband to be the maintenance manager and life went on. We never thought that we would move our whole family out to Kansas and live there. Father Bolduc and we became good friends through the years. He was instrumental in getting us through our terrible car accident in Indiana by assisting us any way he could.

He was always on the go helping someone anywhere and anytime, either spiritually or financially. Father Bolduc was then transferred to Texas where he became the district superior of SSPX. While we lived in St. Mary's with Father Bolduc as the pastor, I worked with him in the little office and my daughter worked as his secretary. Father also had a little office and sleeping quarters, and there he resided. He was so humble and kind to everyone and when the finances were getting low, he would sell one of his antiques. He told us of the time when he met St. Padre Pio and the saint told him to leave the *Novus Ordo* seminary and go with SSPX.

We lived in St. Mary's for twenty-five years. After this, we moved back to Michigan and heard that Father was saying Mass in the Irish Hills. We started attending his Masses—always during the week. This church was through the generosity of Miss Elizabeth Cook. In his later years, he developed cancer and went through the treatments that were painful for him and died in 2012 (the same year as my husband). He did call me up and said the thirty day Gregorian Masses for my husband. What a priest, so loving, so caring, so thoughtful.

We also visited his location at St. Michael's in Green Bay, Wisconsin, and he treated us with the best. His rectory and surroundings for himself were so meager, almost living in poverty. He was always there for our small group.

I had heard that he founded seventy-two chapels in the U.S. in addition to St. Mary's in Kansas. He wanted to buy St. Vincent's in Kansas City, Missouri, but when they found out he was with the SSPX, the deal could not go through. He hired or found a parishioner of St. Vincent's and they purchased the church for the SSPX for such a small price. He had a way of doing these things. He always said that if God wanted us to continue his work, he will provide, and it always came true.

As you know, he was in the antique business and made quite a bit of money and used the money to finance the things he needed for the church. So many stories, so many converts, and so gentle and kind to everyone.[277]

Midge Hanrahan—1967

In the early 1970s, a few traditional Catholics asked Fr. Bolduc if he would come to Kansas City to bring the Tridentine Mass to those who desired it. He came to Kansas City every other Tuesday and said Mass in a parishioner's basement. Close to one hundred people would attend the Mass at times. He would hear confessions, make sick calls, and give spiritual direction. He would take time to visit with people.

He played an instrumental role in setting up many chapels. He helped to spread traditional Catholicism across the United States from one parish to another. With the chapels, he also opened schools. He purchased altars, communion rails, and stations of the old St. Joseph's Hospital in Kansas City—these items were moved to the chapel in Dickinson, Texas. He also purchased St. Mary's in Kansas and St. Vincent de Paul in Kansas City. He picked the location for St. Vincent's because he knew a highway was going to be built that would facilitate access from the north and south. He was instrumental in laying the foundation for the spread of the SSPX in the United States. When Fr. Bolduc was in town, they would drive around the city saying rosaries and place packets of holy items and medals around town. It would take three hours to circle the city.

---

[277] Mrs. Redding letter – 1-5-2018 (source 52)

Fr. Bolduc's pockets were always open to those in need. He was always a gentleman and always polite to those around him. Fr. Bolduc considered that his resources were a gift from God to be used for the salvation of souls. Fr. Bolduc was not given to idle conversation but did have a pleasant sense of humor.

Fr. Bolduc always turned to God to solve the various challenges that would arise. He trusted in Divine Providence and God would provide. The parishioners felt confident that he could successfully complete any project he encountered.

Donna Zyrowski

Donna worked as a secretary for Fr. Bolduc in 1981. Her parents (the Reddings) had moved to St. Mary's in June of that year and requested that she come with them and fill the secretary position. Before she left for St. Mary's, she practiced her shorthand skills that she had acquired in high school four years ago. She had just graduated from college and figured she was good enough to fudge her way through it if needed. That proved to be an overstatement as they were many times when she had to go back and ask Father to fill in a phrase or word that she could not decipher from her shorthand. Father was always very generous and never complained.

One particular item she remembers is when the ladies of the parish were replacing Father Bolduc's t-shirts. They certainly revered him and were looking for a way to raise money for the altar guild. They were selling the shirts for $7 each and she remember thinking she better get one because they could be "relics" someday. She still has the shirt and is waiting for that possibility!

Another incident she remembers was the kindness of Father Bolduc. She worked for Father Bolduc on her twentieth birthday, which was on September third, the feast of St. Pius X, a big feast day at St. Mary's. When he found out it was her birthday, he went up to the flower shop in town and presented her with six beautiful orange roses! She was so taken by the thoughtfulness that she saved those roses and still has them today.

She felt that Father Bolduc had to be a saint, he seemed so very holy to her. Every chance she had, she saved items from her job as his secretary such as notes that he wrote to her asking her to do particular calls or jobs. Father and Donna did continue to correspond after she left and got married, and she has saved those letters as well.

In her opinion, Father Bolduc was a unique and very holy priest. She remembers his collection of antiques and in particular a slot machine that was the very "first" one ever invented. Father found out that her family was in the business of raising bison and sent her an article about his own bison farm and his honeybees as well.[278]

Ellen Belderok

Ellen was married to Herman Belderok, who worked at Fairchild Aviation on the F104 electronics in Farmingdale, New York. Herman's parents were in Westberry, Long Island, in 1972 and it was there that Herman and Ellen met a Father Gommar dePauw who said the Traditional Latin Mass.

In *The Angelus*, they read about the new school starting up in Kansas, and Herman decided to fly out there, but they got a message that the Immaculata has burned down so he did not go. Father Bolduc has family in Florida and Herman met Father and they talked, and Father convinced Herman to come out and visit St. Mary's. Herman's found a "mess" there but was impressed that all the basics were there, and Herman became the business/maintenance manager of St. Mary's in 1979. He implemented discipline into the business processes. As an example, several different people were driving into Topeka to pick up supplies, so Herman set up a procedure so only one trip was made each day for supplies.

Herman was also the first sacristan at St. Mary's and trained all the altar boys and was the M.C. Thus, they were able to offer

---

[278] Donna Zyrowski, email from - 2-5-2018

a High Mass. During this period, Herman also held teaching positions at the school.

Since Herman was so involved in aircraft before coming to St. Mary's, he flew Father Bolduc to his various missions on weekends. Ellen was known as "checkpoint Charlie" since she arranged the flight schedules, kept track of flight progress, and made alternate arrangements when weather or other situations arose. Ellen had a flight schedule from the beginning of August to the end of September in 1978—Father flew on forty-one flights, flying on twenty-four of the sixty days, and was in the air for fifty-two hours. His destinations were Clear Lake, Boston, Fort Lauderdale, New Orleans, Topeka, Springfield, Dallas, St Louis, Los Angeles, Oklahoma City, San Antonio, El Paso, Birmingham, Houston, San Antonio, Green Bay, and Tulsa.[279] Ernest Bolduc said that Father had received four plaques from Northwest for over one million miles each.[280] Father would bless the plane with a special prayer each time he got on a plane.

There was the flight that involved Father Bolduc and the Archbishop involving a trip to Post Falls, Idaho, for a church dedication and then a flight to California. As they were flying, the control tower in Spokane directed Herman on another path and Herman said no, he was fine. The tower told Herman to look to the left and Herman saw Mount St. Helen erupting and he asked the tower for what course he should take. The eruption would spew ash clouds 70,000 feet high and cause engine problems. The Archbishop commented that maybe the "Devil doesn't want me to fly to California."

Father Bolduc left St. Mary's in early 1984. It was a shame. He relocated to Dickinson Texas. When Father left Dickinson, he headed towards New Hampshire with all his belongings in a moving truck.

Herman was asked to leave his job at St. Mary's at the age of fifty-four in early 1984 when Father DeLatour arrived. Herman got a job with the FAA in Kansas City.

---

[279] Travel Schedule for Father Bolduc 8-9-1979 (source 43)
[280] Sony recording 2/25—71 minutes, also Million Miles certificate (source 102)

Ellen said that she and Herman did what they did for Father Bolduc and St Mary's for the love of God and not remuneration. It was a labor of love. When working with Fr. Bolduc, there was no standing still, it was always full speed ahead.[281]

Mrs. Mary Gayner

In late 1978, the Gayners lived in Howell, Michigan, and went to the Redford SSPX chapel. Mary's husband Jerry brought his parents down in 1978 and called Mary back in Howell and related that the church was burning. He could not talk he was so emotional. Her son Mark came down for the pilgrimages and he wanted to come back to St. Mary's for school. They moved to St. Mary's soon to have their children attend a good school and to have the traditional Mass. Dave, Jerry's brother, had moved down from Michigan Bell Telephone to Topeka Bell. Father would go to Kansas City and Topeka (Dave's house) to say Mass. Dave was driving around and saw the statue at St. Mary's and started inquiring and found out the campus was for sale. Mary would take dictation for both Father Bolduc and Mr. Belderock (she still has some of her steno pads.) Most of the people at the parish wore long dresses like "Little House on the Prairie". Father would walk through the office, very happy, and sing these contemporary songs. Some of the office workers were scandalized. He had formal dances with an orchestra from Topeka and wanted the boys and girls to be familiar with each other. They had cards and Father would check the cards and if someone would dance with someone too often, he would cross off their name so they could not dance with that person anymore. Father was trying to teach the young students' manners.

The campus was a huge amount of work all the time. Mary was working at Sante Fe railroad and when she was done with that, she would come to St. Mary's and take dictation. Jerry was working on campus cleaning up the infrastructure at St. Mary's since it was very broken.

---

[281] Interview on 4-28-2018 and October 2017

Father Bolduc was so young and worked all the time. He was good with the people and sometimes the people weren't as good back. He was such a fast person in everything he did. I thought very highly of Father Bolduc.

Mark Gayner

At the age of eighteen, in 1978, Mark, Mary's son, moved his grandparents to St. Mary's. Mark loved the people out in Kansas and decided to move to Kansas. Mark worked on the church before it burned down. He was one of the older boys working on campus. Brother Augustine was the coordinator as Father was always traveling to one or more of the remote chapels.

Mark remembers that if you were digging a ditch, Father Bolduc would be down there digging with you. Father was a hands-on person. There was the first breakaway group of ten or more parishioners and Mark was depressed over that. Mark never saw Father upset, or at least that Mark could see. Father explained that since the beginning of the Catholic church, there were always breakaways, and it wasn't a big deal.

Whenever they would go to another church to buy items, they would pose as a lay group in civilian clothes and Father would be addressed as Mr. Bolduc. Being in civilian clothes didn't stop Father from publicly saying the *Angelus* at a restaurant.

Father's eyes had a certain look at them, they were piercing. Depending on what you did, his eyes would have a different look. Mark saw his piercing eyes when he and his friends filled up the old swimming pool by Our Lady's circle. Many city managers showed up due to the lack of city water that was available. Father did see some humor in the situation.

Father was a matchmaker at a dance. He made sure everyone was getting out and dancing.

Saint Mary's has always been the promised land. People would sell everything and move to St. Mary's. They had a great desire to have the traditional Mass, Sacraments, and sermons.

Father Herve de la Tour

Father only spent a few weeks with Father Bolduc in the beginning of 1983 before Father Bolduc left from St Mary's to go to Dickinson, so his acquaintance with him is limited. But Father DeLaTour spoke with many people who knew him well and Father could see that he was revered with gratitude by everyone who benefited from his tireless zeal. From their account, he seems to have been a great priest who sacrificed himself to bring the Catholic Faith to countless souls across the U.S. We also owe Father for the founding of St Mary's College. May God reward His faithful servant.[282]

Bishop Fellay

Father Bolduc defended the SSPX in the Southern part of the US District against the nine who split. He remained faithful.

But Bishop Fellay personally did not have many memories of Father Bolduc and the two memories he did have were unfortunately rather unpleasant. The first one is when we had to remove him from St. Mary's and the second when he left the SSPX. He could elaborate a little bit on that but did not think that it is very useful.[283]

Karl Stromberg

Karl was baptized in 1978 in San Jose, California, by Archbishop Lefebvre, and Father Bolduc was with the Archbishop. Karl is a carpenter and cabinet maker by trade and in 1979, they asked for volunteers to help with the renovation of St. Mary's, Kansas. He took some time off from his job and went out to help. At that time, Father Bolduc spent most of his time in Dickinson and came up to say Mass on the weekends. Karl had been working on the church and one day at noon when he

---

282 Email of 12/10/2017
283 Email from Bishop Fellay on 5/18/2021

was in town, the fire sirens went off. He looked up and saw the smoke on the campus and it was not long before the church was burned down. The next day, Father came up to St. Mary's from Dickinson and we had an unforgettable experience. He said Mass at the top of the stairs of the church right in front while there was smoke still rising from the ashes. We knelt on the stairs going down. It was like an image of what was happening with the *Novus Ordo* movement—The SSPX was saying prayers and offering the Mass as the Church is smoldering in the background. Later on that year, Father had a cornerstone made and Archbishop Lefebvre came and Karl was one of the two men who placed it. Of course, Father had the intention of rebuilding the Immaculata, but that never was to happen.

Karl decided to move to St. Mary's and continue with his help. Father soon moved to St. Mary's and took over the development of the school. Karl thought Father's vision of the college was actually quite prophetic. He envisioned it as a teachers' college to provide teachers for the Society's schools. After he left, the idea was never fulfilled and now we can see that the real difficulty the schools have are getting enough competent teachers. His vision for the property was a quasi-self-sufficient place with a farm.

As for the other elements of Father, Karl is sure everyone knows that Father was known as "Hector the Collector" and that he sold his Rolls Royce to finance his seminary tuition. Karl remembers one time when he brought a bunch of coins to show the boarding boys while Karl was the first house father. Father Bolduc had some golden Papal medallions from the Middle Ages and rather plain looking silver bowl with coins inlaid so you see both sides. Karl distinctly remembers a Greek one with the image of Alexander the Great.

One rather embarrassing event of Karl's was the repair of a chalice. The cup had separated from the stem, and Father asked Karl to fix it. Karl soldered it back together and then took the buffing wheel and polished it until it shone like gold. Well, a week or two later, he walked past the sacristy, and it was kind of greenish looking. When he asked Father what happened, he said that Karl had polished off all the gold. Karl was a recent convert and thought they were solid gold.

Father bought altars from two churches, and Karl and others all got together and removed them. The one in Omaha, Nebraska, was at a perpetual adoration church originally which was run by Father Flanagan (of Boys Town). The two side altars at St. Mary's came from that church. The other church was in St. Louis, a beautiful Romanesque revival church in a dangerous neighborhood. After working all day, the workers would lock ourselves in at night. One night, Father discovered someone on the roof trying to steal the copper and he went out and fired a shotgun in the air and the fellow left right away.

Father only drank water except for one time when he was sick, he drank orange juice as medicine. Karl had moved an old monk down to Florida for Father and met Father's father and mother where they lived in an orange grove, and Karl thinks that is why he drank the juice.

Karl included a newspaper article about the Archbishop being in San Jose on May 24, 1978. It shows Karl being baptized by the Archbishop with Father Bolduc assisting.[284]

Bishop Tissier de Mallerais – 1973

I knew Father Bolduc rather well. He came to Écône Switzerland (Seminary SSPX) to visit Archbishop Lefebvre; it was about the year 1973. He would speak French but with a strong accent of New Orleans and I enjoyed very much to hear him speaking the accent of the Old France.

If I remember correctly, Fr. Bolduc stayed for two years as a seminarian at Écône although most of his studies were at Fribourg. He was ordained a priest at Écône on June 29, 1974; the same day I received the sub-diaconate from Archbishop Lefebvre. Fr. Bolduc seemed to be very pious and simple. He accepted the rule and seemed to agree with Archbishop Lefebvre during his time with the SSPX. For me, he was an example of piety.

---

[284] Letter from Karl – 3/19/2018 (source 120)

Fr. Bolduc was sent to the United States and bought the SSPX house in Dickinson, Texas, with the big adjacent church. After that, with admirable audacity, he bought St. Mary's College in St. Mary's Kansas, the famous Jesuit college and academy.

He was appointed District Superior of the Southwest District of the Society of St. Pius X in the United States. His character was very pleasant but also firm and serious. He was obedient to the Archbishop when the Archbishop decided to use the Holy Week rites of John XXIII, whereas other priests with sedevacantist tendencies refused to accept those rites.

I remember he had been a seminarian before the war or just after the war and that as a soldier stationed in Germany, he frequented Theresa Neumann, a stigmatist lady of the countryside of Bavaria. These visits to Theresa Neumann helped Father maintain his will to become a priest.

I know he had been an antiquarian and had true knowledge of sacred items.

Paul Bryan – 1976

Paul was living in Arkansas with his wife and nine children when he decided that he needed to find a traditional Mass. He had gotten Father Bolduc's number and called him in Houston, Texas. Father Bolduc told him to come to Houston and there would be work for him there. This was a big move for Paul, the well-being of his family was foremost in his mind. Paul mentioned that Father was very helpful with the move. The parish was called St. Jude's and shortly after arrival at Christmastime, 1976, it was evident that the men in charge of St. Jude's were not going to allow Archbishop Lefebvre to take custody of the church. Father Bolduc, after some temporary venues, bought the Queen of Angels church in Dickinson, Texas, which required great amounts of renovation. Paul was working at his job, but his older boys were helping at the church often getting it ready for the first Mass. Father Bolduc was kind of a magician at getting things fixed up.

Paul operated a Dairy Queen and eventually ended up owning four of these in the Dickinson area. Father moved up to St. Mary's and Paul kind of lost track of him. For some reason, Father left the SSPX. Paul had a great respect for Father Bolduc—they had their differences as did others, but it was nothing that was major or that Paul held against him. He was a special person that got things done at the right time. Paul can remember sitting outside of the hall at Queen of Angels and it needed a roof really bad and Father said: "Well get up there and do it." He was the right priest at the right time.

Paul would describe Father Bolduc as very sure of himself, not especially diplomatic, somebody that will get the job done, regardless of what the opposition is. Once he set his mind to something, there was no changing it. He was a good confessor; he was a good spiritual priest—he gave some very good sermons—Paul has seen better and a whole bunch worse. The Mass was the main thing, everything he did was to enhance the holy Mass. Father was a lot humbler than people gave him credit for and if he did take credit, it was humbly. Father was a wheeler and dealer and Paul thought that was okay. Examples of this trait were St. Mary's, Dickinson, and Kansas City.

Paul wants to see Father get credit for the good things he did. He made a lot of people mad but in most cases, it was their fault, not his. As for sixty chapels founded by Father Bolduc, Paul thought that number was maybe a little high if you're counting non-house churches.

Thomas Summers
Saints Peter and Paul Chapel

I have had multiple people read Father's biography and comment that, after reading it, they really didn't feel they knew Father Bolduc well enough. I have written below my thoughts on Father as a person through my lens, which is limited. I have known Father Bolduc since the early 1980's while I was a parishioner and then a coordinator for the Irish Hills, Michigan,

Saints Peter and Paul chapel. I will try to tell you what I know of Father from my time with him.

Father Dwyer, at the fiftieth Anniversary of St. Michael's in De Pere, Wisconsin, said: "Priests are imperfect instruments of God." I need to take that to heart when describing Father Bolduc because he was not perfect like the rest of us are not perfect here below. He was really a great priest and man but like any of us, but he made mistakes. I wrote the biography of Father because he was such an amazing person and I felt others would enjoy learning about him and his efforts to save Traditional Catholicism in the United States.

Miss Elizabeth Cook was a spinster who had a great love for the Traditional Mass. Her friendship with Father Bolduc was one of mutual respect and admiration. She was a nurse who retired to Brooklyn, Michigan, (also called the Irish Hills) in 1971 and started building what she hoped would one day be a seminary. Her monetary resources were very meager, so she purchased forty acres and started building a house. The first year, she lived through the winter in a small room in the basement. It had no windows, was approximately 6'x6' and the heat source was from burning paper in a barrel.She had a dream, and nothing was going to stand in her way. Many people volunteered their time helping build a house that had two small chapels. Every inch of space was used as was every piece of wood. The best built building on the property was a two-car garage that Father Bolduc built.

There were a few squabbles between Father Bolduc and Miss Cook over such things as whether the Sanctuary Lamp had to stay lit all month since it was so costly. It was not unusual for Father to show up and find a new lawnmower or organ. They would discuss where the money was going to come from and invariably Father took out his checkbook. The first Mass was in 1978.

Miss Cook was bedridden for many of her years, but she could look from her bedroom over to the other bedroom where the Bolduc brothers made a cherry coffin. It was always interesting to investigate the coffin to see twelve-quart jars stored in there to save her blood after she died (in case she was a saint). This was Miss Cook's idea.

Father Bolduc had a great love for Miss Elizabeth as evidenced by his letters to her throughout the years. She was a strong and determined Traditional Catholic. She was alone in the home/chapel most of the time and Father took care of her like she was his own mother. Miss Elizabeth treasured her personal talks with Father before the parishioners showed up for once-a-month Mass. Then Father would have confessions with two chairs—one for him and one for the penitent. Father would then vest for Mass on the top of a dresser, and he would come to the chapel to say Mass. The original chapel held around twenty people while the new one held thirty. Father's Masses were always so reverent and spiritual. Some of the parishioners went to a *Novus Ordo* Mass on the off weeks so the contrast strengthened their love of the Tridentine Mass. The sermon was always something that fired you up to be a better Catholic and to love your faith. After Mass, there was a potluck dinner around the basement fireplace with all the families bringing some food. To save money, dinner was served on paper plates and plastic silverware which was often washed and reused.

I took over the sacramental registry after Father died and found one entry in the book along with fifty or so scraps of paper that had not been entered. Father seemed to have so many "irons in the fire" that I am afraid paperwork didn't always make it to the priority list.

When discussing the finer points of the faith, I can always remember Father Bolduc saying, "It's the Mass and the Sacraments that count, the rest isn't as important." That stuck with me when I had come to a poor parish or discuss the rules of fasting. Father never stood on ceremony—his Benedictions spoke for themselves—it was God we were adoring, not the monstrance.

When the consecrations of the bishops happened in 1988, Father and I separated ways as Father was very critical of the Archbishop's decision. We got back together when Miss Cook died, and Father pulled me aside and said he was mistaken and that the Archbishop made the right decision to consecrate the four bishops.

At Miss Cook's funeral (she died at eighty-nine years old) on September 30, 1993, she was buried on a snowy day at a 20' x 20' cemetery on the property. As the casket was lowered into the ground, several snakes came out and slithered on the snow away from the casket. Father Bolduc, kidding about his deceased friend, said "Even the snakes don't want to be down there with her." This may seem insensitive but if Miss Cook would have been alive, she would have enjoyed the humor.

Before Father Bolduc passed away, we were discussing how to improve the property and Father Bolduc said he thought we might want to build a new chapel separate from the house. I mentioned that Miss Cook wouldn't like that, and Father Bolduc said, "You can't rule from the grave." Norm Childs and I were somewhat surprised at that but realized Father Bolduc was right, things change, and then different decisions are made.

After Father passed away in 2012, the house was cleaned out and all valuables stored offsite. It was hoped that one day the chapel could be restarted. A survey was taken of the previous parishioners and funds and interest did not justify the costly upgrading that would have been required to start again. The SSPX did volunteer to provide a priest once a month but that offer lapsed with the lack of interest. The chapel sat empty for five years with no heat and much evidence of trespassers. Mold that was there before expanded its hold on the house. Eventually the chapel, except for the garage, was torn down in late 2017. So sad. Since that time, the property has been sold. Part of the proceeds went to the St. Thomas SSPX seminary in Virginia. Miss Elizabeth would have been happy about that.

The vestments and Mass articles of Miss Elizabeth's chapel were donated to SSPX brothers in Winona Minnesota. They were so appreciative.[285]

---

[285] Miss Cook's obituary and Father's letters to Miss Cook.

Appendix D

Post Society (1984-2012) Testimonials

Father Dwyer

Father spoke at the St. Michael's Fiftieth Anniversary Celebration on October 4, 2020. He is the present pastor at St. Michael's and resides at the Brothers Novitiate in Winona, Minnesota. Before the celebration, there was a High Mass which was conducted at nine am by Father Steven McDonald, first assistant to the U.S. District Superior. After Mass, there was a dinner and then we listened to excellent speakers and watched a slide show presenting the fifty years of St. Michael's history. Below is an abbreviated speech by Father Dwyer.

Father Dwyer has always had a connection with the people of St. Michael's because Father Bolduc was the first priest he knew (Ed. note: Father Bolduc baptized him). He had heard about St. Michael's when he was growing up—the Green Bay people, they have a nice church, and they get Mass on Sundays. It is amazing the impact a priest can have on a person. As a little kid, Father Dwyer used to be glued to Father Bolduc's words and gestures on the altar. He used to tell his dad during Mass that that thing Father Bolduc has wrapped around his arm is called a maniple, the thing he has draped over his shoulder is called a chasuble. His dad got annoyed with him and said to pay attention to the Mass. He just remembers that Father Bolduc was that role model. Some things that he cannot forget were when Father Bolduc had a trip scheduled to Rome in 1988 and at that time, Father Dwyer's grandfather was ailing. Father Bolduc told Father Dwyer's mom that if grandfather took a turn for the worst, please call him. Grandfather took a turn for the worse and Father Bolduc canceled his important trip to Rome and came to Albuquerque and gave grandfather the last rites. He was a very impressive priest, and it is something Father Dwyer can't forget. The impact a good priest will leave with his parishioners is very lasting. Father Bolduc also came in the 90's to administer the sacraments to Father Dwyer's other grandfather and eventually gave him the last rites also.

Some people are very taken with Father Bolduc and were with him the entire way, and Father Dwyer only knew him as a great priest. There were others that said Father Bolduc had failings and made mistakes. They are both right as you can be a good priest and instrument of God and still have failings. That is true for any of us, that's true for Fathers Dwyer and McDonald and even for Archbishop Lefebvre. Think of St. Peter, he was with our Lord for three years witnessing the miracles of Christ and after three years Peter denied Christ, which is amazing. We always think that if someone is holy that they are completely good and no imperfection in them, that is not true. God made us and we are not perfect. The good that he brings about through his instrument, the priest, is really the thing to focus on, the good that is brought about. Some focus on the bad things the priests do, the scandals and such because that is what makes the news. But what about the good that you never hear about, like the stories about Father Bolduc and Father Dwyer's grandfathers? These priests of the Church that we looked up to are channels of grace. God works through them although they are not one hundred percent perfect. He works through them just like he worked through the Apostles, just like He works through any priest in the Church. That is something we all have to remember. Priests say with St Paul: "I planted, Apollo watered but God gave the increase." It is God who is bringing about great things through his instruments the priests. St. Theresa of the Child Jesus said, concerning religious: "God didn't choose me because of how worthy I was, but God chose me." God can work great things through Father Dwyer by my being a docile instrument in his hands. I'm never going to be perfect and none of the priests you know or ever knew are ever going to be perfect. God does great things through the priest as Father Dwyer saw with Father Bolduc, God was doing great things through him, and he influenced Father Dwyer's vocation because of the good things that he did and said in his sermons.

Father Bolduc was also an influence on the priest that was Father Dwyer's mentor, Father Albert Gonzales. Before Father Gonzalez became a priest, he had this idea about wanting to go to the seminary, but he kept fighting it. All of sudden, he decided his vocation was not in the religious state, but he was to have a family. After this decision, Father Gonzalez was going to take a trip in Kansas and went across the railroad tracks and he never saw the train which hit his car and caused great damage to the car. He did not receive a scratch in the accident. He went back to St. Mary's, and he saw Father Bolduc yelling at him from a distance: "Are you going to go to the seminary or not?" Father Gonzalez got on a plane and went down to the seminary in Argentina and became a good priest. That was another example of a vocation influenced by Father Bolduc. It's quite amazing to see how God works through his grace, his instruments for the sanctification of all of us. God does not want perfect instruments; he wants imperfect instruments. He wants to show that He is the one that is working in our souls, not the man.

Father Dwyer was very pleased that his first two missions were at parishes where Father Bolduc served, St. Michael's in De Pere and Our Lady of Victory in Necedah. Father Dwyer does not think it was an accident, it's something quite providential. Father McDonald, when he assigned Father Dwyer at St. Michael's, said that he was going to love the people and Father Dwyer said to himself, "Whatever." It turns out that after two years as pastor at St. Michael's, what Father McDonald said was true. Father Dwyer said he hopes that he receives the parishioner's prayers and might be this good instrument in the hands of our Lord and despite all his imperfections, serve the parish as well as Christ wants him to.

Gerard Garno - Father Bolduc a Saint for Our Time

Divine Providence Leads Searching Souls to Fr. Bolduc

In 1962 the Catholic world was changed by the Council called Vatican Il. Pope John XXIII announced the Council and said it was now time to: "open the windows and let in the fresh air." Later, his successor, Paul VI—along with most serious Catholics—realized that instead of "fresh air" we got the "smoke of Satan." The evidence supported that assessment: vocations dropped drastically, members of clergy and religious orders left their vocations, millions of Catholics left the Church for other religions or no religion, and there was an unprecedented decline in overall belief and practices of Catholicism.

It was into this time of apostasy that Gerard Garno was born, in 1962. Initially, his parents were devout Catholics who prayed the Rosary each evening and kept a statue of the Blessed Mother. They ended up having fifteen children.

Gerard was sent by his parents to the best Catholic schools that existed at that time: He went to St. Joseph's Academy run by the Dominican Sisters of Adrian. The order of nuns was flourishing in the 1950's, with young women giving their lives in droves to be brides of Christ.

As he entered pre-school, the nuns were still in traditional habits and taught in a traditional manner. But as the 1960's progressed, he saw the changes from Vatican Il being implemented: a "New Mass" which was more like a folk or rock type Protestant service; new secular looking clothing that excluded the traditional habits; teaching in the schools that was increasingly secular and liberal with ideas such as Darwin's Theory of Evolution taking precedence, etc.

It was by the time of the early 1970s that his parents announced that the Church was now allowing Bible studies with other types of Protestant Christians, and they began to participate in these. From that point, his family began to lose faith in the Real Presence of Christ in the Eucharist, then they decided to stop going to Mass altogether. In addition, they stopped sending us to Catholic schools. Gerard said, "The apostasy had claimed my family: the entire lot of us became lapsed Catholics and/or heretics that no longer accepted Church teaching."

Gerard himself retained a degree of faith, but no longer thought that the Catholic Church was God's will—he began to think that all denominations were acceptable. Hence, through college he attended an evangelical church. He studied the Bible but at the time didn't realize that it was being taught to him now through heretical Protestant interpretations.

It was in one of the Protestant college groups that he met his wife, Laura. In her past she had an initial encounter with the *Novus Ordo* Catholic Church, but was similar to him in that she was then practicing an ecumenical Protestant type religion. They got married in 1988 and—while Protestant in their theology—they shared conservative morals of the type taught by Traditional Catholicism. They continued to go to Protestant Evangelical churches in the early years of their marriage.

At one point around, 1995, Gerard began to question the fact that the various Protestant groups claimed that the Bible was the sole rule of faith, but they did not agree on what it said. That raised the question as to which group—if any—had the true interpretation of the Bible. In his efforts to resolve that question, he became quite confused because no one had a sufficient answer.

As he prayed for guidance and researched, he learned that the problem was that the Protestant religion rejected the teachings of Jesus that were not contained in the Bible itself, called "Tradition." These are mentioned in the Bible where St. Paul asks that we "hold fast to the traditions passed down to you by word of mouth or by letter" (2 Thessalonians 2:15). He and his wife started attending a *Novus Ordo* conservative parish in the area, but he was still attending Protestant services as well. Then, a Catholic midwife that they had hired told them that there was a Latin Mass being held by a Father Bolduc in the Irish Hills of Michigan.

He decided to visit Fr. Bolduc's Mass. It was all in Latin and was beautiful. After Mass, Fr. Bolduc stayed and spent much time with him. He took all the time necessary to answer all his questions. He explained that the Catholic Church was based upon both Scripture and Tradition, but that the "new" or "*Novus Ordo*" Church had, to a large extent, rejected Tradition like the Protestants had.

When Gerard mentioned that he was still attending Protestant services, Fr. Bolduc became quite quiet and serious. He then said to him in a clear and authoritative manner: "*Extra Ecclesiam Nulla Salus*—Outside the Catholic Church there is no salvation. There is only one True religion and that is the Catholic Religion. This is a dogma of the Catholic Church. You must get out of the heretical Protestant churches. If you do not, and do not fully convert back to Catholicism, you cannot be saved. At the end of your life, if you are not a faithful Catholic in a state of grace, your soul will rest in Hell."

Rather than offending Gerard, this admonishment intrigued and inspired him. He had been born into a Catholic family, had been schooled by the Dominican Sisters, and had never heard this dogma before! He immediately stopped going to Protestant services. Then his wife and he both converted to Traditional Catholicism, and Fr. Bolduc conditionally baptized her (since she had been baptized in a Protestant church). With his help, they determined to raise their children as Traditional Catholics.

Over the next fifteen years Fr. Bolduc became a spiritual director and mentor to Gerard's family and to him personally. Father recommended that he get the books of Archbishop Lefebvre and study them. Each month when Father came to Michigan, Gerard would anxiously await the time they could visit and discuss the questions he had. Father would sit with him for hours and explained the truths of the Catholic faith in a way Gerard had never experienced. He also met with his wife Laura and helped her understand the crisis in the Church as well, and the need to practice Catholicism as it was handed down from the Apostles and the Church Fathers; and to not accept the *Novus Ordo* modernist religion.

Untiring Apostle of Traditional Catholicism

Fr. Bolduc worked unceasingly, and to the point of complete exhaustion while giving every bit of his time and energy to the promotion of the True Faith. He crisscrossed the country continually, serving various communities of traditional Catholics, and starting new chapels wherever possible or necessary. He was sometimes so exhausted from these travels that when Gerard was with him, he would literally fall asleep while they were talking. He never complained, however, and when Gerard mentioned that maybe he should slow down, he simply said: "No, most people don't push themselves hard enough." He never held anything back in his unflagging service of Our Lord.

Fountain of Virtue

As is characteristic of all saints, Fr. Bolduc excelled in the practice of virtue. Whenever there was someone in need, he would find a way to help them. For example, in the mid-1990s when Gerard's family was growing, and it was apparent that they would have many children (they went on to have a dozen), he encouraged him to consider the practice of law. He wrote a stellar letter of recommendation, and thereafter Gerard was admitted to several law schools. Throughout that time, Father was there to provide spiritual, moral, and financial support.

Moreover, while Fr. Bolduc practiced unceasing zeal for overcoming modernist errors, he did so in a way that was always cheerful but never undignified or giddy. When correcting error, he did so gently and never did exhibit the "bitter zeal" to which we as Traditionalists can be prone. He never showed anger or condemnation but rather love and gentle exhortation. When asked about his cheerful and loving approach, he simply explained a timeless truth exhibited by Our Lord Jesus Christ Himself: "You draw more flies with honey than vinegar."

Further, he never spoke ill of those who offended him. To illustrate, he had been the District Superior of the SSPX in the United States. He told Gerard that at one point the SSPX had decided to let him go from the Society as there were apparently some disagreements. However, he always spoke highly of the SSPX and its members, including its founder, Archbishop Marcel Lefebvre. He spoke of their virtues and praised the good they had done and never ceased to give credit to Archbishop Lefebvre for saving the Church from total destruction by the modernists.

Supporter of Catholic Families

At one point Gerard's family struggled with the fact that they only had one Mass a month with Fr. Bolduc. They also had a *Novus Ordo* parish in the area that had an "indult" Mass on a Thursday evenings, but the rite was not pure and had elements of liberalism in the liturgy, preaching, and parish life. Father encouraged them to move near a SSPX chapel. They took his advice and moved near St. Joseph's Church in Armada, Michigan, in 2000. Still, Father continued to provide support and counsel to Gerard's family. He would write letters and offer Masses for them, when possible.

Champion of Catholic Orthodoxy

In the course of their interactions with Father, he showed that he was extremely theologically astute and also was aware of all points of view within the Church. He knew of all the various factions and groups within the Church and was always available to discuss their positions.

However, he never strayed the least bit into liberalism on the one side or to excessive rigidity and unwarranted dogmatism on the other. If there were differing views on areas of controversy, he would be careful to mention each and explain majority and minority positions from the standpoint of Tradition. For example, he sympathized with Sedevacantism and told Gerard that Archbishop Lefebvre even considered it. He explained that he spent much time with the Archbishop and was his bodyguard at one time; and when Pope Paul VI took some shocking modernist positions, that the Archbishop shook his head and said: "He cannot be the Pope; he cannot be a Pope!" Still, Fr. Bolduc followed the Archbishop's practical position of recognizing the Vatican II popes as popes, albeit bad and liberal ones.

Father was unwavering in his support for the importance of the Sacrament of Baptism as necessary for the salvation of a soul and to bring it into an initial state of grace. He never adopted the slightest novel or liberal positions in any area and was unwavering in his ability to guide souls back to the orthodox Catholic positions.

Supporter of the Arts

With an undergraduate degree in music, Gerard was able to share much in common with Father as he had a strong interest in and support for the arts. For example, when he heard that Gerard was researching and writing a book on Gregorian Chant, he invited him to bring his family to stay at his home in New Hampshire. While there, he gave Gerard full access to his extensive library, including many books that were extremely helpful in his research. When it came time to leave, he lent Gerard numerous volumes that were used to finish the project successfully. He also gave Gerard a tour of his wonderful art collection, including rare paintings, jewelry and art that went back hundreds of years. Included in that collection were interesting artifacts such as Napoleon's pistol; a book written by Henry VIII (before he apostatized) which earned him the title of "Defender of the Faith" from the Pope, and numerous rare chalices, including one that was owned by Pius X.

Father of Vocations

Fr. Bolduc was an inspiration for vocations. To illustrate, when he heard that Gerard's son Jonah was interested in going to a special Catholic school, he offered to support him as a benefactor. He faithfully sent monthly donations until Jonah graduated. Upon graduation, partly due to the good example of Fr. Bolduc, Jonah decided to become a priest and entered a SSPX seminary. Thereafter, Fr. Bolduc came to Michigan and took Jonah with him as he said Mass and brought the Blessed Sacrament to the sick. He taught Jonah many things. He provided an excellent Catholic example of a priesthood devoted to God and His Church, an untiring servant of Our Lord and a stellar *Alter Christus*. This inspired Gerard's son and now Jonah continues in the footsteps of Fr. Bolduc and strives to emulate his life of love and sacrifice in a priestly ministry.

Pro-Life Hero

Ever aware of the evils of the modern age such as abortion and euthanasia, Fr. Bolduc was not only firmly committed to teaching the long-term solution, which is the Social Reign of Christ, the restoration of the Catholic Church and the re-building of Christendom, but he took active measures to remedy the situation here and now. For example, at one point he told Gerard that he was involved in an adoption ministry to save as many of these little ones from abortion as he could. To do this, he had made arrangements with various pro-life groups that if they could find unwed mothers who are willing to give their children up for adoption rather than abortion, he would locate Catholic families to place those children, and cover the expenses. On numerous occasions when Gerard was spending time with him, he would say to Gerard, "We have saved another baby." It is unknown exactly how many children he was able to save and place in loving Catholic homes, but it is known that he worked tirelessly to do what he could as acts of true mercy, charity, and justice.

Farmer and Advocate of Rural Life

Because Gerard and Father were both raised on a farms, they shared many hours discussing the agricultural life and its benefits, especially for Catholics and the Church. Father told Gerard that he had purchased various tracts of land and was hopeful that he could establish a farm community for Traditional Catholics. He shared his ideas of having common equipment and shared community life for which the surrounding properties would be used for the support of individual families. In addition, he encouraged and helped Gerard get established and reconnect with Gerard's own farm background. He flew Gerard's family to visit his own farm in New Hampshire; there he showed them all his barns, equipment, and animals—including some bison! He discussed his farm, and agricultural methods and traditions, which went back generations in his family. Needless to say, Gerard's family was intrigued and inspired by the experience.

Zealous for Souls

At one point Gerard's father-in-law was suffering from brain cancer. He was an atheist who had no interest in religion. However, he came to live with Gerard's family since he needed the help and support. Unfortunately, the cancer took its toll and he had to be admitted to a nursing home. Gerard's wife baptized him when he was unconscious fearing he would die shortly; thus, Gerard went to visit him and when he was conscious, explained to him that he had been baptized and explained the effects of that on his soul; this included the prospect of separation from God in eternity and of hell, and the joyous anticipation of Heaven for the faithful Catholic. Gerard ended by asking him if he was glad that he was baptized; he nodded his head "yes!" (he had tubes in his mouth and couldn't speak explicitly). Thus, they knew that he was a willing Catholic at that time. He lapsed back into unconsciousness thereafter and never was conscious again.

When the facility called Gerard's family to let them know that Gerard's father-in-law was near death, they sought a priest to give him the last rites. Unfortunately, no priest was willing, as he was not a parishioner anywhere. When they explained this to Fr. Bolduc, he said: "I will go and give him Extreme Unction." He flew into Michigan and, after saying Mass, asked Gerard to take him to his father-in-law. He gave him the last sacraments in the midst of that lonely and forgotten room of the nursing home; an act of charity to a soul that had lived an evil secular life, but who—the evidence showed—had repented at the end and was worthy of eternity. Only Fr. Bolduc was willing to minister to that near forgotten soul, something for which Gerard's family is eternally grateful. When Gerard asked Father why he was willing to go to such lengths to administer the sacraments, he said: "The highest law in the Church is the salvation of souls." That is the motto he lived by.

Faithful to the End

In about 2009 Fr. Bolduc told Gerard that he was diagnosed with cancer. At that time, he became more tired and was able to travel less. Still, Gerard would pick him up at the airport and drive him to his various locations when he came to Michigan. On the last occasion Gerard saw him, in 2012, he was emaciated and weak, and could not move very well. Yet he continued on in the service of the Lord and the Church! They spent numerous hours together; he discussed the need to maintain Catholic orthodoxy, to keep pursuing the Social Reign of Christ, and exhorted Gerard to never give up fostering the farm life for the benefit of the Catholic family. He told him he had made a final general confession and indicated that he was ready for the next life. Gerard drove him to his final destination of the Mass center in Irish Hills, Michigan. They arrived and were greeted by Thomas Summers. There Gerard knelt and received the last blessing from Fr. Bolduc. Gerard heard Father had died in his sleep two days later. Gerard cried as he thought that he would never see him again and would have to live in this vale of tears without him. Only the hope that he would see him in the next life was consoling. Gerard is quite sure that Fr. Bolduc is now in the company of the Saints, as he was one himself. Thus, it is always an option for us to privately ask his intercession; after all, he was an exceptionally holy Catholic priest who knew how to minister and save souls in an age of apostasy—a true Saint for our time.

Gary Pauly – De Pere, Wisconsin

Gary learned about St. Michael's in 1986 when he gave a Muslim man a pamphlet on Fatima and the man gave Gary directions to St. Michael's. The Muslim man knew about St. Michael's because he had married a Traditional Catholic. Gary and his family went to St. Michael's shortly thereafter and the priest from India said that this was his last Sunday. Father Bolduc kept trying to get a priest to take care of St. Michael's, but it never was to be until he died. The next weekend, Father Bolduc took over saying Mass at St. Michael's. At the same time, Mrs. Dwyer from Necedah wanted Mass there and Father started taking care of both the chapels full time.

Remembrances

Gary had many remembrances of Father Bolduc that he related. There was a *Novus Ordo* lady who was around thirty-five and married, who was trying to get an annulment. She came to Fr. Bolduc and asked for help, as she was not able to accomplish this on her own with her limited means and education. The diocese would not grant the annulment and she would now have to fight for it in Rome, and it was going to cost two thousand dollars. Father Bolduc offered to pay the bill. The annulment did not happen, and she paid Father back. Gary said, "Think about it. She was a *Novus Ordo* Catholic and he still helped her." Father Bolduc helped everyone.

Another remembrance of Father Bolduc involved a man and a woman who got married and her first husband died. She was traditional Catholic, and her next husband was a "Baysider" and not traditional. They were married by Father Bolduc and after so many years, he was not getting along with the sons or her, and wanted to get divorced. The reason for the divorce was that the marriage was not actually done because the diocese did not recognize Father Bolduc as a priest. When it went to court, the lady's lawyer asked the monsignor whether Rome recognized Father Bolduc's priesthood and sacraments—especially matrimony. The monsignor then had to say yes to all those questions. When Father Bolduc heard the monsignor's answers, he was smiling. The divorce did not go through.

A brother and three sisters, in their sixties, were all living in the same house. Father would go over there for confessions, and they'd all be sitting on the same couch. The brother would start telling his sins and one of the sisters would say that the brother had forgot a certain sin and the brother would say, oh yes, and then tell Father that sin also.

Father Bolduc could talk to anybody and make them feel comfortable. There was this old army guy who had not been to Confession for years. His friend asked him if he would see

Father for Confession and he agreed to it for his friend's sake. On meeting him, Father asked: "How are your K-rations?" The army fellow perked up and said: "Oh, you're one of us." Father asked the fellow would you like to go to Confession and the army fellow said not really since he had done some nasty things and it wouldn't pay for him to go to Confession. Father just kept on going and said, what could you have done that was so bad and the fellow started letting down his guard and telling Father. Father said that is not so bad, I've heard worse. The fellow kept giving examples. When he was done, Father asked him if he was sorry for his sins and the fellow said yes and Father said that he was absolved of his sins.

God just took care of Father Bolduc. The St. Pius X pectoral cross came to him from a lady in an antique store. He had helped her fix her shelf that had broken and then organize parts of the shop. She bought it to Father's ordination and surprised him.

Gary remembered Father Bolduc telling him that when Father visited Padre Pio after the Armed Services, Padre Pio told him that he would join the Marist order to study for the priesthood.[286]

Consecrations

Archbishop Marcel Lefebvre was asking for Rome to allow the consecration of a bishop for the Society of Saint Pius X. He was asking as a good filial son of Rome and they seemed positive. At first, they said to send them names of the possible candidates, followed by the request to send some more possible candidates followed by requesting more time to study this. The excuses for providing another bishop to the Society just multiplied. Finally, the good Archbishop decided they were waiting for him to die, so he set a date and consecrated four bishops. It was almost ten years before Gary sorted all this out. He was buried like most people with half-truths, twisted truths and fancy ecclesiastical verbiage.

When the Archbishop consecrated the bishops in 1988, Father Bolduc was very critical of the Archbishop. Father

---

[286] Gary Pauly 5/28/2017 email

Bolduc perhaps, knew more than Gary did, but Gary was not satisfied with what he was getting from the media. Father's thoughts were that the Archbishop was in great danger of falling into heresy or schism. To get a better idea of what was going on, Father and another priest bought tickets to Rome. It was toward the end of the summer that they spent two weeks in Europe. When in Rome, they saw Cardinal Ratzinger, Cardinal Mayer and others. Cardinal Mayer was giving out celebrets to say the Latin Mass at the time, so he gave one to Father Bolduc. Father had not asked for it. The celebret gave him permission to say the Latin Mass anywhere without the permission of the local Ordinary. After returning home, at some point in time, the Diocese of Green Bay asked to talk to Father Bolduc. The issue of the celebret came up and they told Father that he could not say the Latin Mass without the permission of the bishop. He informed them that his celebret wasn't limited by the permission of the local bishop because Cardinal Mayer gave him a celebret that gave him permission to say the Latin Mass anywhere without permission of the local bishop. I suppose this brought pressure back on Cardinal Mayer. So when word got out of Cardinal Mayer giving out such celebrets, he was pressured by liberal bishops to ask for the celebrets back that he had given out. Someone demanded that the celebrets state "with the permission of the Local Ordinary." Cardinal Mayer called Father Bolduc asking that he return the celebret that he had given him. Father said he hadn't asked for it, and that he would keep it. The Cardinal was very sad on the other end of the phone. We cannot imagine the amount of pressure put upon the poor Cardinal Mayer, because he was trying to do something very good in Rome.[287]

As time went on, Father became less convinced that the Archbishop had made a mistake. He arranged for a Father Gregory Hesse, a renowned canon lawyer, to come to De Pere in 1998 to talk to the parishioners about the consecrations. He talked about why Archbishop consecrated the bishops, how he did it completely by the Canon Law, and how Rome was waiting

---

[287] Gary's email of 12/10/17

for the Archbishop to die. Father Bolduc was now convinced that the Archbishop did the right thing. In 1998, Father Bolduc arranged with Bishop Williamson to do ninety-plus Confirmations for parishioners of St. Michael's and Necedah. Until this happened, Gary and others were in a quandary: how to get the Sacrament to those that needed Confirmation. Gary arrived at 3:30 am at St. Michael's and Father was up and Gary said, "We need to get our kids confirmed by the Society bishops." Father Bolduc agreed and arranged the date and location. Of course, Father Bolduc didn't go to the Chicago confirmations, because Bishop Williamson and Father Bolduc were not on the best terms. Fathers Williamson, Bolduc, and Finnegan had all been in the seminary at the same time.[288]

St. Michael's New Church

Father had the new church built in De Pere in 1998/1999. At the dedication, there were three Masses going at the same time said by Fathers Serges, Gonzales, and Bolduc. Before that new church was built, they had the old chapel (garage) and they kept expanding on it from twenty-four to forty-four feet wide in 1994. The chapel was full, and they then built the new church that was one hundred-fifty feet by forty feet. Three years ago, they remodeled the old church (garage) into five classrooms.[289]

Minnesota Retreat House

Father Bolduc desired a retreat house in the wilderness where groups could have retreats. After a few scouting trips, a site in Roosevelt, Minnesota, was selected for St. Joseph's Retreat House. This site is approximately a ten hour drive from De Pere. He built and paid for this building for his gratitude to St Michael's Parish for all the years he was there and perhaps other reasons unknown to us. He wanted families from St Michael's to use it. He died before the finishing touches were put on the building. The first men's retreat was held there by Fr. Duverger in January of 2013.

---

[288] Gary Pauly interview 12/8/17—Sony 2/5 (12-8-17), Sony 3-2 (2019)
[289] Gary Pauly—2/8/2018 interview

Bill Drew—11-21-2022—Facilities and project coordinator—St. Mary's.

Bill was a resident of Wisconsin and dating a daughter (Bridget) of Fran Ullmer. Bill's family were somewhat non-practicing Protestants. The family had prayers before meals and bedtime and were semi-moral but without any Sacraments. They infrequently went to Church. When the relationship was getting more serious, the daughter told Bill that she would not marry anyone who was not Catholic, and she would want to raise the children as Catholics. Bill's only exposure to Catholics was the local church in Pulaski, Wisconsin, that was extremely liberal. Bill had a whole list of why he would never become Catholic. She suggested that Bill talk to her priest at St. Michael's, Father Bolduc. The meeting was set up and Bill was ready to put this priest in his place—"He better be ready because I have a long list of questions for him."

They met and Father asked Bill what he did for a living and at the time, Bill was constructing cement silos. Father talked about the different silos he knew throughout the country and that he was a farmer when he was growing up. Father had a great way of talking to anyone and getting them comfortable. Bill went through the questions—every question Father answered to Bill's satisfaction. The hot topic was that Bill heard about Confession to a person and how could this person take the place of God? Bill asked Father—"What gives you the right/power to do all this: turn the bread into the real presence of God, to forgive someone of their sins?" Father responded that that was a good question and then answered Bill: "I was ordained by a bishop who was ordained by another bishop, and you can follow a trail all the way back to the Apostles." Bill said that hit him and he was shocked that he was questioning this powerful person that is a successor to Jesus Christ. This made sense to Bill and Father cited the Bible quote about "whose sin you shall forgive..." Father said that priests were heavenly physicians that were here to administer God's graces like a physician administers medicine. Bill said it was so simple and that this was the beginning of his conversion. The discussion was powerful; Bill started going to Mass and quit working on Sundays. Father Bolduc married Bill and his wife after Bill's Baptism (the Lutheran baptismal records couldn't be found). Father also baptized all fourteen of Bill's children before his death in 2012. They named their male children after strong men, so they named their last child after Bill's stepfather James and the middle name was Hector, after Father, which he greatly appreciated. Father said, "I've been a priest for twenty-three years and I don't have a namesake—so this is my boy." He had James Hector's picture in the rectory. Father told the children that he was so proud of him.

Bill considered Father to be part of the family—Bill would do anything for him and knew Father from 1990-2012. Bill worked on his regular job in the morning and then in the afternoon would work on the new church in De Pere for over two years. As time progressed, Bill's job on the farm and his business demanded more and more time. He didn't have enough time to also do all the projects that Father would ask of him. The last thing that Father asked him to do was to repair an aspergillum where the handle leaked. Bill didn't quite get it fixed by the following Sunday High Mass, as it was a difficult welding project. Bill's son, Chuck, told Father that the aspergillum was not fixed, and Father told Chuck to go get the mustard bottle (yellow from the store) that they stored the holy water in. Father came to the bottom of the altar, like nothing happened, the bells ring, and Father turns around, serious, with a very slight smile, and starts down the aisle blessing the parishioners with the holy water in the mustard bottle. Father was very sick since he was less than a day from death, but he still had his can-do attitude and a small smile at the awkwardness of the situation. After Mass and catechism, he came over to the family van and gave James a Bolduc farms hat with a buffalo on it. He wanted to have James protect his naturally dark hair from the sun.

Bill went on to describe Father Bolduc. Holy and fatherly, he had never met anyone, let alone a priest, like him. Holy because of his perspective and he always saw the positive in things. Holiness of strength, solid, and a great sense of duty to his parishioners. He was a priest first, a man's man. When Bill read Father DeSmet's biography, he thought of Father Bolduc: rugged and not afraid of anything. Father was strong in what he believed and not like today's heroes who are soft. One of Father's heroes was John Wayne. He was active with a "let's conquer this," "save the Church" attitude. He respected justice and had a tough road.

Bill was in Green Bay, Wisconsin, and owned a business and had a dairy farm in Pulaski, Wisconsin. They had fourteen children and were successfully home schooling their children. Six months after Father Bolduc died in 2012, Bill went to a retreat and in one of the private consultations, the priest understood that the farm was very helpful in raising their children but said that the children needed more, they needed a social environment. After analyzing the pluses and minus of boarding the children at one of the Society's schools, the family decided that they had to move to St. Mary's. Bill was asked by Father Beck to head up a new position titled, "Facilities and Project Director."

Bill said that now, after working at St. Mary's for seven years, he believes that if Father wouldn't have used the "Immaculata burning" money to get St. Mary's on a good footing, we wouldn't maybe have a St. Mary's.

Bill has enjoyed following Father at St. Mary's. Bill commented that he had done a lot of projects at St. Michael's in De Pere and Father and he worked well together—they had a similar mindset. After listening to Father's stories of St. Mary's over the years, Bill wondered what St. Mary's was like. Bill feels honored to follow in Father's footsteps. After Bill's retreat, he received a message from Our Lady that motivated him to move to St. Mary's. Bill thanks God for this opportunity to work for the betterment of St. Mary's. Bill thinks Father Bolduc would be extremely pleased with what Bill is accomplishing at St. Mary's. This was Bill's vision—his apostolate is extremely important and we all need to take care of it, make it look like we're here to stay in business. The new Immaculata is fulfilling Father Bolduc's promise in 1978: "We will rebuild." Bill wanted to make the campus a place for learning, and it was not that when he first arrived to bring his family to St. Mary's. It is extremely humbling to know that Our Lady allowed him to be part of her project here at St. Mary's and under her protection.

James, now in 2022, is in eighth grade and is one of the sacristans. The family goes from two years of age to twenty-eight years old. Fourteen in all. Three girls are married—seven grandchildren and one son just got married. Almost all at St. Mary's, with a few in Wisconsin.

One story Father talked about was Our Lady's crown with all the jewels. As thanksgiving for all of our Lady's blessings, Father collected jewels for a crown from parishioners. He was going to take those jewels to Germany to have a crown made. He hadn't thought about customs and the difficulty getting a bag of jewels (in his suitcase) through customs—you weren't allowed to move these valuables through customs. He went to the airport in Germany and went to the customs conveyor, put his bag on the conveyor, said a prayer, and the cameras xray didn't show the bag of jewels.

Bill talked about Father needing money for improvements at chapels and calling home to Ernest to have him sell certain treasures so he could accomplish the project. His treasures were tools to help his churches and sometimes people in need. He was very charitable.

Mrs. Kristena Zaraza

Kristena has been married for twenty-eight years and has eleven children, six are girls and five are boys. One had a nickname of "Bingaling" and when Father called, he would ask how "Bingaling" was doing? They have sixty acres with eight acres tillable. They have a chapel that is almost finished and a cabin that they used as a home while they built their existing home. Father pushed them to finish the chapel—"You know there is not much time in this world left."

They wanted to raise their kids in the woods and be trained to live without electricity and water. They presently drive three hours to the Brothers Novitiate (in Winona, Minnesota) each Sunday for Mass and the Sacraments. They got to Tradition by a very difficult path. Kristena's mom was Catholic, but she left the faith. Kristena was a Lutheran and her husband was not practicing any religion. When they lived in Southern Wisconsin (by the Illinois border), they had friends of her husband that were Traditional Catholics, and they would talk about their faith. When Kristena had their third child, she and her husband started talking about key life issues like "why are we here, what is our purpose." They went to the Church in Mukwonago with Father Welsh.[290] After two years of preparation, her husband and she were conditionally baptized into the Catholic Church.

She met Father Bolduc by providence when they ordered a "Rural Life Prayer Book" from Catholic Family News in 2008. Father Bolduc responded to the request for the book with a request that the Zaraza's tell him what they thought of it. Kristena was excited that he was a priest and he emphasized the need to have families live on the land and grow some of their own food. They started a correspondence by mail and when he came up to the Zaraza home[291] in July 2008, he gave them the Sacraments.

Father spent the night in their one room cabin in the woods. It had no electricity or running water and an oil lamp for lighting, and he said he loved it and he even overslept! They were to have Mass at seven am and by nine am they sent their son down to check on him. Father told them he had a very peaceful night's sleep. As the years went on and they became closer and closer, they had a great love and fondness for each other. Father was their priest, confessor, and friend. He sat at the table getting peas out of the pods as he liked to help with the chores. Kristena still makes homemade breads and would always try to have warm homemade bread for him after Mass. He would love it and eat two or three slices. Father enjoyed

---

[290] He was a SSPX priest and went independent. There was a previous priest called Father Schneider but when they forced him to the Novus Ordo Mass, he retired.

[291] This is a 4 ½ hour drive from DePere, Wisconsin.

crusty bread and cheddar cheese. He would often call them on Sunday evenings to see how they were getting along.

He bought them many material things but the greatest gift he brought them was the Sacraments and spiritual friendship that will last forever. He came out to their place at least twice a year. He always desired to come out more often, but time and health would not allow it.

When cancer came back to Father Bolduc, he had Mrs. Pauly drive him up so he could tell Kristena in person. She felt that they had one of the best Masses that day. Many offerings were made, and many tears were also shed. She believes that was in April or May. He died four months later.

Later, Kristena received two letters that Father Bolduc had sent.[292] In the May 30, 2008, letter, Father summarizes his life and then talks about why he believes the Zaraza family are smart to stay on the farm. "You are wise to live on a small farm. I hope you can make a go of it. With the present economics and political situation in this country and in the world, being on a farm is the best way to insure for your future. It is also healthy and safe for your children. I try to encourage other Traditional Catholics to do just what you are doing, please continue."

In the June 25, 2009, letter, Father has some other thoughts for the Zaraza family. One comment was evident to all of us that know Father: "My schedule here doesn't leave much time to myself. I am on the go always." Further down, he counsels them on Sunday work: "I was glad to learn that you had gotten some hay in. It is not sinful for those who farm to have to take in hay on Sunday. This is especially so when it would have gotten wet." Father related a few gospel stories such as the donkey in the pit story.[293]

---

[292] Letter—Kristena Zaraza—2/22/2018 (source 121)
[293] Letter—Kristena Zaraza—2/22/2018 (Source 113) and Sony recording 3/6

Gregory Pauly

Greg is the youngest son of Gary and Mary Pauly and is presently around thirty-one years old and is the head server at St. Michael's in De Pere, Wisconsin. He was baptized by Father Bolduc and remembers his First Holy Communion as it was a very special day. Greg was home schooled and, around ten years of age, he liked to go with Father on sick calls as they got to go out to eat. He realizes now how much of a privilege that was to travel with the priest. After Greg got his driving license, he would drive Father to the sick calls and remote chapels for Mass. At the beginning, Father would spend once a month in De Pere and as time progressed, he would spend almost the whole month in Wisconsin.

Father didn't let on about his impending death. Greg remembers some of his health issues with various drugs like Lipitor, his extensions during the Consecration were very low and he could hardly kneel with his bad legs.

Father loved the children and would have treats even as the parents rolled their eyes about all that sugar. He would bring extra food with him when he visited the large families.

Father was very selfless. As soon as Mass was done, he would be gone on his sick calls and come back late. If someone needed the last rites, he would adjust his schedule and make the person with the last rites the priority. There was no down time with Father Bolduc. If he had free time, his wheels would start turning to find something to do like the retreat house in Minnesota.

Greg remembers Father relating that in the Army, they did sleep tests and most of the soldiers became non-functional at five or less hours of sleep and Father was fine with three hours of sleep. And as we all know, he was very productive with only three hours of sleep. Greg related that when you were driving Father to sick calls, he would often doze off until the next stop.

Father was always there to help people. He was selfless, looking to help others and not worrying about his own needs.

He was also reliable, if you called up at the last minute, an emergency, he would do everything to try to help you.[294]

---

[294] See audio recording of interview—Greg Pauly 10/8/2000

Appendix E
Timeline

1936   Birth June 21[295]

1942-1954   Education Grades K-12[296]

1958   Elected President of the National "I like Ludwig Club"[297]

11959-1962 US Army (age 23-26)[298]
            2/5/1959 Entered Army. Visited France, Spain, N. Africa, Greece, India, Turkey
            4/1961 + 7/1961 Visited Teresa Neumann
            7/25/1961 Left Germany for California
            4/4/1962 Left Army

1962   Vatican II opens under John XXIII

1963   6/1963 Bike trip through Europe and Nordic Countries[299]
            9/1963 Padre Pio Visit[300]

1964   Entered Marian Fathers Seminary 9/1964

1965   St. Procopius College 9/1965

            Vatican II Closes

---

[295] Birth source holy card and Father Bolduc background (source 31), Baptized 6/28/1936.
[296] *Ibid* and diary
[297] New Hampshire paper—11/29/1959 Hector Bolduc Head—I Love Ludwig (Source 23)
[298] Brief Background of Father Bolduc—date unknown (source 31)
[299] Local newspaper—around 1963—Hector Bolduc's Bike ride through Europe 7/16/1963 – 7/31/1963 (Sources 25 and diary)

[300] Diary - 9/13/1963 – 9/20/1963

1966	Xaverian University—Washington—1966
1967	Catholic University, Oblates of Mary Immaculate, Mount Saint Marys Seminary and Consortium,
1970	SSPX founded.
1971	December visit to Écône
1972	January—Mosaics in Italy, Greece, Turkey, Austria, Hungary
	February—Back to Washington D.C and seminary
1973	Trip to Greece, Egypt, Ethiopia, France, England, Holland, Germany
	October—entered SSPX seminary at Écône .
1974	Ordained—6/29/1974.
	Assigned to Armada, Mi. Seminary
	Archbishop's declaration—November 21
1976	August—Archbishop's suspension
	Father Kelly—U.S. District Superior
1977	July 10th—Queen of Angels in Dickinson dedicated— source 16.
	Father Ward leaves SSPX in January
1978	Angelus Press is founded in Dickinson TX.
	U.S. District separated into NW (Fr. Kelly) and SW district (Fr. Bolduc)
	June 23rd—St. Mary's College becomes property of SSPX.
	October—JPII election
	November 8—Fire at Immaculata chapel

Trad. Catholics of New Hampshire (TCNH)—Articles of Agreement

1979	Seminary moves to Ridgefield CT. from Armada

September, Grades K-10 opens at St. Mary's.

September—Father Bolduc buys the family farm using TCNH for title.

Seminary moves to Ridgefield, Connecticut from Armada, Mi.

1980   May 1, St. Vincent De Paul church purchased in Kansas City.

1981   August—additional 400 acres are purchased from KATO in St. Mary's

August—St. Mary's College opened.

October 2—Three SSPX sisters/nuns arrive at St. Mary's.

1982   Father Bolduc is relieved of command at St. Mary's over Christmas break.

1983   April—Nine priests are dismissed (Oyster Bay Nine)

February—SW District headquarters moves back to Dickinson.

1984   March—Father Bolduc leaves Society

May—Father Laisney, US district Superior

April 27,1984 Charles Bolduc ("pops") dies

October—Pope John Paul II issues an "indult" with heavy restriction but opening a little the door for some Traditional Masses[301]

---

[301] Provided by Father Laisney in Version 7 biography correction.

1988	June 30, Four SSPX Bishops consecrated
	Priestly Fraternity of Saint Peter (FSSP) established
1989	New church on homestead in Gilford—*Immaculate Conception*
1990	Aurore Bolduc—Father's mother dies December 7th.
1991	March 25 Archbishop Lefebvre dies
1998	Father Bolduc has Wisconsin parishioners confirmed by SSPX bishop
1999	April—purchase back of 177 acres of Bolduc farm
	June—25th anniversary of Father Bolduc's priesthood
	St. Michael's in De Pere, Wisconsin, dedicated.
2007	*Summorum Pontificum* issued by Pope Benedict.
2012	Sept 10th—Father Bolduc dies.
2020	Three churches/properties of TCNH deeded over to the SSPX (De Pere, Necedah, Gilford). Other properties of TCNH sold.
2021	*Traditiones Custodes* declared by Pope Francis severely curtailing the Latin Mass.
2023	May third, New Immaculata, St. Mary's, KS, dedicated.

Appendix F
Online Content

I wanted to provide a web page with content that wasn't possible with a printed book. It is fantastic material that I hope you will enjoy. The name of the website is frbolduc.com.
Go to the website and enjoy its content as described below. Someday, I would like to put tags in the book itself that would take you to the appropriate online content but that will probably be for someone else to accomplish.

Content

- Videos of Father's Mass, sermon, PBS special on the Bolduc family, a historical presentation, and Father's funeral Mass in Wisconsin.

- Selected audio recordings of Father's sermons from 1974 to 2000's.

- Source documents referred to in the biography.

- Padre Pio writeup.

- Pictures collection.

If you would like to send a comment to the author, please address it to: fatherbolduc@gmail.com

Printed in the USA
CPSIA information can be obtained
at www.ICGtesting.com
LVHW051513110923
757848LV00022B/296/J